Searching for the Common Good

Religion – Wirtschaft – Politik

Schriftenreihe des Zentrums für Religion, Wirtschaft und Politik
Herausgegeben von
Prof. Dr. Martin Baumann, LU / Prof. Dr. Paul Dembinski, FR / Prof. Dr. Gerd Folkers, CH / Prof. Dr. Markus Huppenbauer, UZH / Prof. Dr. Jens Köhrsen, BS / Prof. Dr. Antonius Liedhegener, LU / Prof. Dr. Jürgen Mohn, BS / Prof. Dr. Wolfgang Müller, LU / Prof. Dr. Georg Pfleiderer (Vorsitz), BS / Prof. Dr. Konrad Schmid, UZH / Prof. Dr. Jörg Stolz, LAU

Band 19 – 2018

Mathias Nebel, Thierry Collaud (eds.)

Searching for the Common Good

Philosophical, Theological and Economic Approaches

Die Deutsche Nationalbibliothek lists this publication in the Deutsche Nationalbibliografie; detailed bibliographic data is available in the Internet at http://dnb.d-nb.de

ISBN 978-3-290-22047-1: Pano Verlag
978-3-8487-4019-2: Nomos Verlag (Print)
978-3-8452-8301-2: Nomos Verlag (ePDF)

British Library Cataloguing-in-Publication Data
A catalogue record for this book is available from the British Library.

ISBN 978-3-290-22047-1: Pano Verlag
978-3-8487-4019-2: Nomos Verlag (Print)
978-3-8452-8301-2: Nomos Verlag (ePDF)

Library of Congress Cataloging-in-Publication Data
Nebel, Mathias / Collaud, Thierry
Searching for the Common Good
Philosophical, Theological and Economic Approaches
Mathias Nebel / Thierry Collaud (eds.)
232 p.

ISBN 978-3-290-22047-1: Pano Verlag
978-3-8487-4019-2: Nomos Verlag (Print)
978-3-8452-8301-2: Nomos Verlag (ePDF)

1st Edition 2018

Contents

Thierry Collaud

Introduction

The book that these lines introduce originated in an international colloquium on the common good that was held in Autumn 2015 at the University of Fribourg. Some participants were asked to develop their talks in writing, and these were supplemented by other essays (M. Keys, M. S. Kempshall). The resulting book, nevertheless, was not meant to be the acts of a colloquium; rather it was composed as an anthology of different perspectives on a common good that can only be a dynamic, multiform, and always elusive good.

If it is possible and even necessary to think about the common good today, this thought must be nourished by the rich philosophical and theological reflection that precedes us. Several of the essays collected here shed light on this indispensable genealogy. The necessary point of departure is found in Greek and particularly in Aristotelian philosophy; we are interested in seeing how it was taken up and remodeled on the one hand during the Greek patristic period, which is extremely important for Christian and particularly for Orthodox social ethics (C. Tsironis), and on the other hand in the medieval world in its cholastic version (M. S. Kempshall), and more specifically in the Thomistic one (M. Keys). These medieval syntheses pave the way for the modern version and for the contemporary inquiry about the common good. Now the distinctive characteristic of this inquiry is the doubt that grips it concerning its very object. Reflection on the common good has been a major element in philosophical reflections from Antiquity to the medieval period, but does it still have any relevance today? This question arises inevitably in a society marked by liberalism in which the just takes precedence over the good. Isn't the good that results from the demand for justice then reduced to a formal framework that opens up and maintains the space in which individuals can best achieve their singular goods, in other words, their preferences? The *good* is then fragmented into a multitude of goods. In economic liberalism, economic growth is associated with the means offered to each individual to have the most freedom possible in choosing his initiatives and making his life decisions. It becomes the marker of the common good.

Nevertheless, the question of the common good resurfaces when economic growth runs out of steam. Although in fact the three generations that spanned the twentieth century had the impression of a constant improvement in their standard of living, the curve charting the growth of available material goods has probably peaked. Some people began to realize this in 2008 when the whole system was shaken by a major crisis that revealed its flaws and the injustices inherent in an exclusive pursuit of "egocentric efficiency" (P. Dembinski). Can there be then a developing common good when the goods that can be accumulated by each individual diminish and the gap widens between those who possess and those who are in need? Add to this the parallel exhaustion of the democratic system which is supposed to guarantee freedom yet finds itself reduced to the people's ability to elect leaders without a long-term plan who promise change in a circular fashion. Maybe this is what makes so urgent the question about a good that is something other than the quantifiable good, as Amartya Sen elaborates in his idea of capabilities (M. Bonvin) or else about a commonality that goes beyond individual interest. In this sense it is invaluable to discover the economic reflections that are capable, not of revoking the market, but of making it a "civil" place, a place that contributes to the construction of a common, of the civitas (S. Zamagni). In addition there will be a reflection on poverty and vulnerability that also illustrates a recognition of the other which prevents us from dissociating vital needs from dignity (J. C. Huot).

By way of contrast, these references heighten our awareness of the current loss of interest in the common good. Isn't this connected with the disinterest in commonality that is the legacy of modern political reflection, in which the community is only an instrument with which to regulate the interactions of individuals and to manage distribution? The question that was thought to be obsolete, and yet is the basic question, is whether, prior to procedural and functional justice, a *political good* in the strong sense of the term exists, whether there is such a thing, for the community or communities to which we belong, as a *telos*, a prospect, a goal toward which we can go. Reconsidering an old, forgotten question is dangerous, particularly this one, because the prospect on the horizon can be confused with nostalgia for an idealized beginning (M. Nebel). If we give in to this false nostalgia, we run the risk of withdrawing into an identity, of reconstructing an imaginary commonality, an a-temporal commonality a commonality that we supposedly possessed and supposedly allowed to degenerate, but which, in a burst of identity, we will be able to bring back. There is no need to explain the danger of this movement.

To think about the common good is to think about the good of a community as a single body and not as an aggregate of individuals. In its identification of the community with the Body of Christ, Christianity provides us with the paradigm of social corporeality (Th. Collaud). To state the good of this community, singularized this way in its corporeality, is to state its "good life" and the junctures between this common life and the personal lives that are pursuing their goodness too. This brings us back to Paul Ricoeur's definition of ethics, which accords with the definition of the common good that we find in Jacques Maritain: "The 'good life' with and for others, in just institutions,"[1] can unfold only within "the good human life of the multitude."[2]

These points for reflection are the subject matter of the essays in this book. It is made up of three sections: an historical section, an economic section, and a philosophical-theological section. These discussions pose three additional questions that will not be addressed explicitly yet underlie the whole reflection, and by way of introduction we ask them as keys to reading that will stimulate interpretation. We mean the questions about the boundaries of our communities, about the tension between the universal good and the particular goods, and finally about the need to return to the common good in a political philosophy that fully accomplishes its mission.

Boundaries

Contemporary discussions about the desirability or undesirability of globalization focus on boundaries, posing simultaneously the questions about their use and their misuse. Globalization frightens people because it seems to dissolve the ties that support us and cause us live in a homogenized world. Now anxiety always generates defense mechanisms: openness will be countered by self-enclosure, community by immunity,[3] by racism, live-streaming communication by identity politics and isolation. In other words, when boundaries have or seem to have disappeared, people draw new ones that are stronger and more visible. But then there are many risks that they might become lethal, defensive boundaries that mark separation instead of the living, necessary boundaries that allow passage and contact, like the membrane of a cell. Will our encounters be made by armor that clashes or by skin that touches?

1 Paul RICOEUR, *Oneself as Another*, Chicago and London, University of Chicago Press, 1992, 172.

2 Jacques MARITAIN, *The Person and the Common Good*, New York, C. Scribner's Sons, 1947, 43.

3 *Cf.* Roberto ESPOSITO, *Community, Immunity, Biopolitics*, New York, Fordham University Press, 2012.

From this perspective, the question is still also that of the common good *of others*. This realization *of other commons* in other places is of fundamental importance in order to avoid the trap of the opposition civilized/barbarians. The whole history of slavery and of colonization tragically illustrates this forgetfulness of the other and reduction of him to a useful object. It is a denial of his ability to be human and to build a commonality that is at the same time similar to ours because it is human, but different because no concrete form of social organization exhausts the riches of a human community. The reflection on the common good must necessarily be a reflection on common *goods* in the plural and on their necessary intersections. This reflection can then serve as a wake-up call, in the sense that Levinas understands it, to recognize *the other* who comes to "core-out [*dénoyauter*]" self-centeredness that denied him and to "trouble" our heart, to extract it from a placidity and a somnolence that are lethal too.[4] A fine example of these wake-up calls is reported to us by Bartolomé de Las Casas in his *History of the Indies*. In the sixteenth century, the Dominican Friars of San Domingo suddenly became aware that the common good of the Spaniards, conceived of essentially as conquest and enrichment, was being attained by denying the *commonality* of the Indians: "You kill them, so that you may extract and obtain more and more gold every day," as the preacher Antonio de Montesinos said. Unfortunately it almost took the decimation of the indigenous population to bring about this awakening and an end of the self-centeredness. "Are they not men?" the Dominican friar asked, do they not have a social life and therefore their own common good, apart from the Spaniards? "Tell me, by what right or justice do you hold these Indians in such cruel and horrible slavery? By what right do you wage such detestable wars on these people *who lived mildly and peacefully in their own lands*?"[5]

We see therefore how the presence of the other, which arises in a society that has lost its homogeneity, stimulates reflection on the common good by obliging us to redefine our own *good* and to recognize at the same time the presence of other common goods, but also the emergence of a more global *commonality* that proceeds from the encounter with the particular goods.

4 Emmanuel LEVINAS, *Of God who comes to mind*, Stanford University Press, 1998, 59.

5 Montesinos is quoted by Bartolomeo de LAS CASAS in his *History of the Indies,* New York, Harper & Row, 1971, chap. 4-6. The English version of the excerpt cited here is by Benjamin KEEN (ed.), *Latin American Civilization: History and Society, 1492 –the Present* , Boulder CO, Westview Press, 1991, 71-72.

From the particular to the universal: common goods

The boundaries are porous and urge us to acknowledge others in their own identity and in their goods. Along the spectrum from the individual person to the global community there is a multitude of places where the common good is spelled out. That implies two requirements for interpretation. First, it is a matter of pinpointing what *good* and what *commonality* we are talking about. Every intersubjective relational system seeks its *good*. We can thus differentiate the good of the person, the good of the family, the good of local and national communities, etc. In doing so we see that the complexity of the discourse about the common good is increased by the fact that there is not one unique common good that is to be identified, but that the notion of common good relates to different communities. Secondly, we are led to see the impossibility of absolutizing a particular good, and the constant tendency toward the prospect of a universal common good. As we said, the *good* that we identify for a concrete community is always confronted with the *goods* of other communities whose relevance we recognize. The very process of this recognition leads us to include ourselves with the other in a universality of good which, ultimately, always precedes us. When La Casas recognized that there is a common good for the Indians other than that of the Spaniards, he relativized each of these two goods so as to refer to the good of a more generic human community, a brotherhood resulting from a common humanity and more particularly from the relation to a common Creator.

The common good and political philosophy

Finally this complexity leads to the obligation to think. Speaking about the common good, while taking into account its topological non-closure and its overflowing universality, challenges us to undertake a work of political philosophy and theology.

Referring to the common good can be risky, as we have mentioned. The risk lies in the modern inversion of the relation between what is common and what is proper. What is common becomes a threat to what is proper to the individual, or else it turns into something exclusive that is proper to a collective with which some people identify. But to reject any reference to the common good, in other words to reject a common requirement transcending individual choices, in relation to which these choices must position themselves, is just as risky. It condemn the self-deciding ego to futility, as Charles Taylor demonstrates. On the contrary, he says: "Only if I exist in a world in which history, or the demands of nature, or the needs of my fellow human beings, or the duties of citizenship, or the call of God, or something else of this order *matters* crucially, can I define an identity for myself that is not trivial. Authenticity is not the enemy of demands that emanate from beyond the self; it supposes such demands."[6]

In order to be authentic human beings, it is therefore necessary to deploy our choices in relation to "a horizon of essential questions," in other words, in a model that gives a coherent image of the world and of the human communities that take their place in it. Like any model, this one must be thought through, supplemented, and revised or reformed based on its confrontation with reality. This is the work of political philosophy and theology. It is necessary also for these disciplines to dare to think beyond the self-limitation of a philosophy which, according to Habermas, forbids itself "to elaborate a coherent image of the world" because of the "post-metaphysical postulate"[7] The German philosopher then assigns to political philosophy the restricted role "of analyzing our understanding of the world and of ourselves" while relying on rational arguments. But since there is understanding of the world, is the function of political philosophy limited to validating or critiquing the reasonableness thereof, or does it instead have the task of helping to produce an image of the world that is coherent and open, an image of the world that not only validates its current forms but opens a horizon of meaning and stimulates individual and communal ethical creativity? Political philosophy, if it wants to be something other than a form of sociology, must be a forum for audacity, it must dare to propose models of understanding the world, even if it means constantly reexamining and reworking them. Isn't reading the essays collected in this book precisely an opportunity to open our minds beyond formal arrangements so as to think, in advance, of what the good is and what commonality is for the human person and for the community?

6 Charles TAYLOR, *The Malaise of Modernity,* Toronto, House of Anansi Press, Ltd., 1991, 40-41.

7 Jürgen HABERMAS, Michaël FÖSSEL, "Critique et communication: les tâches de la philosophie. Entretien avec Jürgen Habermas," in *Esprit* 8 (2015), 40-54.

Historic overview. Recalling the richness and complexity of a notion and its selective transmission to modernity

Matthew Kempshall

The Language of the Common Good in Scholastic Political Thought

By its opportune choice of phrasing, an invitation to 'delineate the problem' of the common good seems to allow a welcome degree of both negative and positive freedom - to avoid the presumption of any definitive solution and to present instead an outline which will necessarily be open to further refinement and qualification. In accepting such an invitation, two approaches naturally present themselves. The 'problem' of the common good can be surveyed in terms of its historiography, that is, it can be analysed in terms of how a specifically medieval conception of the idea has been handled by more modern scholarship, chiefly but not exclusively in relation to the individual and the individual good. The result would provide a commentary on so-called medieval 'corporatism' and the emergence of natural 'rights', on the neo-Thomist distinction between individual and person, and on a broadly Protestant analysis of the birth of a 'lay' or 'secular' spirit in the centuries before the Reformation.[1] Alternatively, the notion of the common good can be scrutinised historically, that is, it can be viewed within the history of political and ethical thought and from a particular methodological perspective which concentrates on an idea, less as a reified abstract noun with an agency all of its own, and more as a means of thinking and writing that could be deployed in a series of specific situational and historical contexts, thereby reflecting not only a broader conceptual

1 For these themes, see for example Otto Von GIERKE, *Political Theories of the Middle Age*, Cambridge, CUP, 1900; Brian TIERNEY, *The Idea of Natural Rights – Studies on Natural Rights, Natural Law and Church Law 1150-1625*, Atlanta, Scholar Press, 1997; Janet COLEMAN, "On the Limits of Obedience and the Avoidance of Sin according to Late Medieval and Early Modern Scholars", in Virpi MÄKINEN and Petter KORKMAN (Eds), *Transformations in Medieval and Early-Modern Rights Discourse*, Dordrecht, Springer, 2007, 3-36; Theodore I. ESCHMANN, "Bonum commune melius est quam bonum unius. Eine Studie über den Wertvorrang des Personalen bei Thomas von Aquin", in *Mediaeval Studies* 6 (1944), 62-120; Antoine Pierre VERPAALEN, *Der Begriff des Gemeinwohls bei Thomas von Aquin - ein Beitrag zum Problem des Personalismus*, Heidelberg, F.H. Kerle, 1954; Georges de LAGARDE, *La naissance de l'esprit laïque au déclin du Moyen-âge*, 3rd edn., 5 vols., Louvain, Éditions Nauwelaerts, 1956-70; Walter ULLMANN, *Principles of Government and Politics in the Middle Ages*, London, Methuen, 1961, 231-279.

framework but also the specific intentions and strategies of individual authors.[2] It is the second of these approaches which the title of this paper is designed to reflect and on the assumption of two fundamental premises. The first is an understanding that use of the term 'language' is understood permissively, that is, as an acknowledgment of the several possibilities that were open to medieval writers when they were choosing between the - often very different - ways of construing the phrase 'common good' that were on offer to them, and where their decision was, in turn, conditioned by the precise contexts for which that language was intended to be instrumental.[3] The second is an understanding that the semantic precision with which this language was developed and deployed by scholastic philosophers and theologians in particular reflects the fact that it was these writers, perhaps more than any other group, who were able to explore the notion of the common good with unprecedented clarity and rigour and even, as a result, *themselves* 'delineate the problem'.

An Oxford nominalist is perhaps inevitably drawn to concentrate on one empirical instantiation of a concept or an idea in action, both in theory and in practice. In this case, the example - perhaps paradigm - is provided by Godfrey of Fontaines. Godfrey is a particularly interesting scholastic writer on whom to concentrate precisely because of the mixture of influences on his thought: he taught as a secular master, that is, as a member of the clergy but not of a religious order, and was therefore not necessarily tied to any one particular 'school' of thought; he studied at Paris under both Thomas Aquinas and Siger of Brabant and, as a result, was not only critical of the condemnations of 1277 but remained thereafter a defiantly close expositor

2 Matthew S. KEMPSHALL, *The Common Good in Late Medieval Political Thought*, Oxford, OUP, 1999.

3 For this conceptual range, see, for example, Theodore ESCHMANN, "A Thomistic Glossary on the Principle of the Preeminence of a Common Good", in *Mediaeval Studies* 5 (1943), 123-165; Peter HIBST, *Utilitas Publica - Gemeiner Nutz – Gemeinwohl*, Frankfurt, Peter Lang, 1991; Jean GAUDEMET, "*Utilitas publica*", in *Revue historique de droit français et étranger* 29 (1951), 465-499; Theodore HONSELL, "Gemeinwohl und öffentliches Interesse im klassischen römischen Recht", in *Zeitschrift der Savigny-Stiftung für Rechtsgeschichte, Romanistische Abteilung* 95 (1978), 93-137; Michael H. HOEFLICH, "The Concept of *utilitas populi* in Early Ecclesiastical Law and Government", in *Zeitschrift der Savigny-Stiftung für Rechtsgeschichte, Kanonistische Abteilung* 67 (1981), 36-74. For contextual range, see, for example, Pierre MICHAUD-QUANTIN, *Universitas, Expressions du mouvement communautaire dans le moyen-âge latin*, Paris, Vrin, 1970, and more recently, Elodie LECUPPRE-DESJARDIN, Anne-Laure VAN BRUAENE (Eds), *De Bono Communi – the Discourse and Practice of the Common Good in the European City (13th-16th c.)*, Turnhout, Brepols, 2010.

of Aristotle.[4] Godfrey is also an interesting thinker because of the way in which his ideas were articulated over a period of some two decades in the 1280 s and 1290 s, chiefly as part of an extended - and dynamic - debate with other scholastic philosophers and theologians, most notably Henry of Ghent, another secular master, and the Augustinian James of Viterbo, the course of which can be traced in a series of quodlibetic questions that were delivered publicly at the university of Paris.[5] Godfrey is not just a second-generation scholastic writer, in other words, a philosopher and theologian who was in a position to test the ethical and political ideas of Albertus Magnus and Thomas Aquinas, analysing the lacunae and weak-spots in their initial syntheses of Aristotelian natural philosophy and Christian patristic theology, but he is also someone whose evolving ideas can be traced in the course of their development through the give-and-take of academic disputation and in response to external political events.[6]

So what do Godfrey of Fontaines' writings reveal about the terms in which the notion of 'the common good' came to be conceived by scholastic philosophers and theologians and, just as importantly, the ways in which these writers came to differ in their interpretation of how it should be analysed and understood? First and foremost, Godfrey took up and developed an association that had been made by both Albertus Magnus and Thomas Aquinas, namely the connection between the idea of the common good in human society and a metaphysical principle of goodness in the universe. Godfrey did so by expanding upon the idea of analogical predication, that is, the principle that individual goods participate in universal goodness by analogy - they are 'part' of goodness in the sense that they depend on it for their existence and are directed towards it as their goal.[7] The result was a broad theoretical model for explaining how the good of individual human

4 John F. WIPPEL, *The Metaphysical Thought of Godfrey of Fontaines - A Study in Late Thirteenth Century Philosophy,* Washington, Catholic University Press, 1981.

5 HENRY OF GHENT, *Quodlibeta*, ed. Vitalis ZUCCOLIUS, Venice, 1613; *Opera Omnia*, ed. Raymond MACKEN*et al.*, Leuven, 1979; GODFREY OF FONTAINES, *Quodlibeta* I-XV, eds. Maurince de WULF *et al.*, Louvain, 1904-37 (Les Philosophes Belges, II-V, XIV); JAMES OF VITERBO, *Disputationes de Quolibet* I-IV, ed. Eelcko YPMA, Würzburg, 1968-75.

6 KEMPSHALL, *op.cit.,* Chs. 8-9.

7 Eg. AQUINAS, *Sententia Libri Ethicorum* (Leonine edn., Rome 1969) I.7; *Summa Theologiae* (Leonine edn., Rome 1888-1906) Ia 6.3-4; Ia 26.3; Ia IIae 34.3; IaIIae 90.2.; Cf. John F. WIPPEL, *Metaphysical Themes in Thomas Aquinas.* Washington, Catholic University of America Press, 1984; ID., "Thomas Aquinas and Participation", in ed. John F. WIPPEL, *Studies in Medieval Philosophy.* Washington, Catholic University of America Press, 1987, 117-158.

beings could be understood to be always included within the common good of the human community and thus a framework in which to place Aristotle's trenchant comparative terminology from book I of the *Nicomachean Ethics*: «For even if the good is the same for an individual as for a *polis*, that of the *polis* is obviously greater and more perfect to obtain and preserve. For while the good of an individual is desirable, what is good for people or for polities is nobler and more divine».[8]

In emphasising the analogical predication of goodness in all individual things, Godfrey of Fontaines relied upon Aquinas' explanation of how the common good could be described as 'superior' to the individual good in qualitative (perfectius, melius, divinius), and not just quantitative (maius), terms.[9] In doing so, however, Godfrey effectively sidelined an alternative model for understanding the relationship between individual goods and the common good, one which Aquinas had also articulated and again drawn from Aristotle, in this case from book XII of the Metaphysics: «We must also inquire how the nature of the whole [universe] contains the good and the highest good, whether as something separate and self-subsisting or as the order of its parts. Or is it in both ways, as an army does? For the good of an army consists both in its order and in its commander, but mainly in the latter; for he does not exist for the sake of the order, but the order exists for him. And all things, both plants and animals..., are ordered together in some way, but not alike; and things are not such that there is no relation between one thing and another, but there is a connection. For all things are ordered together to one end».[10] According to this so-called twofold, or 'dual', order (duplex ordo), parts of a whole are formally ordered towards one another but also towards an exterior good - typically, in the case of the metaphor of the army, individual soldiers have a relation

8 ARISTOTLE, *Nicomachean Ethics* I.2 1094b7-10, ed. René Antoine GAUTHIER, Brussels-Leiden, 1972 (Aristoteles Latinus, XXVI.3), 142: « *Si enim et idem est uni et civitati, maiusque et perfectius quod civitatis videtur et suscipere, et salvare. amabile quidem enim et uni soli, melius vero et divinius, genti et civitatibus* ».

9 AQUINAS, *Sententia Libri Ethicorum* I.2. Cf. ALBERTUS MAGNUS, *Super Ethica Commentum et Quaestiones* I.2, Bernhard GEYER, Wilhelm KÜBEL (Eds), *Opera Omnia*, Münster, 1951-, vol. XIV.1, 11; *Ethicorum Libri Decem* I.3.14, ed. Auguste BORGNET, *Opera Omnia*, 38 vols., Paris, 1890-9, vol. VII, 48-49; KEMPSHALL, *op.cit.*, Chs. 1-2.

10 ARISTOTLE, *Metaphysics,* XII.10 1075a11-15, ed. Gudrun VUILLEMIN-DIEM, Leiden, E.J. Brill, 1995, 266.

towards one another but also towards their commander and towards a shared goal of military victory.[11]

The availability of this second model - from Aristotle's *Metaphysics* - and Godfrey of Fontaines' explicit preference for the first - from Aristotle's *Ethics* - provides the first generalisation which might be made about a specifically scholastic analysis of the common good, namely that, at the most fundamental level, the concept could be construed in two ways, *either* as an all-inclusive principle of goodness *or* as a structure of mutual relations. Translated into straightforwardly human and political terms, this meant that the common good of the human community could be understood *either* as the perfection of moral virtue to which all human associations should aim *or* the more limited and instrumental goal of peace, concord and security which will make that moral perfection possible. The availability of alternative models, of *two* ways of conceptualising the common good of human society, is an important point to emphasise. Its significance becomes particularly apparent when Godfrey of Fontaines is compared with his sparring-partner Henry of Ghent, where it is a striking feature of their exchanges that, whereas Godfrey consistently appeals to the common good of the human community in terms of its all-inclusive goodness, Henry shows much greater willingness to conceive of this good as something more limited and material, and even as a common good within which the individual good might *not*, in fact, be included.[12]

In essence, the difference between these two conceptual models is reflected in a fundamental semantic distinction - between the common good when it is considered as *bonum commune* and the common good when it is considered as *communis utilitas*. This linguistic differentiation had a precise frame of reference in Aristotelian terminology, which was taken, once again, from the *Ethics*, in this case the distinction that was drawn between three categories of goods - the morally worthy, the useful and the pleasurable - and, by extension, between the different types of human association to which these goods could give rise. On the one hand, Aristotle argued, there are natural associations, such as the household and the *polis*, which are based on moral worth or virtue; on the other, there are those associations

11 AQUINAS, *Sententia Super Metaphysicam* XII.12, ed. Roberto BUSA, *Thomae Aquinatis Opera Omnia*, Stuttgart-Bad Cannstatt: 1980.

12 HENRY OF GHENT, *Quodlibet* IX.19, 293-295. Cf. George de LAGARDE, « La philosophie sociale d'Henri de Gand et Godefroid de Fontaines », in *Archives d'Histoire Doctrinale et Littéraire du Moyen Age* 14 (1943-45), 73-142; ID., *La Naissance de l'esprit laïque*, II Ch. 8; KEMPSHALL, *op.cit*, Ch. 6.

which are based on utility or pleasure alone and are designed merely to secure mutual and temporary material self-interest. «Those who love one another for the sake of utility,» he writes, «love the other person, not in himself, but only in so far as they will obtain some good for themselves from him.... So those who love for the sake of utility are fond of the other because of what is good for themselves, ... not in far as the person they love is who he is, but in so far as he is useful... These friendships, then, are incidental, since the person is loved, not in so far as he is who he is, but in so far as he provides some good. Such friendships are thus easily dissolved..., when the parties to them do not remain unchanged; for if one party is no longer... useful, the other stops loving him. What is useful does not remain the same, but differs according to different circumstances. So when the reason for their being friends has gone, the friendship is dissolved as well, since it existed only for that reason».[13]

In discussing the precise nature of the relationship between the common good and the individual good, both Godfrey of Fontaines and Henry of Ghent were drawn to examine the principles of identity and superiority which were set out in book I of the *Ethics* and, by extension, proceeded to discuss the inclusion or non-inclusion of the individual good within the common good of the human community. In doing so, however, both Godfrey and Henry were also drawn into a more detailed analysis of one further passage from Aristotle, namely the account of civic self-sacrifice which had been put forward in book IX of the *Ethics*. «It is true also of the good person,» Aristotle writes, «that he does a great deal for his friends and his country, and will die for them if he must; he will sacrifice money, honours, and in general the goods for which people compete, procuring for himself what is noble. He would prefer a short period of intense pleasure to a long period of mild pleasure, a year of living nobly to many indifferent years, and a single noble and great action to many trivial ones. Presumably this is what happens with those who die for others; it is indeed a great and noble thing that they choose for themselves.... In all praiseworthy actions, then, the good person is seen to assign himself the larger share of what is noble».[14] In the case of self-sacrifice, in other words, Aristotle seemed to argue that, in the process of laying down their life for the common good (that is, for the common good of happiness and the life of virtue), the individual will thereby secure their own greater (*maius*) or greatest (*maximum*) good. In doing so, and in using this sort of terminology, his argument clearly invited

13 Aristotle, *Nicomachean Ethics,* II.3 1104b30-1; VIII.2 1155b17-21.
14 Aristotle, *Nicomachean Ethics,* IX.8 1169a11-b2.

a debate over how such a principle could be made consistent with the 'greater and more perfect' common good in book I of the *Ethics*. When the individual lays down their life, are they, first and foremost, giving priority to their own greatest individual good - namely a supreme act of virtue - rather than the common good of the human community which will then result from their action?

Godfrey of Fontaines and Henry of Ghent were both agreed that the act of self-sacrifice which was described in book IX of the *Ethics* constitutes an individual's expression of the virtue of love (*caritas*) or, in Aristotle's own terms, friendship (*amicitia*).[15] Where Godfrey and Henry disagreed, and disagreed profoundly, is on how this virtue actually operated within a hierarchy of goods in Creation - what was usually termed in scholastic theology the 'order of love' (*ordo caritatis*). For Henry of Ghent, the *ordo caritatis* comprised a hierarchy of love of God, love of self and love of neighbour. In his view - and for support he appeals directly to book IX of the *Ethics* - the common good of the human community is simply the result or consequence of an individual's self-love being properly directed towards God.[16] For Godfrey of Fontaines, by contrast, the *ordo caritatis* comprises love of self, love of neighbour and love of God, but with love of the common good being interposed between neighbour and God. Godfrey justifies this insertion by appealing to the transformative nature of love which, he argues, necessarily goes beyond Aristotle's definition of friendship as love for another individual or for a second self. Instead, Godfrey argues, individuals are motivated by love of self and love of neighbour but also by love for what unites and transforms the two individuals, namely their shared or common good of virtuous activity and ultimately their shared or common good in God. The love of true friendship, therefore, involves more than two individual goods, more than just reciprocal self-interest - it actually involves a third good, namely union or communion in a shared or common good of a life of virtue. As a result, for Godfrey, an individual has a greater love for the common good than for their own individual good because their individual good is always included in the common good and depends on it for its existence - the individual good will indeed result from an act of self-

15 For the latter, see Bénédicte SÈRE, *Penser l'amitié au Moyen Age: étude historique des commentaires sur les livres VIII et IX de l'Ethique à Nicomaque (XIIIe-XVe siècle)*, Turnhout, Brepols, 2007.

16 HENRY OF GHENT, *Quodlibet* IV.11, f. 160 r.; XII.13, 67-79.

sacrifice but, in the performance of this virtuous action, the individual will still love the common good more.[17]

Godfrey's detailed analysis of the relative priority of individual good and common good in the act of self-sacrifice opened up still further points of disagreement with Henry of Ghent, but it also drew him into a sharp exchange with James of Viterbo, who had succeeded Giles of Rome as the Augustinian master in theology at Paris. According to James of Viterbo, book IX of Aristotle's *Ethics* demonstrates that human beings will always have a greater *natural* love for themselves than they do for the common good, whether that common good is identified in the human community or in God. Only grace, or rather the gracious love of *caritas*, will enable humans to love the common good more than themselves. As far as James was concerned, therefore, what Aristotle's *Ethics* proved was that greater natural love always follows greater union or unity and, in this regard, there is no greater natural unity than that of an individual human being with themselves. Like Henry of Ghent, therefore, James of Viterbo concludes that, in an act of self-sacrifice, the individual shows a greater natural love for himself than for the common good which will thereby result as a consequence of his virtuous action.[18]

Godfrey's response to this line of argument was to maintain that individuals have a greater unity or conjunction with what serves as the cause of their own being or goodness. In the process, however, he was also moved to analyse a fourth and final passage from Aristotle, once again from the *Ethics* but on this occasion taken from the beginning of book V: «Justice is, in a sense, complete virtue, not without qualification but in relation to another person… And it is complete virtue in the fullest sense because it is the exercise of complete virtue. It is complete because he who possesses it can exercise his virtue in relation to another person, not only himself…. Justice, in this sense, is not a part of virtue, but the whole of virtue».[19] These brief remarks formed the starting-point for an extensive - and indeed exhaustive - discussion by Godfrey of the sense in which general or legal justice can be said to be all virtue. Justice is the same as virtue, he argues,

17 Godefroy of Fontaines, *Quodlibet* VI.10, 182-218; X.6, 318-325. Cf. Thomas M. Osborne, *Love of Self and Love of God in Thirteenth-Century Ethics*. Notre Dame, University of Notre Dame Press, 2005.

18 James of Viterbio, *Quodlibet* II.20, 202-214.

19 Aristotle, *Nicomachean Ethics*, V.1 1129b26-1130a14, V.2 1130b5-1131a9, 454-457: "*iustitia virtus quidem est perfecta sed non simpliciter sed ad alterum… in iustitia autem simul omnis virtus est, et perfecta maxime virtus quoniam perfecte virtutis usus est… iustitia non pars virtutis sed tota virtus est*". Cf. Aquinas, *Sententia Libri Ethicorum,* V.2-4.

but it differs from it in essence; it is not a part of virtue but complete virtue. In the process, Godfrey analyses one last model for understanding how the common good can be the same as the individual good but also different, how it is made up of all individual goods but is also more than just their aggregate. Justice is general, Godfrey states, because, rather than have a substance or subject-matter which is peculiar to itself, it uses the actions of all the particular virtues; the goal of this justice is the good of the community and it orders all the actions of the other virtues towards this end. The common good of general justice is, Godfrey concludes, common by virtue and by aggregation because it is an integral whole which contains the good of every particular virtue. General justice, in short, is a single virtue in terms of its essence and its goal, but it is all the virtues, or all virtue, in terms of its substance or subject-matter.[20] Book V of the *Ethics* thereby provides Godfrey with the means of refuting the claim that greater love for the common good can only be understood as an act of grace, of Christian *caritas*, and not of natural human love. For Godfrey, to love another individual with reference to the common good should be classified as an act, not of friendship, but of general justice. Friendship, he explains, is a moral virtue which, strictly speaking, is limited to being exercised towards one or a few individuals. The act of loving the common good of a human community should accordingly be classified as an expression of the moral virtue of general justice. It may be an act of *caritas* when it is performed by a Christian but it can still be considered to lie within the natural capacity of all humans when it is treated as an act of general justice.[21]

In the course of his exchanges with Henry of Ghent and James of Viterbo, Godfrey of Fontaines sets out, in effect, no fewer than four broad theoretical frameworks within which the common good of the human community could be conceived and analysed by scholastic theologians. Each one of them was rooted in the exposition of a problematic passage in Aristotle and each one of them required a position to be taken in a particular debate which it prompted: (i) as the metaphysical order of goodness in Creation; (ii) as the material order of peace and security; (iii) as the good which is identical with the individual good and which includes it as a whole includes its part; and (iv) as the virtue of general justice which is the same

20 Godfrey of Fontaines, *Quodlibet* XIV.1, 303-317. Cf. John F. Wippel, "Godfrey of Fontaines' Quodlibet XIV on Justice as a General Virtue – Is it Really a Quodlibet?", in ed. Chris Schabel, *Theological Quodlibeta in the Middle Ages – the Thirteenth Century*, Leiden, E.J. Brill, 2006, 287-344.

21 Godfrey of Fontaines, *Quodlibet* XIII.1, 169-184; XIV.2, 320-338.

as, but also different from, all the individual virtues of which it is comprised. If nothing else, Godfrey's debates with Henry and with James suggest that, when it came to the ethical and political consequences of 'the common good', both the language of inclusivity and the analogy of part and whole were scrutinised in great detail and their applicability to human communities was considered not only with great care but also, and just as significantly, with no little disagreement. This conclusion therefore constitutes the second generalisation which might be made about the 'problem' of the common good. Where apparently 'corporatist' language is invoked, and the individual good is said to be included in the common good as a part within a whole, this is not done lightly. It reflects a sophisticated analysis of the way in which goodness operates communicatively in the universe and how this goodness is accordingly the object of both the human intellect and (in the form of the virtue of love as its characteristic expression) the human will. Where such 'corporatist' language is *not* invoked, or where its applicability is specifically denied, where the individual good is thought not to be included in the common good or where the part is said to have a closer unity and association, or a greater love, for itself than it does for the whole, then this, too, reflects a sophisticated analysis of the different types of good that the human community can represent or embody and the different types of love that should therefore govern an individual's relationship towards all things other than, and intermediary between, themselves and God.

Godfrey of Fontaines' detailed and wide-ranging analysis of the common good was precipitated by scholastic commentary on the meaning of certain key passages from newly-translated texts of natural philosophy by Aristotle, most notably the *Ethics* and the *Metaphysics*. It is always worth being reminded, however, that these Aristotelian texts often provided a helpful and convenient set of terms and distinctions for ideas and debates which, in other respects, *already* had a currency - and a history - and with which scholastic writers were themselves familiar. This principle certainly applies to the notion of the common good, and nowhere is it more pertinent than in the case of Augustine.

Augustine famously structured a large part of his argument in the *City of God* on an analysis of the significance - and consequences - of Cicero's definition of *res publica*. According to Cicero, a *res publica* is what pertains to the people, where 'people' is defined, not as every grouping of human beings, irrespective of the way in which they have been gathered together, but as a multitude whose association has been produced by a common sense of what is just (*iuris consensu*) and by shared utility (*utilitatis communione*).[22] Without justice, Augustine concluded, there can be no true *res publica* and, since true justice comes from Christ, the *res publica* of pagan Rome had been, in fact, no such thing; indeed, it deserved to be called nothing more than a particularly successful band of robbers.[23] In turning the authority of Cicero against the self-perception and self-description of pagan Rome, Augustine propagated a highly influential definition of political legitimacy. What is sometimes a little less readily appreciated from the *City of God* is that, when Augustine put forward a definition of *res publica* which *would* be applicable to pagan Rome, he dropped from Cicero's formulation not only the prescription of justice (*consensus iuris*) but also the insistence on a common good or shared utility (*communio utilitatis*). The *res publica*, Augustine states, is a multitude whose association is produced by a harmonious sharing in the objects of its love (*rerum quas diligit concordi communione sociatus*).[24] The reason Augustine did so was because of a very strict understanding of the verb *uti* - to use something as a means towards an end - and, by extension, of all its linguistic derivatives, *utilitas* included. Shared goods are thus defined as being 'used', as opposed to abused, *only* if they are directed towards the ultimate goal of fruition in God. Strictly speaking, therefore, there could be no shared 'utility' in a human community, no *communis utilitas*, if that association did not direct this 'common good' towards God.[25]

This, at least, is the theory and yet, in practice, it is clear that Augustine found it hard to restrict his own deployment of the phrase *communis utilitas* to such a correctly-ordered common good. Instead, the phrase *communis utilitas* became synonymous with the sort of shared benefit which, he argues, will always characterise the mixed communities of the elect and the damned

22 CICERO, *De Re Publica* I.39, ed. James ZETLZEL, Cambridge, CUP, 1995, 53: « *est igitur... res publica res populi, populus autem non omnis hominum coetus quoquo modo congregatus, sed coetus multitudinis iuris consensu et utilitatis communione sociatus* ».

23 AUGUSTINE, *De Civitate Dei* II.20-1, Bernard DOMBART and Alphons KALB (Eds) (*C.C.S.L.*, 47-48), 51-55, XIX.21 687-689. cf. Robert A. MARKUS, *Saeculum - Religion and Society in the Theology of Saint Augustine*, Cambridge, CUP, 1970.

24 AUGUSTINE, *De Civitate Dei*, XIX.24, 695-96.

25 Oliver O'DONOVAN, "Augustine's City of God XIX and Western Political Thought", *Dionysius* 11 (1987), 89-110. Cf. Marcia COLISH, *The Stoic Tradition from Antiquity to the Early Middle Ages*, 2 vols, Leiden, Brill, 1990, I 89-104, 126-158; II 142-238; Oliver O'DONOVAN, *The Problem of Self-Love in Augustine*, New Haven, Yale University Press, 1980; ID., "*Usus* and *fruitio* in Augustine *De Doctrina Christiana* I", in *Journal of Theological Studies* 33 (1982), 361-397.

that necessarily form the lot of *all* human associations, Christian as well as non-Christian, at least until the Day of Judgment. What Augustine's *City of God* bequeathed to the Middle Ages, in other words, and well before the introduction of a Latin translation of Aristotle's *Ethics*, was a conception of the common good which was susceptible to at least two interpretations: in its strictest sense, the common good represents the peace and harmony (*pax et concordia*) which can only be derived from a proper orientation towards God; in its looser sense, the common good represents what Augustine called 'the qualified agreement of wills' (*quaedam compositio voluntatum*), a compromise which represents the most that can be expected in a sinful world, not as a direct means towards a higher end, but simply as a remedy or barrier against the worst consequences of wicked human behaviour.

The sensitivity of medieval writers to this ambivalence in Augustine can be traced in a number of different authors from the ninth to the twelfth centuries.[26] Its particular significance for thirteenth-century scholastic writers is exemplified by Albertus Magnus when he maps it onto the distinction between *bonum honestum* and *bonum utile* with which he was already familiar from book III of Cicero's *De Officiis* but which he now found crystallised in Aristotle's *Ethics*.[27] Some human associations, Albertus argues, are based on utility *without* being ordered towards the life of virtue - these are communities whose laws are instituted in order to guarantee that there is no injustice rather than to ensure that people act through reason, where concord is defined simply as the absence of discord and contention rather than as agreement on the common good of virtue. Albertus ends up, in fact, conceding that true concord might not exist, in reality, within *any* human community, either because human beings tend to love one another more than they love a single, common goal, or because individuals tend to associate for the sake of a good which is simply pleasurable or useful, or because they tend to agree only on a good which is useful to the political community. As a result, it is only a qualified type of concord, the harmony which is produced by what Albertus terms 'political friendship', that can

26 See, for example, RUFINUS, *De Bono Pacis*, Roman DEUTINGER (Ed.), Hanover, Hahsche, 1997. Yves CONGAR, "Maître Rufin et son *De Bono Pacis*", in *Revue des Sciences Philosophiques et Theologiques* 41 (1957), 428-444, and, more generally, Matthew KEMPSHALL, "*De Republica* I.39 in Medieval and Renaissance Political Thought", in Jonathan POWELL and John NORTH (Eds), *Cicero's Republic*, London, University of London Press, 2001, 99-135.

27 See note 13.

serve to unite imperfect human communities. This sort of peace is defined simply as the absence, or the opposite, of sedition.[28]

As far as Albertus Magnus was concerned, in other words, concord and peace were terms which could be deployed, as Augustine had done, in either a strict or a loose sense: on the one hand, the common good of a perfect human community is the concord of correctly-ordered love between individuals which is directed towards the pursuit of virtue and happiness; on the other hand, the common good of an imperfect human community is the concord of political friendship which is ordered towards the material utility of peace and stability. Peace, likewise, can be given either a full or a limited definition: either it is the correctly-ordered love between human beings which directs them ultimately towards God or it is a lowest common denominator between good and wicked people. The peace which is defined simply as tranquillity, as the absence of conflict, is distinct from the peace which is defined as the correct relation of human beings towards one another and towards God. An exterior material framework within which individuals can then pursue their individual ends is a different conception of the common good from the ordering of human beings towards their true end of the life of virtue and eternal happiness.

Albertus Magnus' account of the different types of peace and concord within human associations accordingly provides a third general point which might be made about the scholastic understanding of the common good. A distinction between two types of common good, between *bonum commune* and *communis utilitas*, between moral virtue and material utility, is a distinction which was clarified and sharpened by the (re-)introduction of Aristotle's *Ethics*. Up to a point, this distinction can therefore serve as a broad rule of thumb with which to differentiate the perfectibilist teleology of the Aristotelian *polis* from the pragmatic and sombre realism of the Augustinian mixed community. This is true, however, only up to a point. Aristotle's *Ethics* may have tightened up the terminology, but its analysis effectively clarified an ambivalence that was already present in Augustine's *City of God*. The choice of *which* underlying definition of the common good to adopt remained as open to individual writers as it had been before – moral worth *or* security, the strict *or* the loose understanding of utility, true peace and concord *or* simply a minimal guarantee of order. It is the continuing availability of such a distinction to scholastic philosophers and theologians which is, in many respects, just as significant as the consequences of a particular writer opting for one definition over the other. Those consequences,

28 ALBERTUS MAGNUS, *Ethicorum Libri Decem*, VIII.1.1, 517-518. Cf. KEMPSHAL, *op.cit*, Ch. 1.

however, could certainly be considerable. As another Dominican, Remigio dei Girolami, and, indeed, his fellow Florentine Dante Alighieri both demonstrate,[29] when applied to the relationship between the ecclesiastical and the temporal powers, it was this distinction which allowed them to qualify what might otherwise seem to be the strictly logical consequences of a Neoplatonic hierarchy of ends: on the one hand, there is the common good of peace and material security which is the responsibility of political authority and, on the other, there is the common good of eternal beatitude which is the responsibility of the Church, but in the middle is the common good of moral virtue and the correctly-ordered love (or what Dante terms 'freedom') of the individual moral agent.[30]

Godfrey of Fontaines' analysis of the common good was conducted, in the main, as an extended debate with Henry of Ghent and James of Viterbo as colleagues within the faculty of theology at the university of Paris. What is such a striking feature about the arguments put forward by Godfrey, Henry and James, however, is the extent to which all three theologians also invoked a notion of the common good as the defining principle of a more practical political ideology which, in this respect, went well beyond the confines of the schools. Godfrey of Fontaines discussed the toleration of moneylending, for example, of unjust sentences of excommunication, of pluralism, absenteeism and the dismemberment of Louis IX's corpse, as issues which could all involve the common good outweighing considerations of an individual good.[31] In the course of the 1280 s and 1290 s, three questions in particular came to concentrate Godfrey's attention on the more concrete applications of the common good and, in each case, to broaden the range of authorities on which he based his argumentation, from Aristotle and Augustine to canon and Roman law. The first topic concerned the right to dispense from the law, a matter which had long been the subject of discussion by canon lawyers but which, in the 1280 s and 1290 s, came to focus on

29 Remigio de' Girolami, *De Bono Communi and De Bono Pacis*, Emilio Panella (Ed.), *Dal bene comune al bene del comune – i trattati politici di Remigio dei Girolami*, Florence, Nerbini, 2014; Dante, *Monarchia*, Trans. Prue Shaw, Cambridge, CUP, 1995.

30 Kempshall, *op.cit*, Chs. 11-12; Id., "Accidental Perfection: Ecclesiology and Political Thought in *Monarchia*", in Paolo Acquaviva and Jennifer Petrie (Eds), *Dante and the Church – Literary and Historical Essays*, Dublin, Four Courts Press, 2007, 127-171; Id., "The Utility of Peace in *Monarchia*", in John Barnes & Daragh O'Connel (Eds), *War and Peace in Dante – Essays Literary, Historical and Theological*, Dublin, Four Courts Press, 2015, 141-172.

31 Godfrey of Fontaines, *Quodlibet* I.11, 29-30; IV.11, 264-272; VIII.9, 86-98; XI.10, 51-53; XII.9, 114-117; XII.15, 129-132.

the right of the pope to dispense from conciliar decrees, and in particular from the decrees of the Fourth Lateran Council, after Martin IV declared in the bull *Ad fructus uberes* that the mendicant orders could receive confession from individuals that had not been made, or did not need to be repeated, to their parish priests or bishops. This was an issue on which Godfrey of Fontaines and Henry of Ghent, as secular masters, had very strong views, not least after the papacy made a concerted attempt to halt any further discussion of the subject by theologians at the university of Paris.[32] The second concrete issue was that of taxation and, once again, this raised a topic that had already been subject to legal commentary, although this time in Roman as well as canon law, namely an individual's right to property and, in particular, the right of both ecclesiastical and temporal powers to claim and dispose of the temporal property of their churches and their individual Christian (and indeed non-Christian) subjects.[33] Thirdly, and as the political and ecclesiastical crises of the 1290 s caused by Philip IV's wars in Flanders and Aquitaine and his bitter disputes with Boniface VIII gained an increasingly urgent public and polemical significance, the issues of both dispensation and taxation became subsumed within a much broader discussion of the precise means by which rulers of both ecclesiastical and political communities should be held accountable for their governance.[34]

The point to make here - and this is the fourth and final observation which might be made about the scholastic notion of the common good - is that, on all three of these practical political issues, there is a marked and substantive measure of agreement between Godfrey of Fontaines, Henry of

32 Yves Congar, « Aspects ecclésiologiques de la querelle entre mendiants et séculiers dans la seconde moitié du XIIIe siècle et le début du XIVe », in *Archives d'Histoire Doctrinale et Littéraire du Moyen Age* 28 (1961), 35-151; Palémon Glorieux, « Prélats français contre religieux mendiants. Autour de la bulle *Ad fructus uberes* 1281-90 », in *Revue d'Histoire de l'Église de France* 11 (1925), 309-331, 471-495; Jürgen Miethke, "Die Rolle der Bettelorden im Umbruch der politischen Theorie an der Wende zum 14. Jahrhundert" in Kaspar Elm (Ed.), *Stellung und Wirksamkeit der Bettelorden in der städtischen Gesellschaft*, Berlin, Duncker und Humblot, 1981, 119-153.

33 Joseph R. Strayer, "Consent to Taxation under Philip the Fair", in Joseph R. Strayer, Charles. H. Taylor, *Studies in Early French Taxation*, Cambridge, Harvard University Press, 1939, 3-105; ID., "Defense of the Realm and Royal Power in France", in ID., *Medieval Statecraft and the Perspectives of History*, Princeton, Princeton University Press, 1971, Ch. 18; Elisabeth Brown, "Taxation and Morality in the Thirteenth and Fourteenth Centuries - Conscience and Political Power and the Kings of France", in *French Historical Studies* 8 (1973), 1-28.

34 Georges Digard, *Philippe le Bel et le Saint-Siège de 1285 à 1304,* Paris, Librairie du Recueil Sirey, 1936; Joseph R. Strayer, *The Reign of Philip the Fair*, Princeton, PUP, 1980.

Ghent and James of Viterbo. These theologians may have disagreed with one another, and disagreed quite profoundly, in their conceptual understanding of the relationship between the individual good and the common good, but when it came to the way in which the common good could, and should, be used as the litmus test of legitimacy for all government, temporal as well as ecclesiastical, they argued more or less as one. All three theologians were agreed, for example, that laws are, by definition, instituted for the sake of the common good and, as a result, any act of dispensation must always secure the same goal; otherwise, the decree is not valid.[35] Godfrey of Fontaines sets out the consequences of this principle with particular clarity. Indeed, what is notable about Godfrey's position is the way in which he drew on a knowledge of canon and especially Roman law in order to spell out its practical implications for making popes and kings accountable for their stewardship of the goods that were at their disposal. Strictly speaking, Godfrey argues, ecclesiastical property belongs to the church as a whole, whereas temporal property belongs to individual subjects, but, in each case, those people who have been charged with governing the community have to ensure that this property is used for the benefit or good of that community.[36] What is striking here is the way in which Godfrey took the legal language of common necessity and common benefit and combined it with the political language he had found in Aristotle's *Politics* and in particular the discussion in book III of whether it is better to be governed by good laws or by a good ruler.[37] Godfrey accordingly argued that it was not enough for rulers, be they popes or kings, merely to *claim* the presence of urgent or pressing necessity (*magna et evidens necessitas*) in order to justify extraordinary actions such as acts of legal dispensation or exceptional levies of taxation, or merely to *appeal* to a clear or evident utility in order to legitimise their commands. Instead, these rulers needed to *prove* that this was the case.[38]

To be, not a lord (*dominus*), but a protector or steward of the community (the term Godfrey uses is *procurator*), to dispense common goods correctly

35 Eg. GODFREY OF FONTAINES, *Quodlibet* IV.11, 264-272; X.17, 391-394; HENRY OF GHENT, *Quodlibet* II.17, 111-116; VII.24, 167-232; XII.31, 3-268; JAMES OF VITERBIO, *Quodlibet* I.17, 207-215; II.21, 215-223; III.19, 243-247. Cf. KEMPSHALL, *The Common Good*, Chs. 7, 9.

36 GODFREY OF FONTAINES, *Quodlibet* VII.14, 395-396; XII.3, 93-95; XII.19, 147; XIII.5, 222-229.

37 *Aristotelis Politicorum Libri Octo cum vetusta translatione Gulielmi de Moerbeka*, ed. Franciscus SUSEMIHL, Leipzig, 1872, III.15-17 1286a7-1288a29, 220-36. Cf. PETER OF AUVERGNE, *Quaestiones super libros Politicos*, ed. Christoph FLÜELER.

38 GODFREY OF FONTAINES, *Quodlibet* XI.17, pp. 76-78.

or to ensure that individual goods are used properly, is a function and an office which requires both transparency and scrutiny. The way in which this occurs, according to Godfrey, takes one of three forms: a ruler can legitimately impose a burden on his subjects either through the consent of the whole community, or through a law instituted by wise persons and in accordance with reason and prudence, or through the counsel of wise, just and prudent individuals (individuals, Godfrey adds, who are not foreigners or aliens, who are natives of the ruler's country but who, by the same token, are also not members of the ruler's household or his close associates). Consent, good laws and wise counsel are thus all means to the same end, namely to guarantee that the common good remains the only legitimate goal for those placed in authority over others. Failure to provide such proof, or due process for this proof, gave a ruler's exactions the legal status of pillage or plunder (*rapina*) and, as such, required immediate legal restitution. Such failure also gave a ruler's expropriated subjects at least a theoretical right, not just to reprove and correct, but also to disobey. Godfrey's two qualifications to the latter are, first, if the subjects are able to do so (*si possent*), a capacity on which he does not, unfortunately, elaborate, and, second, that the issue must first be discussed by 'prudent men', a category for which he clearly has in mind bodies such as the college of cardinals, a council of the whole church, or the assemblies of nobles, clergy, townsmen and university doctors that were such a feature of Philip IV's rule in the late 1290s and early 1300s. Once this second proviso has been met, Godfrey's position is clear. Obedience is conditional upon the common good. A ruler only rules, he writes, by virtue of the whole community, and this should be understood in the sense that the ruler's goal must always be to secure the common good of that community. To argue otherwise, Godfrey warns, is advocate cowardice, to condone the rule of tyrants and to transform free subjects into slaves.[39]

Godfrey of Fontaines, Henry of Ghent and James of Viterbo, in sum, may have disagreed on the precise theoretical relationship between the common good and the individual good in human associations, in part because of the range of different definitions and different models that were available to them from their different interpretations of Aristotle. When it came to the practical political applications of the idea of that common good, however, they developed a consistent idea of legitimation which, in the hands of Godfrey in particular, entailed a more and more explicit analysis of the centrality of consent, counsel and accountability in governance.

39 Godfrey of Fontaines, *Quodlibet* XI.17, pp. 76.

By obliging rulers to *prove* that any exceptional actions on their part were indeed justified by clear benefit to the community or by the common good, Godfrey put forward a justification of the role of counsel and consent which had profound consequences for both temporal and ecclesiastical rulers - in this respect, at least, the pope was no different in his relationship to the Church than a bishop was to his cathedral chapter, or indeed a king in his relationship to the community of the realm.[40]

So where, finally, does a synecdochal approach to Godfrey of Fontaines leave a specifically 'scholastic' understanding of the notion of the common good and the language in which this analysis was conducted? In theoretical terms, it suggests, perhaps self-evidently, that, at the most fundamental level, medieval writers possessed a series of different models, a range of conceptual paradigms, to which they could appeal. Choosing between these alternatives presupposed adopting a particular position on a number of further issues which were, in turn, open to disagreement and debate and from which they were inseparable - the priority of natural self-love within the *ordo caritatis*, for example, or the relationship between general justice and particular justice within the human community. At the heart of a writer's decision to invoke one model rather than another lay a choice between regarding the political community as the articulation of a higher ideal of goodness or accepting it as a more limited framework of at least relative peace and security. Even then, however, when it came to more concrete issues of taxation and obedience, writers could still find themselves disagreeing on the metaphysics of goodness but finding common ground in their politics. Ultimately, a scholastic understanding of the notion of the common good demanded - and received - sensitivity to the precise situational context in which the language of the common good was actually being invoked or deployed. To draw such a conclusion is not to equate the instrumental use of language with the malleability of a waxen nose.[41] What it does suggest, however, is that the traditional plate-tectonics of 'corporatism' and 'individualism', of 'hierocracy' and 'secularisation', or of 'Augustinianism' and 'Aristotelianism', might need to be modified, if not replaced, with a rather more subtle appreciation of the care and sophistication with which medieval writers could themselves identify and delineate the problem presented by 'the common good'.

40 Cf. JOHN OF PARIS, *De Potestate Regia et Papali* , VI-VII, XXIV-V, ed. Jean LECLERCQ, *Jean de Paris et l'ecclésiologie du XIIIe siècle,* Paris, Vrin, 1942, pp. 185-190, 254-259.

41 ALAN OF LILLE, *De Fide Catholica Contra Haereticos*, in *P.L.*, CCX, cols. 305-422, col. 333.

Mary M. Keys

Politics Pointing beyond the Polis and the Politeia: Aquinas on Natural Law and the Common Good

Contemporary political theory, faced with problems flowing from the individualism encouraged by large-scale republics and modern liberal democratic forms, has increasingly seen the need to combine its commitment to rights with deeper reflection on shared goods, responsibilities, and virtues. Within this context, Aquinas's theory of common good (*bonum commune*) has received increasing attention, not from antiquarian interests but with a view to enriching the resources currently available for political theory and civic practice.

This essay contributes to this project by offering a précis of the book *Aquinas, Aristotle, and the Promise of the Common Good.*[1] The idea for the book began with an interest in Aquinas's way of relating the personal good of individual human beings with the common good of their societies, and with a conviction that in Aquinas's theory moral virtue formed the chief nexus between the two. While the project began by considering the role of human or civil law in the task of education in virtue, civic and also moral, upon reflection on the differences between Aquinas's and Aristotle's accounts of the virtue of magnanimity, it expanded to include the import and implications of Aquinas's theory of natural law as it relates to ethics, politics, and common goods.

As work on the book progressed a strong undercurrent developed in its narrative and argument: that regardless of their religious beliefs of lack thereof, political theorists today ought to take Aquinas and his theories of virtue and natural law seriously and be open to the possibility that they may contain much that is true. Here there are serious obstacles to be overcome. First among these is the common conviction among political theorists that faith and reason are at loggerheads; that instead of *fides et ratio* we can have only faith *v.* reason. On this model, one must choose between a life of piety and faith and a life of full-fledged philosophic inquiry. Natural law, or at

1 See Mary KEYS, *Aquinas, Aristotle, and the Promise of the Common Good.* Cambridge: Cambridge University Press, 2006. An earlier version of this essay appeared in Holger ZABOROWSKI (Ed.), *Natural Moral Law in Contemporary Society*. Washington: The Catholic University of America Press, 2010, 170-194.

least Aquinas's formulation of it, is in consequence rejected as an illegitimate attempt to bridge the unbridgeable gap between faith and philosophy. A corollary opinion considers that most Christian thinkers in medieval times are philosophically inferior to their ancient mentors and perhaps also to their modern counterparts. Finally and more narrowly, there is the monolithic and inadequate understanding of the medieval "commentary" genre as an exclusively interpretive enterprise, attempting to get at the original intent and *only* the original intent of the writers such as Aristotle whose works are commented upon. This in turn yields a broadly shared impression that Aquinas and his confreres took a doctrinaire approach to Aristotle, revered as "The Philosopher"—a sort of *ipse dixit* attitude that kills dialectical inquiry and deadens the life of the mind.

This book and more briefly this essay argue that Aquinas's works are important for political theorists to engage on the closely interrelated topics of virtue, law, and the common good; and that it does not suffice to read Aristotle, Aquinas's chief philosophic mentor, on these themes. Aquinas's thought and his account of natural law are valuable for political theorists in view of the needs in current national and international affairs as well as in contemporary academia and political philosophy. Aquinas's work is especially significant for its openness to discovering and living out truth via both faith and reason, and to the cosmopolitan, transcendent, religious, and political dimensions of human life. Aquinas offers a robust theory of the foundations of political life, a theory that points beyond the *polis* and the *politeia*, beyond the singular political community and its form of government or "regime." Aquinas does not merely repeat or unconditionally accept Aristotle's judgments in practical philosophy and in other matters knowable through the inquiry of human reason; nor alternatively is Aquinas original in places only by muddling or oversimplifying Aristotle's pristine philosophic reason, chiefly by inappropriate importations from Divine Revelation.

The thesis of this essay is twofold: first, that Aquinas knowingly develops and in some respects deviates from Aristotle's theories of natural right and ethical virtue, and that he sees natural law as revealing important truths about *political* action and *political* virtue, not least that the common goods that they seek point beyond the *polis* and the *politeia*; and second, that Aquinas's accounts of certain ethical virtues are in consequence more capacious and indeed more fully human than Aristotle's corresponding accounts. The argument has three parts, the first treating Aquinas's commentary on Aristotle's account of natural right in the *Nicomachean Ethics*; the second on Aquinas's response by way of natural law to problems in Aristotle's regime-relative political science and account of political virtue as developed especially in Book III of the *Politics*; and the third, an illustration of the first two parts of the argument with an explication of Aquinas's revision of Aristotle's virtue of magnanimity, by paradoxically positing humility as its "twin virtue" (*duplex virtus*) rooted in natural law and conducing to both personal and common goods.

I. Natural Right and Natural Law: Aquinas's "Tendentious Glosses" on Nicomachean Ethics V.7[2]

In *Thomism and Aristotelianism* Harry Jaffa argues a position contrary to the argument of this essay.[3] On Jaffa's reading, Aquinas clearly imputes to Aristotle his own understanding of the inclination to moral goodness or virtue, and his corresponding account of indemonstrable first principles of practical reason and precepts of natural law. Aquinas does this, moreover, because he gets the *Nicomachean Ethics'* chapter on natural right wrong: he reads Aristotle in Patristic. Jaffa's assessment of Aquinas recalls Rousseau's famous critique of earlier enlightenment thinkers, who thought they depicted natural man but painted civil man instead.[4] Like Hobbes, Locke, and others who according to Rousseau did not go far enough to reach the true account of nature and the natural man they were seeking—who were too conditioned by social conventions and insufficiently radical in their thought for the task at hand—so Aquinas wanted to uncover pure philosophic wisdom through the original meaning of Aristotle's texts, but in the end read them through a distorting lens fashioned by his Christian faith and the late classical and patristic traditions.[5] Aquinas sought natural or pagan ethics, but painted Christian ethics instead. And Christian ethics, Jaffa rightly stresses, is in crucial respects quite different. As Jean-Pierre Torrell expresses it, to identify Thomistic and Aristotelian ethics "is to forget that

2 The phrase "tendentious glosses" is borrowed from John I. JENKINS, "Expositions of the Text: Aquinas's Aristotelian Commentaries", in *Medieval Philosophy and Theology* 5/1 (1996), 39-62.

3 Harry JAFFA, *Thomism and Aristotelianism: A Study of the "Commentary" by Thomas Aquinas on the "Nicomachean Ethics"*. Chicago: University of Chicago Press, 1952, 167-188.

4 Jean-Jacques ROUSSEAU, *The Discourses and Other Early Political Writings*, ed. Victor GOUREVITCH. Cambridge: Cambridge University Press, 1997, Exordium [5].

5 Cf. Leo STRAUSS, *Natural Right and History*. Chicago: University of Chicago Press, 1953, 157-158.

between their two moralities lies the entire difference added by the Gospel."[6]

This essay cannot address here all the nuanced points of interpretation and critique made by Jaffa in his concluding chapter on "Natural Right and Natural Law." Instead, it must suffice to summarize three of Jaffa's most important arguments concerning Aquinas's *Commentary on "NE"* V.7, the famous and notoriously difficult chapter on the natural and the legal right or just, as two distinct parts of political justice. This essay will then offer three objections to Jaffa's conclusions, in support of the contention that in developing his theory of natural law Aquinas is consciously laying new, deeper and broader foundations for ethics and political science.

Jaffa begins his chapter by summarizing Aquinas's account of natural law in the *Summa Theologiae* [*ST*]. He then argues that in the *Commentary on the Nicomachean Ethics* [*Comm. NE*], Aquinas writes this same natural law teaching into his interpretation of Aristotle's quite different account of natural right. On account of Aquinas's glossing Aristotle's natural right theory with shades of natural law and also because of Aquinas's failure to criticize Aristotle explicitly concerning what philosophic reason can know about human actions and ethics, Jaffa concludes that "it is only reasonable to assume that Thomas understands his own natural law doctrine to be identical, in principle, with the moral doctrine of Aristotle."[7] Jaffa points out several passages in *Comm. NE* where Aquinas offers what John I. Jenkins (1996) aptly terms "tendentious glosses" on Aristotle's text. The first group of these remarks, Jaffa argues, wrongly imputes to Aristotle's natural right teaching Aquinas's own theory of a natural inclination to moral virtue, hence to practically reasonable action in accord with a law written by nature on the mind. By contrast, Aristotle's natural right regards objective states of affairs or moral facts, not moral psychology or moral agency.[8]

A second salient objection that Jaffa makes is to Aquinas's explicit mention, in his exposition of natural right, of the naturally known, indemonstrable principles of practical reason, which Aquinas also elaborates in the *ST* as the foundation of natural law. Jaffa concludes from this anomaly that "Thomas apparently takes Aristotle's statement, to the effect that what is naturally right or just does not depend on opinion, as an outright endorse-

6 Jean-Pierre TORRELL, *Saint Thomas Aquinas: The Person and His Work*. Washington, D.C.: The Catholic University of America Press, 1996, 228; cf. Servais PINCKAERS, *Sources of Christian Ethics*. Washington, D.C.: Catholic University of America Press, 1995, 188-189.

7 JAFFA, *op.cit*, 168.

8 Ibid., 169-171, 174.

ment of his own doctrine that there is a natural habit of the understanding [*synderesis*], by which *we know* what is, in principle, right and wrong according to nature."[9] Third and last for the discussion here, Jaffa writes that Aquinas, without foundation in Aristotle's text, qualifies the Philosopher's unequivocal statements that natural right is entirely changeable, as malleable (or in Aquinas's Latin text of the *Politics*, similarly malleable) as legal or positive right. Again, Aquinas does so along the lines of his own natural law teaching: there are first principles of natural right that are unchangeable, because the essence of our human nature is unchangeable. While these hold always and everywhere, there are also secondary principles or more specific conclusions from the first principles that fail to hold in a few cases, due to the mutability of concrete human actions and circumstances. Again, Jaffa claims, this is a clear misreading of Aristotle's text, attributable ultimately to Aquinas's faith in Divine Revelation and his Catholic theological presuppositions.[10]

Jaffa is right to find important elements of Aquinas's theory of natural law in the *Commentary on "NE"* V.7, on natural and legal right. He is further correct to note that readers of the *Comm. NE* can take away an erroneous understanding of key aspects of Aristotle's ethical thought, *if* they read all of Aquinas's glosses as endeavoring to clarify precisely what Aristotle meant, and only what Aristotle meant; *and if* they further assume that Aquinas, as such an influential and careful commentator, always (or virtually always) got Aristotle right. Jaffa's point of departure is the keen concern that many mid-twentieth century readers of Aquinas's works—some of the only scholars who at that time took the contemporary relevance of classical political philosophy seriously—did in fact hold all these assumptions. He wishes in *Thomism and Aristotelianism* to complicate the picture especially with regard to the second premise, that Aquinas's commentaries are wholly accurate, or at least the best available accounts of Aristotle's literal, intentional meaning. Jaffa thereby seeks to clear a path to a fresh examination of Aristotle's texts and of alternative commentary traditions, to reinvigorate a genuinely Aristotelian ethics and social science for contemporary life.[11]

There are, however, problems with Jaffa's overall reading of Aquinas's texts and appraisal Aquinas's intention. Jaffa's approach is too one-dimensional, perhaps inspired by a generous desire to give Aquinas the benefit of the doubt in this regard: so devoted a student of the Philosopher could not

9 Ibid., 175 (emphasis in original).

10 Ibid., 179-193.

11 Ibid., 4-7.

have intentionally distorted Aristotle's teaching, virtually the embodiment of natural reason regarding ethics, in his *Commentary on the "NE"*. It would therefore seem most probable that Aquinas did so unconsciously, so immersed was he in his task as a theologian that he could not help understanding Aristotle's words in a deeply Christian sense.[12] Contrary to this assumption, however, there are clear textual indicators that in the *Comm. NE* Aquinas consciously goes beyond Aristotle's intentional meaning in his explication of natural right, and that he is fully aware that his account of natural law differs in important respects from Aristotle's foundational understanding of natural right.

First, Jaffa describes the question on natural law in the *Summa Theologiae* (*ST* I-II 94) without noting that Aristotle's *NE* is nowhere cited where it should be—indeed, it is almost not cited at all—if it were a major source of Aquinas's account of the naturally known first practical principles and the accompanying inclinations to moral virtue and religion. Likewise Aquinas makes no mention of Aristotle or the *Nicomachean Ethics* in the earlier article *ST* I-II 91, 2, where Aquinas first inquires into the existence and nature of natural law. This is odd, given that Aquinas in his article on the precepts of natural law explicitly cites Aristotle's *Metaphysics* on the existence of indemonstrable first principles of speculative reason.[13] Why would Aquinas not also call readers' attention to the *Nicomachean Ethics* with equal directness on the matter of first practical principles, especially given that this article is a key part of the section of the *Summa Theologiae* on the moral life and the virtues? It is even odder since, as Jaffa rightly observes, these crucial elements of Aquinas's argument in *ST* I-II 94, 2 are also part of the elaboration of Aristotle's natural right in Aquinas's *Commentary* on *NE* V.7. These seem salient facts for ascertaining Aquinas's intention and appraisal of his own theory in relation to Aristotle's.

In his summation of Aquinas's *Summa Theologiae*, Jaffa fails to call attention to the one citation of the *Nicomachean Ethics* in the question on natural law. In a subsequent article of question 94 (*ST* I-II 94, 4), Aquinas explicitly refers to Aristotle's text on "the naturally just" and incorporates it in to his dialectical inquiry regarding natural law. He does so, however, primarily in the context of an "objection." This *argumentum* and Aquinas's reply merit attention, and will elucidate some important features of Aquinas's *Comm. NE* that Jaffa does not discuss. Aquinas's question here is "[w]hether the

12 See Ibid., 168, 188.

13 See AQUINAS, *Summa theologiae*, trans. Fathers of the English Dominican Province. Allen, TX: Christian Classics, [1911, 1920] 1981), I-II 94, 2.

natural law is the same in all human beings?" The second objection he raises to affirming this proposition runs as follows: "Further, 'Things which are according to the law are said to be just,' as stated in *NE* V. But *it is also stated in the same book that nothing is so universally just as not to be subject to change in regard to some men*. Therefore even the natural law is not the same in all men" (emphasis added). To this Aquinas replies: "This saying of the Philosopher is to be understood of things that are naturally just, not as general principles, but as conclusions drawn from them, having rectitude in the majority of cases, but failing in a few."[14]

Two features of these passages seem especially important: First, in formulating this objection (*argumentum*), Aquinas, as it were, "cuts and pastes" together two different comments from the *NE,* on the legal just and the natural just, respectively. But in his *Comm. NE* V.7, Aquinas consistently and faithfully reflects Aristotle's own separation of *nomos* from *physis*, of law or convention from nature. Even when he incorporates elements of his understanding of natural law into this *Commentary*, Aquinas never once uses the precise term "natural law." This is another strong indicator that Aquinas is aware of and indirectly acknowledges the absence of a full-fledged natural *law* theory in Aristotle's *NE*, as indeed in classical Greek thought generally.

Second, it is critical to note how Aquinas introduces his reply to Aristotle's trenchant "objection" based on the mutability of natural right. He does not say, "what the Philosopher means is" or "the correct literal interpretation of Aristotle's words is…." Rather, in a deliberately ambiguous and open way Aquinas writes, "*The saying* of the Philosopher *is to be understood…*" (emphasis added). He does not, as he often elsewhere does, point to any other passage of the *NE* or another work where Aristotle actually says what Aquinas will say in elaboration or clarification. One can paraphrase Aquinas's reply thus: "The words of the Philosopher are true if understood in this way, and so we should understand them thus."[15] Turning to the text of the *Comm. NE*, one finds Aquinas almost always using similar formulae when he goes beyond Aristotle's express statements or likely literal meaning, glossing passages in terms of his own understanding of the deepest truth, of the fuller reality they signify in his own estimation. He does not try to pass off his theory as Aristotle's, but neither is he only expounding the Philosopher's express understanding with every elaboration in the *Commentary*. Here are some examples of Aquinas's introductory clues, from some of the passages Jaffa finds most objectionable: *Est autem con-*

14 Aquinas, *ST* I-II 94, 4, obj. 2 and ad 2.

15 Cf. Jenkins, "Expositions of the Text: Aquinas's Aristotelian Commentaries", 39-62.

siderandum, quod iustum naturale est ad quod hominem natura inclinat: "It is to be considered, however, that the natural just is that to which nature inclines man" according to a "twofold nature": material and sensible, in common with the other animals and specifically rational.[16] *Est tamen attendendum quod quia rationes etiam mutabilium sunt imutabiles…*: "It is nevertheless to be noted that, since the essences of mutable things are immutable," the primary principles of natural justice are likewise unalterable.[17] *Est autem hic considerandum, quod iustum legale sive positivum oritur semper a naturali, ut Tullius dicit in sua rhetorica*: "However, it is to be considered here that the legal or positive just is always derived from the natural [just], as Cicero says in his *Rhetoric*."[18] Even when Aquinas follows a direct paraphrase of Aristotle with a specifically Thomistic gloss and no similar preface, he almost always refrains from saying what he often says elsewhere: "Aristotle manifests"; "Aristotle proves"; "Aristotle shows us his intention"; "here the Philosopher raises (or resolves) a doubt."[19]

This evidence indicates that Aquinas's *Commentaries* are intended not only to clarify the Philosopher's literal meaning and reveal the richness of his thought, but also at times to correct, supplement, or point beyond Aristotle's exact account. In Aristotle's own spirit, Aquinas attempts to "save the appearances" whenever possible and credit all he considers true in the Philosopher's sayings—as he does regularly with his other interlocutors as well—even while showing what more he thinks needs to be said or what should be differently understood. In this instance, Aquinas takes the truth

16 AQUINAS, *Commentary on Aristotle's "Nicomachean Ethics"* (Comm. NE), trans. C. I. Litzinger. Notre Dame: Dumb Ox Books, 1993. V, 12 n. 1019; cf. ID, *ST* I-II 94, 2.

17 AQUINAS, *Comm. NE* V, 12 n. 1029; cf. ID, *ST* I-II 94, 4-5.

18 AQUINAS, *Comm. NE* V, 12 n. 1023; cf. ID, *ST* I-II 91, 3 and 95, 2.

19 One subsequent formulation of Aquinas in this context was noted after the publication of Keys (2006) that seems more problematic for the argument stated here. In *ST* I-II 95, 2 Aquinas inquires "*whether every human law is derived from natural law.*" Three "objections" to this derivation come from Aristotle's *Ethics* V.7, while the *sed contra* arguing in its favor is taken instead from Cicero, as one might have expected along the lines of this essay's argument and the texts cited above. In response to objection 1, however, Aquinas replies to Aristotle's statement that "*the legal just is that which originally was a matter of indifference*" (which the natural law most definitely is not) as follows: "*the Philosopher is speaking (philosophus loquitur) of those enactments which are by way of determination or specification of the precepts of the natural law*" (AQUINAS, *ST* I-II 95, 2, ad 1; emphasis added). Due to constraints of time, this essay can for now only note the existence of this complication, which might be resolved along the lines of Jenkins's argument and the interpretative argument here, but which also is more difficult thus to reconcile than the other relevant passages here quoted and discussed.

of natural right to comprise also and especially its interrelation with natural law. Parts of Aristotle's account must be jettisoned or reinterpreted in order to incorporate this insight. Aquinas indicates some of them in the *Commentary*, while reserving the full account he has to offer and even the non-Aristotelian term "natural law" for his *Summa Theologiae*. The fact that Aquinas rarely takes open issue with Aristotle does not indicate that Aristotle's authority always in his view holds, even on the terrain of natural or philosophic reason. Aquinas's commentaries are living works of dialectical inquiry, not simply historical studies.[20]

II. Natural Law and the Problem of Regime-Relative Political Virtue

In his *Commentary on the "Politics"* [*Comm. Pol.*], Aquinas follows with care Aristotle's investigation in the opening chapters of *Politics* III into the meaning of "citizen" and the excellence proper to citizens. Across the most varied regimes, that person is a citizen who shares in or is eligible to share in deliberation and decision-making in the city. The citizen is thus one who either has or can have an active role in running the regime, administering its justice, and helping to guide policy with a view to its welfare. Aquinas repeatedly stresses that according to Aristotle, political- or citizen-virtue is properly defined *relative to the regime*. Just as a ship's diverse crew members all act well by contributing to its preservation and safe voyage to port, so a city's diverse citizens all contribute to the regime's persistence and well-being, though in different ways and according to various functions. Their common excellence or virtue as citizens is always a function of the regime governing their polis, just as the decision as to who is or is not offered citizenship in a city depends on the nature of its current regime. A person qualifying for citizenship in democratic Athens, for instance, might well fail to meet Sparta's property qualification for citizen-sharing in the regime.

Aquinas's comments further highlight the regime's role as the "form" of the city, in a sense analogous to Aristotle's and Aquinas's teaching on the soul as the form of the human body (the example is this essay's, not Aquinas's). The regime crafts the city's specific identity and holds it

20 For a fuller discussion of Aquinas's relation to Aristotle in matters philosophical, see Mary KEYS *Aquinas, Aristotle, and the Promise of the Common Good*, especially 70-74. This section of this essay is in general much indebted to Jenkins's "Expositions of the Text: Aquinas's Aristotelian Commentaries", which helped to assess more comprehensively some perplexing features that were noted and partially addressed in Aquinas's *Commentaries* on Aristotle's *Ethics* and *Politics*.

together: it is its principle of both unity and common action, the glue, as it were, that holds the association of citizens together in common life. When the regime changes the city is in the most significant sense "other" than it was, despite the fact that the city's territory and population may be virtually the same as they had been previously.[21]

One strength of Aquinas's *Commentary* is the way it elucidates the tension latent in the first five chapters of Aristotle's *Politics* III between citizenship as defined by law or *nomos* (civic status issued by and exercised with a view to the regime in power—*de facto* or realist citizenship, as it might be called today), and citizenship as it should be by nature or *physis*, according to the chief needs of any city and with a view to achieving its fullest common good (natural or *de jure* citizenship, as it might be called, in the sense of *jus naturale* or natural right).

Both definitions are in some sense a product of what polities all have in common.[22] In the first case, each city has some regime in place, the right to participate in the activity and administration of which captures the core meaning of citizenship. In the second case, all political societies are in need of governance from persons possessing *phronēsis* or *prudentia*, practical wisdom with a view to the preservation of the common life and the community's flourishing amidst changing and often difficult circumstances. On the first count, citizenship is defined by the regime's permission to participate, normally expressed in a general legislative code concerning citizenship requirements and regulating the filling and administration of offices. On the second count, the citizen is defined pointedly by Aristotle as one *who knows* (cf. *Pol.* III.4; *Comm. Pol.* III, 3 n. 375 [12]),[23] the person who possesses the political wisdom required both to carry out well the many tasks involved in public office and to be ruled well in turn. It is a strong perennial possibility, to say the very least, that these two "groups"—the citizens according to nature and the citizens according to law—may not be the identical.

21 See AQUINAS, Aquinas, Thomas. *Commentary on Aristotle's 'Politics'* (*Comm. Pol.*). Selections from *Comm. Pol.* I and III, trans. Ernest L. Fortin and Peter D. O'Neill. In *Medieval Political Philosophy*, edited by Ralph LERNER and Mushin MAHDI. Ithaca, NY: Cornell University Press, 1962, 2 n. 364 [8].

22 For reflections in contemporary context on natural law and "what political communities have in common" see Ralph MCINERNY, "What Do Communities Have in Common?" in Sander GRIFFIOEN (Ed.) *What Right Does Ethics have? Public Philosophy in a Pluralistic Culture.* Amsterdam: VU University Press, 1990, 47-59.

23 Cf. ARISTOTLE, *The Politics* (*Pol.*), trans. Carnes Lord. Chicago: University of Chicago Press, 1984, III.4; AQUINAS, *Comm. Pol.* III, 3 n. 375 [12]).

Part of the subtle irony inherent in Aristotle's account of citizenship is conveyed in the *Comm. Pol.* through Aquinas's glosses on the rightful, as it were, *natural* claims to citizenship versus the claims defined by positive law. Most people think "natural" or simply just citizenship is defined primarily by birth: birth on this city's soil; birth to citizen parents; birth into a family of this socio-economic class. Aquinas follows Aristotle in appearing at first to cater to these parochial or even prejudiced views of who counts as a "good citizen," a "real citizen," or "genuine citizen," even while challenging their foundational premises on a deeper level. Birth-based definitions cannot in any way apply to a city's founder or founders, or to its first generation of citizens; yet these people more than any ought to be considered full-fledged citizens for instituting their city and establishing and launching its regime. The most serious truth underlying the often comical common opinion on citizenship concerns the *natural* social and civic need for prudence and the other virtues; the need in other words not just for politically or legally rightful participation as defined by the regime, but also and especially for *wise* participation in governance and judging based on the very nature of political society and its normative *telos*, the common good.[24] In this deeper sense the best model of citizenship and civic virtue is not any ordinary citizen, however respectable or even conscientious and honorable he or she may be. As Aquinas's helpful gloss on Aristotle's text reveals, the *citizen* par excellence is rather the outstanding *statesman*.[25]

With regard to the chief question of *Politics* III, chapter 4, whether the virtue of the good citizen and the good human being are the same or not, or whether the good citizen is ipso facto a good person, and vice-versa, there comes to the fore the distinction between ruling and being ruled, between statesmen and ordinary citizens. In regimes that do not promote full ethical virtue or seek the common good of all citizens (such as democracy as defined by Aristotle, oligarchy, and of course tyranny) there is never

24 Another important truth embedded or implicit in such opinions about citizenship and birth is that good statesmen must have genuine affection or love for their people and polity, and that cities need friendship above all else. Birth is one way of improving likelihood of "familiarity" which often—but clearly not always—"breeds affection" in citizens, both among themselves and for their city as a whole and its officials, as well as in rulers for their people. Knowledge without love will not secure the common good or even motivate its attempt, especially in the face of difficulty and danger. Aristotle has emphasized this already in *Politics* II.5; Aquinas also does so in *ST* I-II 105, 3, referring the reader back to *Politics* III. The currently typical legal language of "naturalization" of immigrants merits reflection in this context.

25 Aquinas, *Comm. Pol.* III, 4 n. 383 [7].

a direct correlation between human and civic virtue. Among other regimes it seems that only the best regime, a perfect aristocracy, can unite civic virtue and complete human virtue in those citizens who have the practical wisdom it takes to rule and be ruled well. Writes Aquinas, "…in a certain city, namely that of the best, in which the ruling offices are granted according to the virtue which is that of the good man, the good man and the good citizen are identical, while in other cities…the good citizen is not the same as the good man. Furthermore, the one who is identical to the good man is not any citizen whatever but the ruler [actual or potential] of the city…"[26]

Yet it is striking that neither Aristotle in his *Politics* nor Aquinas in his *Commentary* provides an extant example of a truly aristocratic regime. In virtually all political communities, the majority of the citizens together with their rulers find themselves in this undesirable shared situation: the end that they and their city seek in common, to live well, is defined differently by the city and regime on the one hand, and by human nature and philosophy (to say nothing of Aquinas's Christian theology) on the other. The regime recognizes and reflects a part, but only a part, of the requirements of justice and happiness, easily mistaking and misrepresenting that part for the whole. How then can citizens rightly devote themselves to action for the common good, if in so doing they act for an end the regime establishes and enforces, yet which cannot simply or completely perfect them as human beings? The problem seems especially acute for those citizens who are subjects or ruled by others. If their prudence is merely "true opinion," as Aristotle on his part opines, crafted by the practical wisdom of their rulers and the laws and decrees, how can it even be *true* opinion, when the vision of justice and the public good those rulers impart is itself partial, hence partially defective and false?[27] And if the rulers and future rulers themselves have no time (and perhaps no inclination) to study philosophy, even political philosophy, busied as they are by the practical necessities of civic life, such as training for war, how will even they be able to rise above received opinion or, at best, partial knowledge of the good for humans?[28]

26 Aquinas, *Comm. Pol.* III, 4 n. 383 [7].

27 Cf. Aristotle, *Pol.* III.4, 1277b25-29; Aquinas, *Comm. Pol.* III, 3 n. 375 [12].

28 One of Aquinas's glosses on Aristotle (who is in turn quoting Euripides) underscores this ordinary absence of philosophy from the education of rulers, as commonly conceived and practiced in the real world. Aristotle does not mention philosophy explicitly in this passage—indeed he rarely does so in the *Politics*; yet Aquinas's remark seems on target and illuminating of Aristotle's intention. Cf. Aristotle, *Pol.* III.4, 1277a16-21 with Aquinas, *Comm. Pol.* III, 3 n. 370 [6].

One way around this dilemma would be to redefine civic virtue as in its essence other than regime-relative. Sensitive to regime volatility and the dangers of instability and anarchy, one might still argue that to be a virtuous citizen is to promote the common good as fully and effectively as possible, unimpeded by the regime's truncated and perhaps positively warped version of the social and civic end. Thus to be a good citizen in the antebellum United States, for instance, would often entail work against or at least outside of and in a wholly different spirit than the legal structures and policies of the time, to benefit those persons deprived of citizenship through slavery. Likewise, on this model the best citizen of the former Soviet Union would paradoxically have to refuse first-class citizenship by not joining the Party and by fostering free and truthful (if clandestine) speech, thereby promoting the true human dignity and social trust demolished by the regime. But on second thought, such persons would seem excellent not as members of the USSR but rather as members of a society in many ways oppressed by the regime that defined the USSR, as a political society. It is no accident that as soon as its Marxist-Leninist regime was no more the USSR received a new name—or rather new names, as its empire fragmented and its citizens became citizens of Russia, Ukraine, or one of a dozen other nations.

Following a similar line of reasoning, for Aristotle and for Aquinas as his commentator the regime remains central to a correct notion of citizenship and civic virtue. And for at least this reason, the tension between good humanity and good citizenship must remain. There are many regimes in which to be an excellent citizen is to be a bad human being, and even in decent polities one must rise above the imperfect civic standard and see farther than the regime if one is not to stunt one's full growth as a human being and as a member of society. Neither Aristotle nor Aquinas would deny that this critical distance can be quite difficult, even painful for public-spirited citizens to achieve. On Aristotle's account, moreover, it is difficult to understand how a citizen who does not possess at least those capabilities required of an excellent ruler in the best regime could *ever* achieve such regime-transcendence.

In his *Summa Theologiae*, in contrast to his *Commentary on The Politics*. Aquinas does appear to privilege the generically *social* character of human nature over the regime-relative political in several key respects.[29] One may even say that while retaining an awareness of the importance of regimes and the virtues and vices they require to perdure and tend to promote, Aquinas *redefines* the political or civic character of human nature as more fundamentally in function of human sociality and its ethical requirements.[30] In doing so Aquinas offers readers probing new possibilities for harmonizing human and civic excellence. And, by arguing for the naturalness of humanity's religious character and quest, taking this dimension of humanity more seriously in ethical context than Aristotle appears to have done, Aquinas opens up space for transcendence on the part of ordinary, non-philosopher citizens who are aware (however vaguely) of their citizenship in a universal community under God, and perhaps through grace are cognizant as well of being members of God's own household.[31]

According to Aquinas's foundational natural law theory, by virtue of aiming at the common good and the human good in which moral virtue is central, politics presupposes and foreshadows a human telos more common than any particular political regime can provide for or reflect, and which should serve as the North Star for the compass of political theory. Aquinas's *Commentary on the Politics* nudges the reader towards recognizing the need for a quest for a social and civic standard at once guiding and transcending the horizon of this-worldly regimes. The problem of political virtue and regime-particularity impels Aquinas to seek a political foundation that respects the legitimate, unavoidable requirements of real regimes yet that also assists *all* humans, not just philosophers, in some way to see beyond and transcend them. That foundation is to be found in the first place in Aquinas's account of natural law, and ultimately in the divine Giver of that law. The edifice is "cosmopolis," the universal polity on the order of nature, elevated and perfected to become the City of God in the order of grace and glory. Ernest Fortin expresses the Thomistic difference this way: "[I]n taking over Aristotle's concept of the political nature of man and of human living, Aquinas has modified it profoundly under the influence of Christianity and Stoicism and… the notion of God as a lawgiver in both of

29 John O. RIEDL "Thomas Aquinas on Citizenship", in *Proceedings of the American Catholic Philosophical Association* 37 (1963), 160-61; Kevin WHITE, "The Virtues of Man the Social Animal: *Affabilitas* and *Veritas* in Aquinas", in *Thomist: A Speculative Quarterly Review* 57/4 (1993), 641; Cf. Brian J. SHANLEY, "Aquinas on Pagan Virtue", in *Thomist: A Speculative Quarterly Review* 63/4 (1999).

30 For an example, see AQUINAS, *ST* I-II 113, 1.

31 Cf. AQUINAS, *ST* I-II 94, 2; Ernest L. FORTIN, *Collected Essays*, Volumes 1-3. Lanham, Md.: Rowman and Littlefield, 1996, II:160-161.

these traditions. Civil society...is itself judged by a higher standard to which human actions must conform universally. It becomes part of a broader whole, embracing all men and all cities and is by that very fact deprived of its privileged status as the sole horizon limiting the scope of man's moral activity, setting the goals to which he may aspire, and determining the basic order of his priorities."[32] At least in part, this Thomistic modification of the Aristotelian ethical-political paradigm is a profoundly human and philosophic response to problems of regime-relative political virtue and political science internal to Aristotle's *Politics*.

III. Natural Law, Magnanimity cum Humility, and Contemporary Politics

In *Thomism and Aristotelianism* Jaffa also notes an important dissonance between Aristotle's and Aquinas's respective accounts of a paramount ethical and political virtue, magnanimity or greatness of soul (Greek *megalopsychia*; Latin *magnanimitas*). The difference can be expressed succinctly in this way: Aristotle's magnanimity[33] seems incompatible with deeply felt gratitude and especially with humility, whereas Aquinas's magnanimity cannot exist as a true virtue without the support and collaboration of these two qualities. In the case of humility, Aquinas goes so far as to posit it as magnanimity's "twin virtue" (*duplex virtus*). Yet as Aquinas himself observes, it is far from clear how humility in particular can be compatible with magnanimity, a virtue conducing to outstanding statesmanship: "humility is apparently opposed to the virtue of magnanimity, which aims at great things, whereas humility shuns them."[34]

Jaffa further and rightly refers readers to Christian (or, as he stresses, "revealed") theology as an important source of Aquinas's divergence from Aristotle. Radical doctrines, such as creation *ex nihilo* as a free expression of divine goodness, certainty concerning divine "particular" providence as extending to each and every being, in particular to rational or human beings, and a vision of each human person as *imago Dei* and invited to friendship with God, cannot help but influence the Christian thinker's understanding of moral conduct and ethical excellence. In his postscript Jaffa quotes with approval this pithy summary of the distinction between Thomistic and Aristotelian ethics that can well be applied to their specific

32 Fortin, *op.cit*, II: 160-161, 169.

33 See Aristotle, *NE* IV.3.

34 Aquinas, *ST* II-II 161, 1, obj. 3.

understandings of magnanimity: "Aristotle did not look upon God as Creator nor as exercising conscious government and providence, but regarded Him as the final Cause alone…The virtuous man of Aristotle is, in a sense, the most independent man, whereas the virtuous man of St. Thomas is, in a sense, the most dependent man, that is, the man who realizes truly and freely expresses his relation of dependence on God [i.e., a personal God who governs human affairs]."[35]

It still remains to be inquired, however, whether the foundations of magnanimity humbly conscious of its dependence on God, as well as happily cognizant of its need to look to other human beings and acknowledge their support with enduring gratitude, are wholly and exclusively supernatural. Jaffa implies as much throughout *Thomism and Aristotelianism*, where he indicates that Thomas's revisionist ethic flies in the face of common sense and threatens the very possibility of human or social science. However, Aquinas would maintain that they are not, and moreover he is able to offer plausible reasons for so maintaining based on his foundational theory of natural law. In this discussion this essay cannot attempt a thorough explication of these arguments, much less anything approaching a demonstration of their validity. Its aim is simply to say enough to make the reader aware of some core Thomistic claims and their sources in Aquinas's texts, and to suggest that in some instances at least similar arguments should resonate well with readers today, in the early decades of the third millennium.

Aquinas's natural theology, the high point of his metaphysics, teaches that unassisted human reason is in principle capable of knowing the existence of God and certain of his attributes.[36] Aquinas judges that finite and contingent being *must* be created being, and that reason can attain to this truth; what he judges unknowable in the absence of divine revelation is whether the world was created "in time" or from all eternity.[37] Someone

35 Frederick COPLESTON, *A History of Philosophy*. Vol. II. *Medieval Philosophy from Augustine to Duns Scotus*. New York: Image Books, [1950] 1993, 410-411; cf. John O'CALLAGHAN, "Creation, Human Dignity, and the Virtues of Acknowledged Dependence", in *Nova et Vetera* 1 (2003), 109-40; Alasdair MACINTYRE, *Dependent Rational Animals: Why Human Beings Need the Virtues*. Chicago: Open Court, 1999.

36 AQUINAS, *ST* I 2; I 12, 12; AQUINAS, *Summa contra gentiles*, trans. A. C. Pegis, James F. Anderson, Vernon J. Bourke, and Charles J. O'Neil. Notre Dame: University of Notre Dame Press, 1975, I.10-102; cf. Etienne GILSON, *History of Christian Philosophy in the Middle Ages*. New York: Random House, [1922] 1955, 365-375; Ralph MCINERNY, *Characters in Search of Their Author: The Gifford Lectures 1999-2000*. Notre Dame: University of Notre Dame Press, 2001.

37 AQUINAS, *ST* I 44-46.

thus aware that his or her existence is in this way utterly dependent upon a good, wise, benevolent, powerful, and provident God, and sensitive to the dimension of mystery inherent in a created universe and each of its beings, has the foundation for an attitude of profound philosophic reverence.[38] Such a *natural* modesty or humility is thus in truth a human or ethical virtue, even for "the princes of this world," be they statesmen or, as Aquinas judges, in the highest instance "philosophers."[39]

A difficulty here, however, as Aquinas himself is quick to note, is the trouble that unassisted reason has in reaching metaphysical truths about the world and its ultimate cause. Left to their own devices, only a tiny minority of human beings would have discovered them, after years and perhaps decades of effort; and even then their conclusions would often contain much error admixed with truth. Only the most fortunate of humans, those blessed with quick, penetrating intellects and dogged self-discipline, living in peaceful lands and privileged to enjoy much leisure and learning, would ever have achieved philosophic knowledge of the truths which are essential for leading a good life and achieving happiness—or so Aquinas argues. Hence God in his mercy reveals what the reason of so many would neces-

38 Cf. Paul WOODRUFF, *Reverence: Renewing a Forgotten Virtue.* Oxford: Oxford University Press, 2001, 4. Woodruff's thoughtful and timely recovery of *reverence* as a human virtue. The book's central tenet that certain forms of reverence are good and even indispensable for our social and political lives to be well-ordered and to flourish is persuasive. However, Woodruff seems to argue wrongly when he maintains that *"reverence has more to do with politics than with religion."*

39 Cf. AQUINAS, *ST* I 12, 13, s.c., with 32, 1, ad 1. Thus Aquinas would contest Pierre Manent's claim in *The City of Man* that *"By nature—at least if one isn't telling himself stories—the man who is truly superior necessarily and legitimately disdains the man who is truly his inferior"* (Pierre MANENT, *The City of Man.* Princeton: Princeton University Press, 1998, 200). See also AQUINAS, *ST* I 27, 1, ad 3, where Aquinas notes that the "very nature" of creatures "entails dependence on God"; and Aquinas's treatment of the virtue of religion (*religio*), a moral virtue and a "part" of justice, which inclines its possessor *"to show reverence to the one God under one aspect, namely as the first principle of the creation and government of things"* (*ST* II-II 81, 3, c.), thus following "*a dictate of natural reason*" (*ST* II-II 81, 2, ad 3). Douglas Kries makes a related religious and political observation, concluding that Aquinas considers the best regime of Aristotle's *Politics* to be *rationally* inferior to the polity established by the Mosaic law, insofar as the former fails "*properly [to] take into consideration that aspect of [natural] justice which orders human beings to God in regulating that aspect of justice which orders human beings to each other.*" See Douglas KRIES, "Thomas Aquinas and the Politics of Moses", in *Review of Politics* 52/1 (1990), 102; see also 98-101. For an analogous but not identical argument in contemporary context, see Václav HAVEL, *Open Letters: Selected Writings, 1964-1990.* New York: Knopf, 1991, discussed below near this essay's end.

sarily have failed to grasp, and the reason of none perfectly comprehended.[40]

Against those who fear that Aquinas's emphasis on God's will as the foundation of both creation and revelation undermines the possibility of science, both natural and especially ethical and political science,[41] Aquinas in effect maintains that if the risks of a lapse into an anti-rational fideism are avoided, then the practice of science and the quest for wisdom stand rather to gain and be strengthened.[42] Presumptuous pride—according to Aquinas, one of the vices principally opposed to the virtue of magnanimity[43]—is a great threat to genuine knowledge. It focuses the thinker on an exaggerated image of his or her own excellence, obscuring accurate perception and disposing to over-confidence and rash judgment. Those reasoners, theoretical and practical, who through believing in things unseen yet attested to by divine authority accustom themselves to self-doubt and humility, are more capable of wonder at the otherness of beings; more apt to proceed with due caution and care in their study; and more cognizant of the possibilities for error in their conclusions and unethical misuse of their results.[44] Faith likewise nourishes the difficult, never completed quest for truth and justice and sustains it in hope. Faith thus provides grounds for a noble magnanimity in scholarly as well as civic life.[45]

Yet what of those many readers who do not accept some or all of Aquinas's philosophy of being and his natural theology, to say nothing of his revealed theology? Are they bound to prefer the magnanimity of the *Nicomachean Ethics* to that of the *Summa Theologiae*? Jaffa contends that this is the likely outcome of a comparison of the two theories: Aristotle keeps the ethical and political sphere of human life properly separate from the speculative or theoretical domain, and hence his account of magnanimity and other virtues does not depend on his metaphysics in the same way

40 AQUINAS, *SCG* I.4; ID, *ST* I 1, 1; I-II 99, 2, ad 2.

41 Cf. Larry ARNHART 'Statesmanship as Magnanimity: Classical, Christian, and Modern", in *Polity* 16/2 (1983), 274-276.

42 Cf. AQUINAS, *ST* I 19, 4-5.

43 Cf. AQUINAS, *ST* II-II 130, 2.

44 Cf. AQUINAS, *SCG* I.5.4; ID, *ST* II-II 130, 2, ad 3; 133, 1, ad 4.

45 Cf. AQUINAS, *SCG inter alia* I.2.2; ID. *ST* I-II 40 and II-II 17; II-II 129, 6. For a political theorist's recent reflections on the meaning and import of hope, see Glenn TINDER, *The Fabric of Hope: An Essay.* Atlanta: Scholars Press, 1999; those of a contemporary analytic philosopher, Peter GEACH, *Truth and Hope.* Notre Dame: University of Notre Dame Press, 2001; and for an important twentieth-century Thomist's, Josef PIEPER, *On Hope.* San Francisco: St. Ignatius Press, [1949] 1986.

Aquinas's does. Aristotle's conclusions are therefore in themselves both more accessible and more persuasive to readers today and to their multicultural, multiethnic contemporaries. The heroic *megalopsychia* the classical statesman evinces is much needed in modern times, Jaffa holds. It is the great vice of *Thomistic* Aristotelianism that it obscures such important aspects of the Philosopher's ethical wisdom from needy enquirers in search of a realistic yet ennobling social science.

Yet it is important to note that metaphysics is not the first or foremost teacher of ethics according to Aquinas. There is also the ground-up moral phenomenology beginning from natural law and rooted in what Aquinas terms *synderesis* and *conscientia*.[46] The ethical experience of each human person, Aquinas maintains, evolves in the context of an inborn inclination towards good and aversion to evil. [47] Natural knowledge of the first and very general precepts of natural law enjoins personal, rational reflection on human relationships, social norms, the example and advice given by others, and one's concrete lived experiences, to deepen one's understanding of the requirements of virtue and upright conduct and the connection of these with *beatitudo*, with happiness or flourishing.[48]

Reflecting on the problem of a person's moral responsibility in a political society or culture that (perhaps inevitably) propagates defective views of human fulfillment and ethical conduct, MacIntyre considers Aquinas to hold that the universal experience of friendship in its myriad instantiations offers unique possibilities for ethical growth.[49] Insofar as one is genuinely committed to a friend's welfare, one gradually learns how virtue develops in various kinds of conduct, and by contrast, which actions and attitudes

46 For Aquinas's understanding and explication of *synderesis*, the "natural habit" of the first principles of practical reason, and *conscience*, the application of moral knowledge to the judgment of a particular act, see AQUINAS, *ST* I 79, 12 and 13; I-II 19, 5 and 6; 94, 1, 4, and 6.

47 *"All the inclinations of any parts whatsoever of human nature, e.g., of the concupiscible and irascible parts, in so far as they are ruled by reason, belong to the natural law, and are reduced [from the Latin reducere, to be led or brought back] to one first precept [namely, 'good is to be done and pursued, and evil is to be avoided'], as stated above: so that the precepts of the natural law are many in themselves, but are based on one common foundation"* (AQUINAS, *ST* I-II 94, 2, ad 2). Aquinas thus argues later in the *ST*, for example, for the viciousness of magnanimity's chief foil pusillanimity because it runs contrary to the natural law, that is, to the natural inclination to attempt to accomplish the good that is within one's power, "refusing to do that which is commensurate thereto" (ID., *ST* II-II 133, 1, c.).

48 AQUINAS, *ST* I-II 94, 2; cf. 94, 4 and 6.

49 Alasdair MACINTYRE, *Whose Justice? Which Rationality?* Notre Dame: University of Notre Dame Press, 1988, 179-181, 198-200.

impede concern for and esteem of another's good. In so doing, one comes to an ever-deepening understanding of the requirements of *one's own good* as a human being.

So, one might consider Aristotle's magnanimous man, who is naturally disinclined to rejoice in the good turns others have done him or to acknowledge them after those favors have been returned with interest. Aristotle implies that the *megalopsychos* nonetheless does have friends and is even willing to "adjust" his life to spend time in their company and to meet their needs.[50] Insofar as he comes to esteem his most virtuous companions, his soul-mates, as other selves, he might reflect that just as he appreciates hearing the good he has done recounted and remembered, so his friends likewise appreciate and even deserve to hear their own noble deeds recalled. More than that, he may come to realize that the genuine love and affection he has for his friends should make his being their moral debtor more often than not a pleasant reality. Friendship of the noblest kind issues in a kind of individual self-transcendence that propels toward mutual self-fulfillment. It may be that Aristotle himself hoped that readers who matched the description of the *megalopsychos* (the magnanimous man) in book four of the *Nicomachean Ethics* might be brought to reconsider their excessive concern with superiority and consequent ingratitude, by the time they had studied the lessons on *philia* or friendship in the eighth and ninth books.[51] Such at least is one possible implication of Jaffa's interpretation of the structure of the *Ethics* as one of ethical *ascent* from common attitudes and appearances to deeper truths about the human condition,[52] although we should note as

50 Cf. ARISTOTLE, *Nicomachean Ethics* (*NE*), trans. Martin Ostwald. New York: Macmillan, 1962, 1125a1.

51 Indeed, an invitation to this sort of ethical ascent could be read in two of the chapters following almost immediately on the treatment of *megalopsychia* in the *Nicomachean Ethics*: that on friendliness or affability (ARISTOTLE, *NE* IV.6), and that on truthfulness, defined as the disposition willingly to reveal the reality of oneself and one's character in attitude, word, and deed (ARISTOTLE, *NE* IV.7). For a recent analysis of ethical growth by way of *philia* and its role in Aristotle's political science and theory of the common good, see Thomas SMITH, "Aristotle on the Conditions for and Limits of the Common Good", *American Political Science Review* 93/3 (1999), 628-631. For a parallel discussion of *amicitia* in Aquinas's political thought, see John FINNIS, *Aquinas: Moral, Political, and Legal Theory*. New York: Oxford University Press, 1998, 111-117. Cf. also Lorraine SMITH PANGLE, *Aristotle and the Philosophy of Friendship*. Cambridge: Cambridge University Press, 2002 and James V. SCHALL, "Friendship and Political Philosophy", in *Review of Metaphysics* 50 (1996), 121-141.

52 See JAFFA, *Thomism and Aristotelianism*, 64-66.

well that Jaffa doubts anyone other than a true philosopher could experience the fullness of friendship as described in those passages.[53]

If the experience of friendship can be posited as in some sense universal, transcending the historical or cultural particularities in which it is embodied and by which it is informed, Aquinas's natural law teaching also implies that different socio-political contexts tend to obscure some content of the natural law, and hence of human virtue, even while illuminating other aspects of it. In recent times, the moral sensibility shown by dissenters in the former Soviet Union and its satellites offers strong experiential support—generally from outside Thomist circles and often from non-Christians—for the humanity of humility, and its role in forming the character of the truly magnanimous person capable of contributing to the common good. In a 1984 essay entitled "Politics and Conscience," to give one powerful example, Václav Havel urges jaded modern men and women to recover their primordial awareness of their "life-world" or "the natural world," together with the sense of ethical responsibility that this dimension of humanness enjoins. This task entails recovering the simplicity and capacity for wonder manifested by small children.

They are still rooted in a world which knows the dividing line between all that is intimately familiar and appropriately a subject of our concern, and that which lies beyond its horizon, that before which we should bow down humbly because of the mystery about it… [This 'natural world'] is the realm of our inimitable, inalienable, and nontransferable joy and pain, a world in which, through which, and for which we are somehow answerable, a world of personal responsibility…At the basis of this world are values which are simply there, perennially, before we ever speak of them, before we reflect upon them and inquire about them. It owes its internal coherence to something like a "pre-speculative" assumption that the world functions and is generally possible at all only because there is something beyond its horizon, something beyond or above our grasp but, for just that reason, firmly grounds this world, bestows upon it its order and measure, and is the

53 It is also important to note that the constrained nature of friendship based on a common love of noble deeds, some of which can only be performed by one person or another, is reflected to the end of the *Nicomachean Ethics*: *"One will wish the greatest good for his friend as a human being. But perhaps not all the greatest goods, for each man wishes for his own good most of all"* (ARISTOTLE, *NE* VIII.7, 1159a11-13; cf. IX.8, 1169a18-1169b2). Aquinas might well argue that the divine friendship of *caritas* (see AQUINAS, *ST* II-II 23-33, especially 23, 1 and 3) finally frees all virtuous human friendships to be themselves, so to speak, by loosing the tension created by the all-too-human concern of each friend for his or her own superiority.

hidden source of all the rules, customs, commandments, prohibitions, and norms that hold within it. The natural world, in virtue of its very being, bears within it the presupposition of the absolute which grounds, delimits, animates, and directs it, without which it would be unthinkable, absurd, and superfluous, and which we can only quietly respect. Any attempt to spurn it, master it, or replace it with something else, appears, within the framework of the natural world, as an expression of *hubris* for which humans must pay a heavy price, as did Don Juan and Faust.[54]

In the conclusion of this essay, Havel alludes to the surprising impact of the "antipolitical politics"[55] practiced by dissidents as diverse as physicist Andrei Sakarov, novelist Aleksandr Solzhenitsyn, philosopher Jan Patočka, and Solidarity Trade Union leader Lech Walesa, whom Havel could then describe as a "simple electrician with his heart in the right place, honoring something that transcends him and free from fear."[56] The writings and even more so the lives of these heroes of Central and Eastern Europe have much to teach Westerners, Havel suggests: "I am convinced that what is called 'dissent' in the Soviet bloc is a specific modern experience, the experience of life at the very ramparts of dehumanized power. As such, that 'dissent' has the opportunity and even the duty to reflect on this experience, to testify to it and to pass it on to those fortunate enough not to have to undergo it. Thus we too have a certain opportunity to help in some ways those who help us, to help them in our deeply shared interest, in the interest of mankind."[57] One of the "essential and universal truths" in the dissidents' experience is the personal, social, and political importance of a courageous, magnanimous humility: "We must draw our standards from our natural world, heedless of ridicule, and reaffirm its validity. We must honor *with the humility of the wise* the limits of that natural world and the mystery which lies beyond them, admitting that there is something in the order of being which evidently exceeds all our competence. We must relate to the absolute

54 HAVEL, *Open Letters, 1964-1990,* 250-251.

55 Ibidem, 270-271. Havel loosely defines this concept as *"politics as one of the ways of seeking and achieving meaningful lives, of protecting them and serving them...politics as practical morality, as service to the truth, as essentially human and humanly measured care for our fellow humans"* (Ibid., 269).

56 Or better, in Walesa's case as also in Solzhenitsyn's, *and* in Aquinas's, honoring *Someone* who transcends yet also creates and grounds and governs one's person and indeed the entire universe.

57 HAVEL, *Open Letters*, 269-270; cf. Thomas L. PANGLE, *The Ennobling of Democracy*. Baltimore: Johns Hopkins University Press, 1992, 84-90.

horizon of our existence which, if we but will, we shall constantly rediscover and experience."[58]

From this evidence this essay concludes that Aquinas's natural law-based ethic of humility *cum* magnanimity, understood as essential also for the common good, is not one with which, humanly and philosophically speaking, "the facts [of our moral experience] soon clash."[59] Indeed, still early in a new millennium, our many memories of the past "century of sorrows"[60] suggest that humility constitutes a more central social and political virtue than even Thomas Aquinas may have recognized.[61]

58 HAVEL, *Open Letters,* 267 (emphasis added); cf. Aviezer TUCKER, *The Philosophy and Politics of Czech Dissidence from Patočka to Havel.* Pittsburgh: University of Pittsburgh Press, 2000, 155-161.

59 ARISTOTLE, *NE* 1145 b and ff.; Cf. JAFFA, *Thomism and Aristotelianism*, 22, 27-29.

60 Pope JOHN PAUL II, *Address to the Fiftieth General Assembly of the United Nations Organization,* October 5 1995, § 16-17: *"In order to recover our hope and our trust at the end of this century of sorrows, we must regain sight of that transcendent horizon of possibility to which the soul of man aspires...* We can and we must do so! *And in so doing, we shall see that the tears of this century have prepared the ground for a new springtime of the human spirit"* (italics in original).

61 Cf. AQUINAS, *ST* II-II 161, 1, ad 5. For generous support that made this paper and the book on which it is based possible, the author thanks the Earhart Foundation; the Erasmus Institute, University of Notre Dame; the Institute for Scholarship in the Liberal Arts, University of Notre Dame; the Jacques Maritain Center, University of Notre Dame, the Martin Marty Center for the Advanced Study of Religion, University of Chicago, the National Association of Scholars; the John M. Olin Foundation; the Program on Constitutional Government in the Department of Government, Harvard University, the Strake Foundation, and research assistant Colleen Mitchell.

The common good: still pertinent today? The Economy

Paul H. Dembinski

Building the common good and making it grow

Ten years after the start of the financial crisis in 2007-2008, the world is lapsing into a new 'age of uncertainty' – to borrow the title of a book written by Galbraith in a different context.[1] The ramifications – not to say metastases – of the financial crisis are now undermining the systemic foundations (political, economic and social) that were laid at the end of the Second World War.[2] This 'planetary system' prospered for over sixty years (1945-2007) because it made economic efficiency its main principle of operation and criterion of success. At the same time, it anchored its political ideal in the notion of the 'open society' and 'unfettered mobility' so beloved of liberal philosophers and, in doing so, unreservedly and uncritically embraced technological progress and its promises of a brighter future.[3]

Sixty years on, when the financial crisis broke out, a stunned world discovered that although overall economic performance, measured in terms of gross domestic product, had been unprecedented, its quality and distribution had created huge asymmetries and deep fissures in society. Yet many observers – including some economists – had seen and diagnosed these dysfunctions, in particular the over-expansion of the financial sector; but their warnings had no impact on the development of the system.[4] At the same time, some stage performers, such as Leonard Cohen in 1988, were sounding the alarm in striking words:

Everybody knows that the dice are loaded
Everybody rolls with their fingers crossed
Everybody knows that the war is over
Everybody knows the good guys lost
Everybody knows the fight was fixed

1 John K. Galbraith, *The age of uncertainty*, London, BBC/André Deutsch, 1977.

2 Paul H. Dembinski, *Finance, servant or deceiver? Financialisation at the crossroads*, London, Palgrave Macmillan, 2008; Paul H. Dembinski & Simona Beretta, *Beyond the financial crisis: towards a Christian perspective for action*, Geneva, FCIV Press, 2014.

3 Daniel Stedman-Jones, *Masters of the universe: Hayek, Friedman, and the birth of neoliberal politics*, Oxford, Oxford University Press, 2012.

4 John K. Galbraith, *A short history of financial euphoria*, London, Penguin, 1994; Paul Dembinski & Alain Schoenenberger, *Financial markets – mission impossible?*, Paris, Fondation pour le progrès de l'Homme, 1993.

The poor stay poor, the rich get rich
That's how it goes
Everybody knows …

Before identifying the profound roots of the crisis, we must first answer the following questions. Why were the dysfunctions ignored for so long? Why were they not corrected in time? Why did all the warnings go unheeded by decision-makers, and fail to touch their hearts? One of the most plausible answers is *ideological blindness*. For decades, politicians and economist closed their minds and ears to any argument that might have radically challenged the ideological foundations of the system. As for the tangible facts of these dysfunctions and asymmetries and their impact on people around the world, they were swept aside by a variable-geometry self-justifying discourse. So there was no reason to worry unduly about inequality, for – so we were promised by the ideologists – resources and income would be redistributed naturally, albeit slowly, by the 'trickle-down' effect that Adam Smith had described in *The theory of moral sentiments*.[5] The high-income strata, however selfish, would spend what they earned, and this would eventually reach the less well-off and enrich them in turn. For decades, the dominant, soothing argument was that we should simply wait and let the supposedly natural processes of the market economy run their course.

In 2007-2008, the financial crisis blew all that out of the water. It struck at the very heart of the system, and was so vast that it ripped apart the ideological veil that had concealed the asymmetries inherent in its reality – forcing governments to take emergency action only yesterday dismissed as unthinkable and incompatible with the liberal doxa. Yet for the last ten years, apart from such measures, the Western economic establishment has sat tight, and is still blithely waiting for a return to pre-2007 'business as usual' – refusing to accept (despite the incontrovertible statistical evidence) that the growth of the past decades was financed on credit, and that this was the direct cause of the crisis. By failing to act, and by clinging to the gains achieved (especially in the fiscal sphere), our economic leaders have deepened the gulf between ordinary people and what are now commonly known as the 'elites'. In 2016/17, the British referendum, the US presidential elections and the reshuffling of the political scene in France showed just how dramatically the balance of political power has shifted in Western countries since the crisis. At international level, these domestic problems have helped to undermine the hitherto much-envied establishment.

5 Adam Smith, *The theory of moral sentiments*, New York, Penguin, 2011 (1759).

Geopolitics is back, and the elites' growing inability to cope and lack of imagination are continuing to shake things up.

The pre-crisis logic, based on the pursuit of free-trade efficiency, non-intervention and technological progress, is increasingly unable to maintain the coherence of the system. Alternative, competing logics – such as national or local preferences, increased political control of the economy and technology (especially in the interests of sustainability), or experiments of social and solidarity economy – are gaining ground, and starting to compete with the still dominant logic. The 2007-2008 crisis has thus supposedly begun to undermine – including in people's minds – the prevailing systemic rationality. The system's resources and ability to come up with corrective policies – particularly with regard to debt reduction, growth and taxation – are being exhausted before our eyes.[6] It therefore seems very likely that the pressure of reality is pushing the system to its limits. Without being able to say exactly where the breaking point will be, the system is most probably heading for a new crisis, especially as it is subject to other pressures at the same time. Its size and growing complexity are multiple sources of tension, and meanwhile technological inflation is putting people under almost unbearable pressure.

From the 1970 s onwards, Soviet communism found itself in a similar situation.[7] At the time, the Polish economist Janusz Zielinski, who had a sharp eye for signs of economic exhaustion, glimpsed the limitations of the 'planned' economy: '*It is a historical fact that a given economic system can accommodate quite a broad range of economic policies. It is also clear by now that this range is limited ... At the same time, whatever priorities pursued, it has (the system - PHD) has limitation which do not change with different economic policies.*'[8]

The foregoing suggests that a phase of systemic transformation must be envisaged, at least as a hypothesis. Such a perspective provides a clearer understanding of what current events imply for political, economic and social conceptions of the common good, and their prospects for private action and public policy. This is the purpose of this paper.

The first section will examine the profound causes of the financial crisis, and diagnose a systemic transformation. It will also indicate the opportuni-

6 A typical example is the Greek debt crisis, which all the parties involved (the IMF, the EU and the Greek government) now agree cannot be solved by the current approach.

7 Paul Dembinski, *The logic of the planned economy: the seeds of the collapse*, Oxford, Clarendon Press, 1991.

8 Janusz Zielinski, 'On Systenm Remodelling in Poland : A Pragmatic Approach ', in *Soviet Studies, 30.1* (Jan.1978), p4.

ties that the crisis could offer. The second section will return to the keystone of Christian social teaching: the idea of the common good. The third section will use the principles of this teaching to suggest specific avenues for action that can increase the common good in both quantitative and qualitative terms. The final section will discuss the urgent need to replace 'structures of sin' with 'structures that enhance the common good'.

I. The diagnosis: denial or (ideological) blindness, and systemic transformation

In general, systems break down once the dominant logic can no longer produce, or reproduce, the conditions for their long-term survival. All systems can overcome temporary breakdowns as long as they can quickly restore their inner coherence before things get out of control.[9] To do so, they have three abilities that must, however, be activated coherently, subject to the available resources:

Its *self-justifying* ability, which produces a discourse that serves to justify system's existence and operation both internally and externally. The range of this discourse depends on how it relates to the perceptions and expectations of the people concerned, and the discrepancies from what the system actually achieves.

Its *self-organising* ability – the structural dimension discussed in the final section – enables the system to mobilise organisational resources, within the limits of its operating logic, in order to adapt its goals to the expected results.

Its *self-targeting* ability enables it to refine its goals without violating the limits of its own logic.

In practice, these various abilities are activated – not always coherently – by largely political institutional drivers rooted in legislative, executive and judicial powers.

The system runs into trouble, and may potentially collapse, once coherence and harmony between 'goals, results and expectations' break down permanently. This means that the system must have already exhausted its capacity for adaptation and resilience. Any system is capable of adaptation and resilience, but these will vary from one historical moment to another, depending on internal and external circumstances. The system reaches its

9 Paul H. Dembinski, *Finance: servant or deceiver?*, 78 ff.

limits when it exhausts its resilience without managing to restore the aforementioned coherence.

If the then political leaders fail to pick up the early-warning signals and are slow to intervene before trouble occurs, internal tensions increase and the system exhausts its reserves. Ideological blindness, sometimes verging on refusal to accept reality, thus seriously hampered the 'elites'' perception of the early-warning signals of the crisis – a blindness that is now causing major systemic tension.

This is the culmination of a gradual process that began during the Enlightenment and speeded up astonishingly in recent decades with the help of information technology: the *fragmentation of reality*, and its subsequent *quantification*. This process, which moreover feeds specialisation and hence economic efficiency, has today led to the existence of two realities: a private and unique emotional experience, and the abstract aggregate resulting from conceptualisation followed by quantification.

Koyré explains the starting point of the process as follows: '... *there is something that Newton must be held responsible for – or rather, not just Newton, but modern science in general: the division of the world into two. ... [Science] did this by replacing our world of experienced qualities and perceptions, a world in which we live, love and die, with another world: a world of quantity, of reified geometry, a world in which there is room for all things – except man.*'[10]

The process of fragmentation and quantification, boosted by technological progress, has today moved far beyond the sphere of science. In particular, it is found throughout the economic and financial world. Its spread to every sphere of society has given rise to four confusions that have steadily taken root in the collective and individual mentalities of the world's Western or Westernised 'elites' – whose intrinsic feature is that they are almost entirely immersed, to use Reich's phrase,[11] in the world of signs and symbols. Since these four confusions have been described elsewhere, they need only be briefly mentioned here:[12]

Confusion between the real and the virtual. This is undoubtedly the most significant of the four. The proliferation of technology and the spread of tasks linked to 'symbol manipulation' have accompanied the shift in

10 Alexandre Koyré, *Etudes Newtoniennes*, Paris, Gallimard, 1968, 25-49; see also Israël Giorgio, *La mathématisation du réel*, Paris, Seuil, 1996. For the anthropological consequences, see Bernard Ronze, *L'homme de quantité*, Paris, Gallimard, 1977; Olivier Rey, *Quand le monde s'est fait nombre*, Paris, Stock, 2016.

11 Robert Reich, *The work of nations*, New York, Vintage Press, 1992.

12 Paul H. Dembinski & Simona Beretta, *op. cit.*, 56 ff.

middle-class life towards the virtual (information and images). It is nowadays harder to distinguish between the direct truth of experienced reality and its manifestation on screens and in charts. The virtual has thus become a constituent part of the real, especially in the economic field, where the reality of businesses and processes has been supplanted by their financial expression. This 'financialisation' has exacerbated the confusion between the real and the virtual, and hence increased people's alienation from the real. The illusion is shattered once the individual is struck head-on by events with personal implications. All of a sudden the confusion ceases, and bewildered people are abruptly exposed – without any technical mediation – to full, unadorned reality.

Confusion on the time axis between the future and the present. This confusion is the direct consequence of virtualisation and financial quantification. The spread of financial techniques, particularly credit, has helped blur the once impassable boundary between what is available today and what will – perhaps – be available tomorrow. With the spread of such techniques, burdens that should have been borne today are – easily – postponed until tomorrow on the assumption that continuous, lasting economic growth will allow any debts to be paid back without difficulty. This has undermined respect for commitments and disciplined behaviour.

Confusion between ends and means. This classic confusion has spread easily in a world in which economic activity is subordinated to exchange (a form of fragmentation beloved of Adam Smith) and hence naturally dominated by the all-pervading presence of money. Money, rightly known as a 'general equivalent', has become widely established as an indispensable means of achieving all ends. As a result, the distinction between ends and means has become secondary, for almost all ends, individual or collective, seem to require money.

Confusion between the 'other' and the anonymous aggregate. The personalisation of groups and institutions (businesses, markets, public opinion and so on) with the help of information technology has paved the way for confusion between real people and abstract expressions and conflations of *faceless identities and realities*, the product of abstractions, logarithms and probabilities whose relationship to the real is, by definition, a simplifying one.

Put together, these four confusions make the real inaccessible and create a veritable dichotomy between the perception of the world by the 'elites' – through the prism of the symbols and technologies that form 'their world' – and the daily reality of the great mass of people. Speaking of the Soviet economy, Besançon put his finger on the extreme form of a similar gulf:

'The Soviet economy has been the subject of extensive scientific analysis ... But those who ... have approached the Soviet system through history, literature, travel or immigrants' tales cannot recognise it in economists' descriptions ... as if there were an unbridgeable gap between the system as recorded by the latter, with their measurements and figures, and the other system, without measurements or figures, which has been gradually been built up by instinct, based solely on people's own experience.'[13]

In the Western world, the ideological blindness speeded up and spread after the fall of the Berlin Wall, because the events of 1989-1991 seemed to bear out the logic of the system in the here and now. The fall of the wall sounded its final victory over all potentially competing or alternative logics, especially those inspired by a need of public intervention and regulation.[14] History with a capital H then seemed about to end. At the same time, commercial and cultural barriers were coming down, and nothing now seemed able to halt the emergence of a uniform world in the West's image. The end of geography and the death of distance were prophesied.[15] Technical achievements in transport and telecommunications reduced distance to the mere question of cost, paving the way for a 'flat' world.[16]

Protected from exposure to the real by the growing blindness based on the four confusions, the logic of the contemporary economic system was able to shrug off criticism and so avoid taking the corrective action that a more realistic reading of the situation would have dictated. Not until 2007-2008 were people's eyes suddenly opened to a dizzying abyss of fragility, disparity and asymmetry.[17] Financial destabilisation enabled harsh reality on the ground to pull off the blinkers – at least to some extent. Exclusion and misery are now acknowledged as major problems, the direct result of a performance-based systemic logic – despite generally growing overall economic results. In her largely intuitive essay with its striking title 'Economic horror', Forrester was one of the first to make a direct link

13 Alain BESANÇON, *Anatomie d'un spectre: l'économie politique du socialisme réel*, Paris, Calmann-Lévy, 1981, 9.

14 This was also the time of the 'Washington consensus', the final doxa on the policies to be pursued in developing countries.

15 Richard O'BRIEN, *Global financial integration: the end of geography*, London, Pinter, 1992; Frances CAIRNCROSS, *The death of distance*, Boston, Harvard Business School Press, 1997.

16 Thomas FRIEDMAN, *The world is flat: a brief history of the twenty-first century*, New York, Farrar, Strauss and Giroux, 200; Francis FUKUYAMA, *The end of history and the last man*, London, Penguin, 1992.

17 One of the best illustrations of this blindness is the British Academy answer to Queen Elizabeth II's question 'Why did no-one see the crisis coming?' in 2008. See DEMBINSKI & BERETTA, *op. cit.*, 11 ; The Guardian, 29 July 2009 ;

between growth as prosperity for some and exclusion for others.[18] Today, Pope Francis does not hesitate to extend this analysis, especially when he states 'Such an economy kills.'[19]

As long ago in 1948, Perroux foresaw that what he then called 'capitalism' could run into the aforementioned 'limits of the system', writing : "A way of thinking that is prior and alien to capitalism sustains, for a variable period of time, the framework in which the capitalist economy operates. But owing to the latter's very expansion and success, inasmuch as it receives the esteem and gratitude of the masses and fosters among them a taste for material comfort and well-being, it undermines the traditional institutions and mental structures on which every social order depends. Capitalism erodes and corrupts. It consumes vast quantities of vital energy whose rise it does not control". And he went on : "Political leaders need a rare cool-headedness in their diagnosis, and an exceptional energy in administering the treatment, if they are to detect and ward off this ailment in good time".[20]

Perroux's words clearly suggest that a temporary breakdown or a systemic crisis does not necessarily lead to collapse – although this is a real risk, as in the case of Soviet communism. To avoid this, we need an uncompromising – as Perroux calls it, 'cool-headed' – diagnosis. And it is not enough for the diagnosis to be relevant – it must be timely, before the crisis has undermined the foundations of the system, and it must be accompanied by action that is up to the challenge.

Such were the intentions of the G-20 leaders when, as early as 2009, they made numerous statements and commitments in favour of coordinated action for substantial, necessary and urgent adjustments to the system that would remedy its most glaring injustices. Since then, however, the G-20 has become more circumspect, and the announced changes to the system have

18 Viviane FORRESTER, *L'horreur économique*, Paris, Fayard, 1996.

19 Pope FRANCIS, *Evangelii Gaudium*, 2013, Section 53: '*Just as the commandment "Thou shalt not kill" sets a clear limit in order to safeguard the value of human life, today we also have to say "thou shalt not" to an economy of exclusion and inequality. Such an economy kills. How can it be that it is not a news item when an elderly homeless person dies of exposure, but it is news when the stock market loses two points? This is a case of exclusion. Can we continue to stand by when food is thrown away while people are starving? This is a case of inequality. Today everything comes under the laws of competition and the survival of the fittest, where the powerful feed upon the powerless. As a consequence, masses of people find themselves excluded and marginalised: without work, without possibilities, without any means of escape.*'

20 François PERROUX, *Le capitalisme*, Paris, Presses Universitaires de France, 1948.

been put on hold. Yet time is pressing, for centripetal forces are threatening the fragile equilibrium both locally and globally.

Far from being some temporary incident, the crisis is the symptom of a profound systemic breakdown. Such dysfunctions or breakdowns occur when the challenges facing a system are more than it can cope with. It is unable to reform or find new ways of governance, and its internal contradictions – which are its limits - are such that the its very existence is the main obstacle to a resolution of the crisis. It has now run up against its own limits. To avoid total collapse, it urgently needs to change the systemic course and alter its principle of coherence before some radically alternative logic takes its place and blows up the very roots of the system.

On another plane of analysis, Pope Francis confirmed the urgent need for systemic change when he wrote in Section 218 of *Evangelii Gaudium* '*The dignity of the human person and the common good rank higher than the comfort of those who refuse to renounce their privileges. When these values are threatened, a prophetic voice must be raised.*' Can concern for the common good become the new 'principle of coherence', the logic of a renewed economic system? We must therefore recast the current economic system around a logic that can first put an end to the most flagrant injustices, and then prevent them from occurring in the first place.

II. The common good: an ideal orientation for action

The common good is not an exact socioeconomic and political construction, a kind of 'third way' between capitalism and communism. However, as a keystone of Christian social teaching, it must initially be seen in the light of Christ's words in which, in response to the tempter, he recalls that man does not live on bread alone, but on all the words that issue forth from the mouth of God (Luke 4, 3 and Matthew 4, 4). In his 1963 encyclical *Pacem in terris*, Pope John XXIII emphasises the two complementary aspects of the common good: one terrestrial, one transcendent. Referring to the definition of the common good in his 1961 encyclical *Mater et magistra*, he wrote '... the common good must take account of all those social conditions which favor the full development of human personality ... Consisting, as he does, of body and immortal soul, man cannot in this mortal life satisfy his needs or attain perfect happiness. Thus, the measures that are taken to implement the common good must not jeopardise his eternal salvation; indeed, they must even help him to obtain it' (§ 58-59).

This quotation emphasises the humanly unattainable nature of the common good, whose only perfect expression – as Thierry Collaud recalls elsewhere in this book – is the mystical and mysterious communion with the Body of Christ made flesh that is the Church. This communion goes back to eschatological time,[21] and is called on to be embodied in what Pope Paul VI called the 'civilisation of love'.[22] To Patrick de Laubier, this will be an ephemeral moment in human history but it takes on its full importance in eschatological time. The 'civilisation of love', like the communion and popular joy that welcomed Christ on his triumphant entry into Jerusalem, will be an ephemeral period in human history, succeeded by widespread apostasy in preparation for the saviour's return in glory.[23]

Although the fullness of the common good can only really be understood in the light of faith, its human dimension – the conditions for life in society – remains accessible to anyone of good will who cares for human dignity and wants to see it blossom. The human common good is thus not an absolute that suffices in itself, but an 'ideal orientation' that can inspire and guide the action of men of goodwill, whether believers or non-believers. The point is not to carry out a specific project, but to gradually transform contingent reality by acts of quality guided by principles and values.

The Compendium of the Social Doctrine of the Catholic Church (2004) emphasises the dynamic nature of the pursuit of the common good: a process of permanent development of the 'work in progress' type. This process, this systemic logic, demands the collaboration and active involvement of all:

> 'The common good therefore involves all members of society, no one is exempt from cooperating, according to each one's possibilities, in attaining it and developing it. The common good must be served in its fullness, not according to reductionist visions that are subordinated by certain people to their advantages; rather it is to be based on a logic that leads to the assumption of greater responsibility. The common good corresponds to the highest of human instincts, but it is a good that

21 Eschatological time is a paradoxical time in that it is an early presence in the ambiguity of human history of an everlasting reality – in other words, a presence of what will lie (absolutely and eternally) at the very heart of the ambiguities of the present. See Romano GUARDINI, *Les fins dernières*, Paris, Saint Paul, 1999.

22 Pope PAUL VI, *Omelia del Santo Padre per il rito di chiusura dell'anno santo*, 25 December 1975.

23 Patrick DE LAUBIER, *La civilisation de l'amour selon Paul VI*, Paris, Frédéric Aimard, 2013, 47-48; see also, by the same author, *L'Eglise, corps du Christ dans l'histoire: une interprétation catholique*, Paris, F. X. Guibert, 2005, 137-158.

is very difficult to attain because it requires the constant ability and effort to seek the good of others as though it were one's own good' *(§ 167).*

Further on, the same Compendium sets out the fundamental requirement that is the very essence of the ideal orientation towards the common good: the 'social love' component,[24] another name for the spirit of charity highlighted in the previous quotation with reference to the golden rule. The Compendium says *In order to make society more human, more worthy of the human person, love in social life – political, economic and cultural – must be given renewed value, becoming the constant and highest norm for all activity* (Section 582).

In his encyclical *Caritas in veritate* (2009), Benedict XVI uses the terms 'gratuitousness' and 'gift' to stress the importance of the spirit and the intention with which the act is carried out; these have as much weight in the – human and eschatological – dynamics of the common good as its mere material consequences. De Laubier agrees when he stresses the importance of love received to the dynamics of the common good: '*Without lapsing into millenarianism or utopianism, the social doctrine of the Church may be seen as a non-utopian ideal of a planetary society, provided that* caritas *is given and above all received.*'[25]

Such line of acting in the light of the ideal orientation – gradually and at all levels – is adapted to all times in history, but is particularly relevant in periods of turbulence and darkness, when the overall view is blurred or there is no ideological project. At such times of transformation, some systemic logics are exhausted, whereas others are born and strengthened. For this very reason, the moment of hesitation and uncertainty provides an opportunity for the logic centred on concern for the common good to prevail over the competing ones, including the liberal one. It is clear from the foregoing that the systemic logic of the common good will gain a foothold

24 'It is from the inner wellspring of love that the values of truth, freedom and justice are born and grow. Human life in society is ordered, bears fruits of goodness and responds to human dignity when it is founded on truth; when it is lived in justice, that is, in the effective respect of rights and in the faithful carrying out of corresponding duties; when it is *animated by selflessness, which makes the needs and requirements of others seem as one's own and intensifies the communion of spiritual values and the concern for material necessities…* when it is brought about in the freedom that befits the dignity of men and women, prompted by their rational nature to accept responsibility for their actions. These values constitute the pillars which give strength and consistency to the edifice of life and deeds: they are values that determine the quality of every social action and institution.' PONTIFICAL COUNCIL FOR JUSTICE AND PEACE, *Compendium of the Social Doctrine of the Catholic Church*, 2004, Sections 204-208, quotation from Section 205.

25 Patrick DE LAUBIER, unpublished text dated 1997.

in human reality if, and only if, it is expressed through acts inspired by conscious concern for the common good. It is through these that social love – another way of saying concern for the common good – can be expressed. To help people in their efforts to build the common good, the social doctrine of the Church sets out to '*propose the principles and values that can support a society worthy of man. Among these principles, the solidarity principle to some extent includes all the rest.*'[26]

Principles are thus like road signs that help people of good will to aim their action at the moral good and its social expression, which is the common good.

III. Directions of actions aimed at the common good

It seems that in Chinese two characters can be combined (*wēi-jī*). so as to have a double meaning: crisis as the danger of a breakdown in the old order, and crisis as an opportunity for a new start. Whereas the asymmetries created by the recent failings of the economic system still await appropriate corrective action, the systemic crisis provides a new window of opportunity for action guided by concern for the common good. There is no lack of avenues. We need only take each of the aforementioned architectural principles of social teaching to grasp the wealth and number of projects whose urgency and importance the crisis has helped highlight. All these elements should be able to consolidate first the emergence and then the assertion of tomorrow's dominant logic, focusing on concern for the common good.

As regards the solidarity principle, significant progress should be made on five urgent lines of work, each of which can contribute to the common good.

The first level of solidarity and inclusion is within the family and the community. It is here that 'social love' reflexes should primarily be cultivated and developed among, and by, the people directly concerned. Western societies have seriously lagged behind in this area, whereas new expressions of social love should enable developing societies to halt the current disintegration of the ties that form the basis for any community.[27]

26 Pontifical Council for Justice and Peace, *op. cit.*, Section 580.

27 Pierpaolo Donati (ed.), *Famiglia: risorsa della società*, Bologna, Il Mulino, 2012; Lubomir Mlcoch, *Economics of the family: theories, institutions, policies and values*, Cambridge, Jubilee Centre, 2017.

The second level of solidarity is the labour market and business. 'I'm-all-right-Jack' attitudes and the heightened tension between capital and labour have opened up the way for individualistic selfishness that will not willingly grant anything to others. Employees, management and shareholders have hardened their working relationships to the point where all trace of social love has been eliminated in the interests of harsh economic efficiency. This line of work is a difficult one, but essential if the common good is to be built.[28]

The third level of solidarity is institutional redistribution. Here again, social love has been reduced to a strict minimum, on the one hand by widespread reluctance to pay taxes and on the other by the extreme proceduralisation of social welfare benefits. Trust and discipline are the two faces of the social love that has yet to be developed. This line of action has both domestic and, in the case of development aid, international dimensions, and includes policies inspired by the capabilities approach described elsewhere in this book by Jean-Michel Bonvin.

The fourth level of solidarity is that of gift and philanthropy. Like the widow's mite in the Gospel, the moral impact of gift is incommensurate if it is done in a spirit of charity rather than the pursuit of image or reputation. Actions that expresses concern for the common good through gift and gratuitousness are under way, but are endangered by the pitfalls of instrumentalisation.

A fifth level of solidarity needs to be mentioned: *the debt relationship,* in which the distribution of risk is, by definition, asymmetrical and unfavourable to the creditor. The solidarity principle should therefore also be applied in finance. This would enable risks to be better balanced if the financed project fails (without the creditor being at fault). The crisis has highlighted the problem of countries' sovereign debt, but the problem equally affects both households and businesses.[29]

According to the *subsidiarity principle*, everyone must be allowed a maximum of autonomy, and only the tasks that the lower levels of the social organisation are unable to handle should be transferred to its upper levels. This principle has often been applied in the political field – especially in the European project – but has had almost no impact on the economic field,

28 Philippe De Woot, *Lettre ouverte aux dirigeants chrétiens en temps d'urgence*, Paris, Desclée de Brouwer, 2009; *Repenser l'entreprise*, Brussels, Académie royale de Belgique, 2013; Olivier Favereau & Roger Baudoin, *Penser l'entreprise: nouvel horizon du politique*, Paris, Collège des Bernardins, 2015.

29 Jean-Michel Bonvin (ed.), *Debt and the jubilee: pacing the economy*, Geneva, Observatoire de la Finance, 1999.

where in recent decades the emphasis has been on ever-increasing size of organisations, particularly enterprises.[30] This situation has created dizzying asymmetries between microbusinesses and multinationals in the global economy, with a balance of power that is unfavourable to the former. More broadly, promises of economies of scale have encouraged the concentration of economic activity and the emergence of giant businesses. Does such concentration comply with the subsidiarity principle? Is it essential to the smooth operation of society and the economy?

Finally, another key principle in Christian social teaching is the *universal destination of goods*, whose counterpart is the Christian view of property and the associated rights and duties. In the Christian perspective, property is never absolute but subject to social restrictions, for the purpose of all creation is to serve the common good. The Christian way of seeing things conflicts with today's absolute view of property.

Four lines of work that concern the common good deserve mention here:

The preferential option for the poor. This is a key emphasis that runs throughout social teaching, particularly as regards ownership. Concentration of land, especially farmland, is undermining the basis for survival of entire populations around the world. Today's absolute view of property is creating injustices that can only be mitigated or reversed by concern for the common good, expressed by acts that unlock the bolts of property and broaden access to it.[31]

The question of intellectual property, which is now so prevalent. It raises in a new way the principle of the universal destination of goods. These issues must be examined in terms of the common good, i.e. the good of all, not just those who hold or exploit these rights. A crucial distinction must be made between what is essential, for instance in the pharmaceutical sector, and what is not. In the former case, exclusion by exorbitant prices clashes head-on with the demands of universal destination. Here again, past asymmetries can be remedied, provided that the parties bear the common good in mind.[32]

The question of depletion of resources and ecology overlaps with that of intergenerational justice, and hence the risk of future generations being excluded from access to such resources, on which their survival depends. This thorny

30 Olivier Rey, *La question de taille*, Paris, Stock, 2014.

31 Pierre Coulange, *L'option préférentielle pour les pauvres: parcours biblique et théologique*, Bex, Parole et silence, 2011.

32 Fondation Caritas in Veritate, *Patents on genetic resources?*, Geneva, FCIV Press, 2013.

problem can only be solved if the parties are able to stop focusing on themselves and include in their view of the common good the generations that will follow them. Social love and generosity are essential here too.[33]

The fourth line of work involves 'global public goods' which, like the oceans, the atmosphere and the climate, cannot be appropriated by even the most powerful governments. Organising fair access to these resources for all people is a difficult problem, and none of the proposed weightings for distribution are really satisfactory.[34] Yet every day these global public goods are used by everyone. From micro-actions to macro-decisions, we must create room for application of the golden rule – do unto others as you would have them do unto you – as recommended in the aforementioned Compendium.

IV. Systemic dynamics geared to the common good

Christian social teaching gives a pointer to those who want to put their faith to practical use in their everyday lives. One of its basic principles is involvement in society. In other words, the permanent concern and readiness to contribute to the dynamic development of the common good is not an option for Christians, but an obligation to act wherever they happen to be.

The crisis has revealed the limits of a systemic logic that is solely geared to egocentric efficiency. By weakening this hitherto dominant logic, the crisis has created an opportunity to transform the system around a new logic that can gradually become the new principle of systemic coherence. The logic of the common good could thus take over, helping to pave the way for tomorrow's system, insofar as it is reflected in everyone's daily actions – regardless of the chances that transformation of the system will actually lead to the pursuit of the common good. Christians have a duty to act wherever they happen to be, and to draw their inspiration from the aforementioned ideal orientation. In doing so, they should be able to rely on the aid of people of good will who care for human dignity and the conditions in which it can blossom.

Systemic transformation can get under way if action inspired by concern for the common good takes place simultaneously a four levels of the system: (1) *ideas and world view*, (2) *institutions in the broad sense* (structures, including mental ones), (3) *ways of interacting* (mechanisms), and (4) *individual*

33 Pope FRANCIS, *Laudato si'*, 2015.

34 Inge KAUL, Isabelle GRUNBERG and Marc STERN (eds), *Global public goods*, Oxford, Oxford University Press, 1999.

behaviour. These levels are complementary, so that, in the absence of individual behaviour and decisions inspired by concern for the common good, neither institutions nor ways of thinking will change. Nor will there be any change if a new, transformative, coherence is not gradually brought to existence. If values and ways of thinking (the system's self-justifying abilities) and structures (its self-targeting and self-organising abilities) develop in opposite directions, there will be no systemic coherence, and the system will be no longer be able to work.

The world-view level. The first part of this text discussed at length the ideological blindness that overcame the world in the decades before the crisis. It referred to the deeper roots of this blindness, which lie in the extreme fragmentation of reality into quantifiable but falsely uniform units that fosters the virtual, abstract representation, and commoditisation, of the world.

The aforementioned four confusions were fed by this fragmentation, burdening people's thinking with an idealised view of the world and hence delaying early diagnosis of the crisis. We urgently need to restore a world view that is realistic, i.e. that takes account of the specific features and limitations of fragmentation. This depends on understanding what cannot be cut up into pieces – starting with the view of man as a whole. It also depends on asking questions rather than giving cut-and-dried answers or trotting out useless recipes – the ability to grasp change and challenge things, rather than rely on comfortable certainties. Action at this level depends on renewing technological and economic paradigms, and critically renewing the anthropological foundations of this knowledge and how they are conveyed in political and economic terms. Christians with concern for the common good must become actively involved in professional circles if we are to return to a realistic world view.

The level of institutions and structures. What is an institution? To borrow North's terminology, it is any stable element in a social system, an element that structures social interaction.[35] In this sense, he considers institutions and structures as synonymous. However, although institutions are stable, they are not immobile – not only can they develop spontaneously, they can also be reformed. The social teaching of the Church traditionally emphasises governments' responsibility to create an institutional framework appropriate to the pursuit of the common good. Yet, besides formal institutions, there are quite clearly very many informal ones – such as habits and

35 Douglas North, *Institutions: institutional change and economic performance*, Cambridge, Cambridge University Press, 1990.

mentalities. At the same time, it must be acknowledged that in free societies, in addition to public institutions, there are private institutions such as business, associations or non-governmental organisations which also take part in the dynamics of the common good.

Structural decisions, which lay foundations and reform or alter formal institutions (both private and public), by definition have a naturally greater impact because, directly or indirectly, they affect social interactions or individual decisions. They thus exert leverage on the results produced by the system. Such decisions thus have a key 'architectural' impact on the systemic implementation of the common good. Today's major technological decisions are among the most important such structuring decisions that will shape the life of society for generations to come.

The same is not true of informal institutions; although their impact on decisions and interactions is similar to that of formal institutions – take, for instance, a corruption-based culture – their dynamics are more spontaneous. Most of the time they develop slowly; but there may be periods of faster change, especially because of new technical possibilities. Apart from such breakthroughs, changes take place as a consequence of myriad individual actions and decisions that are insignificant when taken one by one, but structural in the long term and as a whole. Thus our daily acts erect and validate, or on the contrary weaken and erode, informal institutions – which may strengthen or weaken formal institutions, as in the case of corruption.

The importance of the structuring dimension did not escape John Paul II, who emphasised that structures may have a damaging impact on concern for the common good. He thus spoke of 'structures of sin' – structures that were perverse by their nature, because they structured and constrained actions of others to the point of forcing them to behave in iniquitous ways.[36] Such structures are also the work of people – people with the ability to make iniquitous laws, and to create organisations or technologies, or lay down rules, that were incompatible with human dignity, and so on. Such structures were like multipliers of sin, dragging down the people they conditioned often without them being fully aware that it was even happening.[37]

36 Pope JOHN PAUL II, *Sollicitudo rei socialis*, 1987, Section 36.

37 Jacques BICHOT, 'La personne humaine aux prises avec les structures de péché', in Paul DEMBINSKI, Nicolas BUTTET (eds), *Car c'est de l'homme qu'il s'agit*, Paris, Parole et Silence, 129-142; Mathias NEBEL, 'Péché structurel', in Éric GAZIAUX, Denis MÜLLER (eds), *Dictionnaire encyclopédique d'éthique chrétienne*, Paris, Cerf, 2013, 1479-1487. See also Mathias NEBEL, *La catégorie morale de péché structurel: essai de systématique*, Paris, Cerf, 2006.

In terms of the systemic transformation envisaged here towards a logic geared to the common good, it is important to reverse the notion of 'structures of sin' and emphasise the urgent need to invent (and put them place through adequate structuring decisions) institutions – formal and informal, public and private – that are not multipliers of sin, but levers for the common good. These 'structures for the common good' are organisations, laws and regulations that, far from encouraging sin, encourage concern for the common good -- and the social love without which, as we have seen, the common good will remain a dead letter.

The mesosocial level of interactions, mechanisms, etc. As the term indicates, structures provide the backbone for social interaction, but are not themselves social interaction. Mechanisms are routines of interaction, which are influenced – but not determined – by structures. Interaction is the link between the individual decision and the structure or institution. We are talking here of the infra-institutional level that is essential to life in any society. Because of the finer mesh, people's specific dignity is more directly involved at the level of interactions.

Pressure for efficiency has ended up casting most human economic relationships in the mould of *transactions*: the *exchange of equivalents* that Stefano Zamagni refers to elsewhere in this book. Yet, although anonymous transactions – a direct consequence of the commercial fragmentation of the world – may be efficient, for the very same reason they consume the resources needed for future fecundity. The same is not true of *relationships* which, because they are projected in the long term, provide room for unknown and unexpected element and a promise of future fecundity. The ubiquity of transactions in society is thus a potential threat to their own future. What is essential is not to prevent transactions, but to encourage a relational system more able to take account of the various parties' aims, needs and capabilities. These are millions of micro-deeds in which people of good will can express their concern for the common good.[38]

The level of individual action. As we have seen, neither structures nor mechanisms nor a world view based on the pursuit of the common can come about unless people take the initiative. In his 2007 encyclical *Spe salvi*,

38 Paul DEMBINSKI, 'Efficiency vs. fecundity: rediscovering relations', in Domènec MELÉ, C. DIERKSMEIER, *Human development in business: values and humanistic management in the encyclical* Caritas in veritate, London, Palgrave Macmillan, 2012, 98-116; see also Mathias NEBEL & Paul DEMBINSKI, 'Relational thinking and Catholic social teaching', Cambridge, Sallux & Jubilee Centre, 2017; John ASHCROFT, Roy CHILDS (eds), *The relational lens*, Cambridge, Cambridge University Press, 2017; Alain CAILLÉ & Philippe CHANIAL, *Au commencement était la relation … mais après?*, Paris, Découverte-MAUSS, 2016.

Benedict XVI was quite clear about this: '*The right state of human affairs, the moral well-being of the world can never be guaranteed simply through structures alone, however good they are. Such structures are not only important, but necessary; yet they cannot and must not marginalise human freedom. Even the best structures function only when the community is animated by convictions capable of motivating people to assent freely to the social order. Freedom requires conviction; conviction does not exist on its own, but must always be gained anew by the community. Since man always remains free and since his freedom is always fragile, the kingdom of good will never be definitively established in this world. Anyone who promises the better world that is guaranteed to last for ever is making a false promise; he is overlooking human freedom. Freedom must constantly be won over for the cause of good. Free assent to the good never exists simply by itself. If there were structures which could irrevocably guarantee a determined – good – state of the world, man's freedom would be denied, and hence they would not be good structures at all*' (Section 24).

The common good must be linked to the body of Christians' social action. However, to succeed in this, they must constantly solve the dilemmas they encounter in real life. This issue has been discussed elsewhere;[39] but it is certain that the common good requires decision-makers to cease focusing on themselves and pay attention – quite apart from such normal considerations as efficiency and legality – to two more aspects of their actions: *the intrinsic quality of the actions*, which only the decision-maker is fully aware of, and *the impact that their actions will have on those that have to undergo their consequences*, without having been involved in making the decision.[40]

If we can take the prerequisites of the common good into account simultaneously at these four levels of the socioeconomic system, we may hope to recast the system into one with with less asymmetry and injustice. Yet no mechanism, procedure or system can remain geared to the common good in the absence of social love. The common good is not so much a matter of socioeconomic engineering as of *a thousand faces of charity on the move.*

39 Joseph BADARACCO, *Defining moments: when managers must choose between right and right*, Boston, Harvard Business School Press, 1997; Étienne PERROT, *L'art de décider en situations complexes*, Paris, Desclée de Brouwer, 2007; Étienne PERROT, *Le discernement managérial*, Paris, Desclée de Brouwer, 2012.

40 Jean-Loup DHERSE, Hugues MINGUET, *L'éthique ou le chaos?*, Paris, Presses de la Renaissance, 1998.

Stefano Zamagni

The Common Good and the Civil Economy

This paper seeks to elucidate the main features of the civil economy paradigm, whose historical roots go back to the fifteenth century, at the time of humanism. A critical assessment of the fundamental differences between the civil economy (Antonio Genovesi) and political economy (Adam Smith) paradigms is then offered. Finally, attention is paid to the notion of the common good, i.e. the central pillar supporting the construction of the civil economy. It is compared to the notion of total good that, on the other hand, sustains the political economy research programme. The paper concludes by indicating why in the last quarter of a century the perspective of study of the civil economy is progressively gaining ground in both academic and public discourse.

Introduction

What is the link between the civil economy and the common good? More specifically, in what sense does the civil economy paradigm 'speak' the same ethical language as the common good? To answer these questions, we must first explain the meaning and basic principles of the civil economy and, second, specify what is meant by the common good.

Before turning to this, let me mention a sign of the times, typical of the current stage of history and represented by insistent appeals to ethics, as if everything were ethics, that has been replacing the equally insistent appeals to politics typical of the 1960 s and 1970 s, when 'everything was politics'. Yet it is clear to everyone that this focus on the primacy of ethics comes to a halt as soon as specific issues are discussed. This is precisely what MacIntyre conjectured when in his famous *After virtue*,[1] after noting the multiplicity of theories in today's ethical panorama, he concluded that the indisputable use of ethical principles merely served to put an end to the actual ethical debate. In other words, the focus on acknowledging the primacy of ethics does not lead to ethical consensus.

And the consequences are there for all to see. It is a fact that today even the most abstract of economists must admit that if the problems now

1 Alasdair MacIntyre, *After virtue: a study in moral theory*, London, Duckworth, 1981.

facing society – the endemic growth in inequality, the scandal of hunger, the emergence of new social diseases, the outbreak of identity conflicts on top of the existing conflicts of interest, the paradoxes of happiness, the sustainability of development and so on – are to be solved, economic research can no longer shut itself away in a kind of ethical limbo. If, as I believe, it is true that every theory offers a glimpse of reality, economic theory in the proper sense cannot be studied without choosing a viewpoint from which to observe reality. Again, the economic discourse will also continue to expand and increase its own technical and analytical apparatus; but if it does not break out of its self-referential framework, it will be less and less able to grasp reality, and hence to serve any useful purpose. It certainly cannot be denied that this is today the true threat to the discipline. For fear of having to make specific anthropological and ethical choices, many economists prefer to retreat into mere analysis, putting more and more intellectual energy into the use of increasingly sophisticated logical and mathematical instruments. But there can never be a trade-off between formal rigour of the economic discourse, which remains essential, and its ability to explain, i.e. interpret, economic facts – if only because it should never be forgotten that the production of economic knowledge, at the same time as it helps shape and alter economic actors' cognitive maps, also acts on their moods and motivations, in other words on their characters.

What is civil economy?

The civil economy is founded in a tradition of thinking whose roots go back to fifteenth-century civil humanism and continued, with varying degrees of success, up to its golden age, that of the Italian, Milanese and above all Neapolitan Enlightenment.[2] While in Scotland Smith and Hume were defining the principles of political economy, in Naples during the same period the civil economy research programme was taking shape under Genovesi, Filangieri, Dragonetti and others.[3] There are many similarities between the Scottish and Neapolitan-Milanese schools: the anti-feudal arguments (the market seen above all as a means of breaking free from feudal society); the praise of luxury as a factor in social change, without too much concern for the 'vices' of those that consume such goods; a great ability to

2 Luigino Bruni, Stefano Zamagni, *Civil Economy*, Oxford, P. Lang 2007.

3 Antonio Genovesi, *Lezioni di economia civile*, Milan, Destefanis, 1803; Gaetano Filangieri, *Delle leggi politiche ed economiche*, Milan, Destefanis, 1804; Antonio Dragonetti de Torres, *Nuovi saggi di economia politica*, Turin, Boccà, 1927.

grasp the cultural change that the development of trade was bringing about in Europe; the acknowledgement of the essential role of trust in the operation of a market economy; and the 'modernity' of their views of society and the world. Yet there is one profound difference between Scottish political economy and Italian civil economy. While acknowledging peoples' natural tendency towards sociability ('sympathy' and 'correspondence of sentiments' with others), Smith did not believe that such non-instrumental relationality was relevant to the operation of markets: 'Society may subsist among different men … from a sense of its utility, *without any mutual love and affection.*'[4]

Indeed, some passages from both *The theory of moral sentiments* and *The wealth of nations* explicitly stated that benevolent feelings and behaviour complicated the operation of the market mechanism, which would operate far more smoothly the more instrumental the relationships within it were. To Smith, and what would subsequently become the official tradition in economics, the market was a means of constructing truly social relations (there could be no civil society without markets), for it freed people from unchosen vertical and status ties, but was not in itself a place of relationships. Smith did not see the fact that mercantile relationships were impersonal and mutually indifferent as something negative, but as positive and civilising – only thus could the market produce welfare and development. Friendship and market relationships thus belonged to two quite distinct and separate fields; indeed, the existence of market relationships in the public sphere (and only there) ensured that friendships in the private sphere were genuine, freely chosen and detached from status: if a beggar went into a butcher's to ask for money, he would never be able to have a friendship with the butcher outside the market. If, on the other hand, the former beggar one day went into the butcher's or brewer's shop to purchase their wares, that evening he could meet his suppliers for a drink on a more dignified footing, and perhaps become friends with them. To Smith, and the official economic tradition, the market was a place of civilisation – but not of friendship, non-instrumental reciprocity or fraternity.[5]

On these issues, which were central to contemporary economic practice and theory, the civil economy tradition radically disagreed. To Genovesi, Filangieri and Dragonetti in Naples, Verri, Beccaria and Romagnosi in

4 Adam Smith, *The theory of moral sentiments*, Edinburgh, W. Creech, and J. Bell & Co., 1797, II.3.2 (my italics).

5 Luigino Bruni, Robert Sugden, 'Reclaiming virtue ethics for economics', *Journal of Economic Perspectives* 27, 2013, 141-164.

Milan, and then Sturzo and to some extent Einaudi in the twentieth century, as well as more applied economists such as Rabbeno or Luzzatti, or the founder of business economics Gino Zappa (the Italian business economics tradition likewise reflects the older civil economy tradition), the market, the business and the economy were in themselves also places of friendship, reciprocity and gratuitousness.[6] The civil economy did not accept the idea – which today is increasingly widespread and taken for granted – that the market was something radically different from the civil world, which was governed by different principles: the economy was civil, the market was life lived in common, and they shared the same fundamental law, namely mutual assistance. Genovesi's mutual assistance was more than just Smith's mutual advantage: mutual advantage only required a contract, whereas mutual assistance required *philia*, perhaps *agape*.

Today, the civil economy presents itself as an alternative to the economy of the Adam Smith tradition, which sees the market as the only institution that is truly necessary for democracy and freedom; the civil economy reminds us that, although society is certainly the fruit of the market and freedom, there are requirements, based on brotherhood, that cannot be evaded or relegated to the private sphere, in particular philanthropy.

At the same time, the civil economy does not support those who fight the markets and see the economy as being in endemic, natural conflict with the good life, citing falling growth and a withdrawal of the economy from life lived in common. Instead, the civil economy proposes a multidimensional humanism in which the market is not fought or 'controlled', but is seen as a civil place on a par with others, as a feature of the public sphere which, if conceived of and experienced as a place that is also open to principles of reciprocity and gratuitousness, helps to construct the *civitas*.

The economy as if people mattered: this could sum up the essence of the civil economy research programme. To grasp its meaning, let us consider the two opposing ways of looking at the relationship between the economic sphere (which for convenience, and in the broadest sense, we may call the *market*) and the social sphere (the *solidarity* sphere). On the one hand there are those who see in the spread of markets and the efficiency principle the

6 Gian Domenico ROMAGNOSI, *Economia politica e statistica*, Milan, Perelli e Mariani, 1845; Cesare BECCARIA, *Elementi di economia pubblica*, Milan, Destefanis, 1804; Pietro VERRI, *Opere filosofiche e di economia politica*, Milan, Società tipografica de' classici italiani, 1835; Luigi STURZO, *Storia, società ed economia*, Pisa, Istituti editoriali e poligrafici internazionali, 1995; Luigi EINAUDI, *Studi di economia e finanza*, Rome, Società tipografico-editrice nazionale, 1907; Gino ZAPPA, *La determinazione del reddito nelle imprese commerciali*, Rome, Anonima libraria italiana, 1929.

cure for all of society's ills; on the other there are those who, on the contrary, see the advance of markets as the 'desertification' of society, and seek to protect themselves against it. The former view considers the market as essentially *a-social*; according to this view, which harks back to some versions of the liberal ideology, 'society' is distinct from the market mechanism, which is presented as an ethically and social *neutral* institution. The market is called on to be efficient, and to perform the task of creating as much wealth as possible. As for solidarity, it begins where the market ends, when determining criteria for dividing up the wealth produced.

The opposite approach sees the market as essentially *anti-social*. This view, which goes back to Marx and Polanyi and is today most visibly expressed in the various kinds of alternative economies (the 'solidary economy', the 'communitarian economy' and so on), sees the market as a place of exploitation and subjugation of the weak by the strong, and considers that it is a threat to society: in Polanyi's words, 'The market advances on the desertification of society'.[7] Hence the call to 'protect society' from the market, on the grounds that truly human relationships (such as friendship, trust, giving, non-instrumental reciprocity, love and so on) are being destroyed by the spread of market thinking. This view tends to see the economy and the market as dehumanising in themselves, as mechanisms that destroy the 'social capital' on which all genuinely human life lived in common and all sustainable economic growth depend.

The notion of the market/society relationship that is typical of civil economy lies is a radically different perspective from the former two. The central idea is that of experiencing *human sociality*, *within* – not beside, before or after – normal economic life. It tells us that principles different from profit and exchange of equivalents can find a place within economic activity. It thus certainly goes beyond the first view, which sees the economy as an ethically neutral place based solely on the principle of exchange of equivalents, for it is the economic moment itself which, depending on the presence or absence of these other principles, becomes civil or uncivil. But it likewise goes beyond the other view, which sees gift and reciprocity as the prerogative of other moments or spheres in social life, a view that is still rooted, even today, in quite a few expressions of the Third Sector – and that is no longer sustainable, for at least two specific reasons. First, in these times of globalisation the 'two-step' logic (first businesses produce, then the state intervenes to redistribute the wealth) on which the relationship between the economy and society is based (take the welfare state as an

7 Karl Polanyi, *The great transformation*, Boston, Beacon Press, 2001, 3.

example) no longer works, for the basic feature of that logic – the close link between wealth and territory – is now lacking. As a result, businesses are called on to pay attention to the social dimension in the course of their *normal* economic activities. This is the underlying sense of the Corporate Social Responsibility movement:[8] the Council of Europe's Charter on Shared Social Responsibilities is clear evidence of it.[9] Second, the 'crowding out effect'. If the market, and more generally the economy, become places of instrumental exchange *and nothing else*, we are faced with one of today's most worrying paradoxes. According to one of the oldest and best-known economic laws, Gresham's Law, bad money drives out the good one. This broadly applicable mechanism operates whenever, for example, intrinsic motivations (such as gratuitousness) are confronted with extrinsic ones (such as profit): the bad motivations drive out the good ones. Exchange based solely on the pursuit of self-interest drives out other kinds of human relationship. Thus, as it develops, the market – if it is this and nothing else – erodes the preconditions for its own existence, namely trust and the propensity to cooperate.

Indeed, all societies depend on three different principles in order to develop harmoniously and be viable: exchange of equivalents, redistribution of wealth, and reciprocity. All societies are aware of this triadic structure, even though only two of these principles have, time after time, been incorporated into the models of social order that have developed historically over recent centuries – and always with unsatisfactory results. For what happens if one of the three principles is absent? If reciprocity is eliminated, we have a model of social order based on the state/market dichotomy: the market produces, and the state benevolently redistributes according to some criterion of fairness. If redistribution is eliminated, we have the *compassionate capitalism* model (the 'welfare capitalism' of American experience). The market is society's lever and must be free to act without hindrance, as neoliberalism teaches. In this model the market produces wealth, and the rich offer 'charity' to the poor, using civil society and its organisations (charities and foundations). Finally, the elimination or undervaluation of exchange of equivalents produces yesterday's and today's *collectivist* and *communitarian* systems, which attempt to function without contract logic (even at the cost of inefficiencies and disastrous wastages of resources). Well, the central idea of

8 Stefano Zamagni, *Impresa responsabile e mercato civile*, Milan, Il Mulino, 2013.

9 Recommendation CM/Rec(2014)1 of the Committee of Ministers to member States on the Council of Europe Charter on shared social responsibilities (consulted on 20 December 2016).

the civil economy is to aim for a model of social order in which all three principles can coexist, and so find real spaces in which they can operate in practice.

To sum up, civil economy offers a view of economic reality based on three main theses. The first is rejection of the NOMA ('non-overlapping magisteria') principle, first stated in 1829 by Richard Whately,[10] an influential economist at Oxford University and a leading figure in the Anglican Church. According to NOMA, ethical norms have as much impact on economics as they do on the laws of physics. In other words, the economic sphere must be kept *separate* from the spheres of ethics and politics, for it has nothing to do with them. Indeed, the infiltration into the market sphere of values and norms belonging to the other two spheres could jeopardise the pursuit of the market's ultimate goal, which is efficiency. So, if economic discourse seeks to acquire scientific status (understood in a neo-positivist sense), it must sever the umbilical cord that has kept it tied to ethics and politics for centuries. Clearly, the civil economy cannot accept such a principle of separation (which is still dominant), for the obvious reason that the object of the economic problem is human being in its entirety. It follows that economics and ethics reflect one another, and can only be understood with reference to one another. Economics should be kept distinct and autonomous from ethics and politics – but not separate from them.

The second thesis is that a primary task of economic inquiry is also to examine the design of society's institutional order, which cannot simply be taken as something predetermined or 'natural'. So civil economists cannot confine themselves to seeking the optimum adaptation of resources to a given set of rules of play, for the simple reason that not all economic institutions are equally capable of ensuring the same results: one must therefore choose the ones that do most to foster society's civil progress, which will depend both on individual behaviours and on the kind of economic institutions that are selected.

Finally, the third thesis is that the three principles of the market order – exchange of equivalents, redistribution and reciprocity – must be in a multiplicative, not additive, relationship. This means that all three must operate simultaneously if they are to generate virtuous circles. There can be no trade-off between them, for instance by giving up reciprocity to increase the space reserved for exchange of equivalents, or vice versa. In other words, an unmistakable mark of the civil economy is that its ultimate goal is the common good – a concept I will now turn to.

10 Richard Whately, *Introductory lectures on political economy*, New York, Kelley, 1966 (1831).

From the late eighteenth century onwards, under the immense influence of Smith's analysis, the civil economy paradigm was replaced by that of political economy. And it is only in the last quarter of a century that the civil economy approach has begun to re-emerge, after such a long hibernation.

The common good as a category of economic thinking

What are we to understand by the expression 'common good'? A simple but effective way to grasp its meaning is to contrast it with the notion of the *total good*. Whereas the latter can be rendered by the metaphor of an *addition*, in which the items to be added stand for the good of individuals (or the social groups that make up society), the common good is more like a *multiplication*, whose factors stand for the good of individuals (or groups). The meaning of the metaphor is clear. In an addition, the total remains positive even if some of the items cancel out. Thus, if the goal is to maximise the total good (e.g. national GDP), anyone's good (or welfare) can actually be 'cancelled out' provided someone else's welfare increases by more than the other person loses. In a multiplication, on the other hand, cancelling out just one factor reduces the entire product to zero.

In other words, the logic of the common good does not allow trade-offs: one person's good cannot be sacrificed – whatever the person's life situation or social rank – in order to increase someone else's good, for the basic reason that the 'someone else' is still a *human being*. According to the logic of the total good, the 'someone else' is an *individual*, i.e. a subject identified by a particular utility function – and, as we know, utilities can simply be added up (or compared), since they have no faces, or identities, or histories. As Aristotle made clear, life lived in common by human beings is something very different from the mere sharing of pastures by animals. In the pasture, each animal eats for itself and attempts to take food away from the rest. In human society, on the other hand, each person's good can only be achieved by working in common. Above all, each person's good cannot be enjoyed unless it is also enjoyed by everyone else.

Why do the common good and the total good continue to be mixed up, even by experts, creating numerous misunderstandings and leading to many sterile, inconclusive arguments? The most convincing answer is that today's prevailing culture is so imbued with philosophical utilitarianism that even those who, at least in words, oppose it are in practice conditioned by it. Indeed, it should be remembered that Bentham's utilitarian ethics stated and spread the idea that the goal of politics was the *total good* of the nation – and hence that the market (i.e. the economy) and public institutions should not be organised so as to prevent such a goal from being attained.

Of course, as long as utilitarian thinking was circumscribed to the socioeconomic sphere, remedies were (nearly) always found for the inconsistencies it generated, especially regarding the distribution of wealth. Indeed, this is the ultimate meaning of the welfare state, whose philosophical basis is markedly Hobbesian: since the logic of the total good by no means ensures that all citizens can live decently, and since (for obvious reasons) prolonged poverty and serious inequality between social groups hamper the maximisation of the total good, the state is entrusted with the task of intervening *post factum* to compensate those who, for whatever reason, have lagged too far behind in the market race. In recent years, however, the inadequacy of the Hobbesian compromise has been revealed by attempts to extend the logic of the total good to the sphere of what Foucault termed 'biopolitics':[11] a human embryo is sacrificed to enhance, i.e. increase, an individual's welfare; euthanasia is legalised to put an end to the disutility of the patient and those that have to assist her, and so on.

Another consequence of the damaging confusion between the common good and the total good must be mentioned here. It directly challenges the Catholic world, and concerns the reductive way in which the Vatican II Council's dealt with the common good – one of the four founding principles of the Social Doctrine of the Church (SDC). Indeed, *Gaudium et Spes* defines the common good as 'the sum of those conditions of social life which allow social groups and their individual members relatively thorough and ready access to their own fulfilment' (26). As we may note, the common good is not a goal in itself, but merely an instrument for the good of the individual or of groups. The Compendium of the Social Doctrine of the Church, published in 2004 at the express request of Pope John Paul II, put matters right by writing 'The common good does not consist in the simple *sum* of the particular goods of each subject of a social entity. Belonging to everyone and to each person, it is and remains common, because it is indivisible and because only together is it possible to attain it, increase it and safeguard its effectiveness ... No expression of social life – from the family to intermediate social groups, associations, enterprises of an economic nature, cities, regions, states, up to the community of peoples and nations – can escape the issue of its own common good, in that this is

11 Michel Foucault, *Naissance de la biopolitique: cours au Collège de France (1978-1979)*, Paris, Gallimard, 2004.

a *constitutive* element of its significance and the authentic *reason* for its very existence' (164-165: my italics). It may be observed that this definition not only strongly emphasises the originality of the notion of the common good – from which its non-separability descends – but also indicates how it can be achieved. In particular, '[in the democratic State] those responsible for government are required to interpret the common good of their country not only according to the guidelines of the majority but also according to the effective good of all the members of the community, including the minority' (169). So the state interprets, but does not determine or set forth what the common good is, for the state is 'the expression' of 'civil society' (168) and not vice versa, as the various versions of the ethical state would claim.

Here it is worthwhile mentioning the thinking of Antonio Rosmini. After defining the common good as the *goal* of civil society, the famous theologist and philosopher writes 'The common good is the good of all the individuals that make up the social body; the public good, instead, is the good of the social body taken as a whole, or – as some would see it – in its organisation.'[12] In contemporary language, the public good as referred to here by Rosmini is the total good, i.e. the indistinct good of society – as suggested by communitarianism – whereas the common good is the good of the people that live in, and make up, society.

A surely unintended but no less damaging consequence of the confusion of thought regarding the notion of the common good is the fact that the words 'charity' (*agape*) and 'solidarity' were effectively used as synonyms until John Paul II made his clarifying statement. Some examples. The term 'solidarity' occurs 23 times in the 1992 *Catechism of the Catholic Church*, and nine times in the texts published by the Vatican II Council. It is worth noting that *Gaudium et* does not use the former expression *doctrina socialis* to refer to the Social Doctrine of the Church, but rather *doctrina de societate.* This shift in terminology would not even have been noticed had it not been referred to a few years later by Chenu in his influential thesis that the SDC was merely a "Social Teaching of the Church" that did nothing but read those *res novae* ('new things') that 'are points of convergence for many people and, to some extent, express their expectations'.[13]

12 Antonio Rosmini, *Filosofia del diritto*, Roma, Edizione nazionale e critica, Città Nuova, 1997 (1865), Section 1644.

13 Marie Dominique Chenu, *La dottrina sociale della Chiesa: origine e sviluppo*, Brescia, Queriniana, 1971, 53.

An admittedly disconcerting thesis which, for the – altogether praiseworthy – purpose of preventing the SDC from becoming an ideology, not to say a political programme, effectively voided it of its basic principles as well as its practical, guiding function. The gap was subsequently filled in the 1988 encyclical *Sollicitudo rei socialis*, in which John Paul II wrote of the SDC: 'Nor is it an ideology, but rather the accurate formulation of the results of a careful reflection on the complex realities of human existence ... Its main aim is to *interpret* these realities, determining their conformity with or divergence from the lines of the Gospel teaching on man and his vocation, a vocation which is at once earthly and transcendent; its aim is thus to *guide* Christian behaviour. It therefore belongs to the field, not of ideology, but of theology and particularly of moral theology' (41, my italics).

But there is more. In the *Catechism* (2850) we read that the bond that unites us in the Body of Christ is not charity (as *agape*, love), but solidarity. On the other hand, the October 2005 Bishops' Synod in Rome, at the end of its work on the topic 'The Eucharist: source and summit of the life and mission of the Church',[14] published a *Message* in which the term 'solidarity' occurs three times (4, 5 and 13) and 'charity' only once (20). The risks to the Christian message if 'charity' (love) and 'solidarity' are seen as substantially equivalent, and hence interchangeable, notions are only too clear.

This is why it is so important to specify the characteristics of the common good, which must not be confused with either the private good or the public good. In the common good, the advantage each person gains from being part of a given community cannot be separated from the advantage that others gain from it. In other words, each person's interests are realised *together* with other people's – not *against* them (as with the private good) or *regardless* of them (as with the public good). In that sense, 'common' is opposed to 'one's own', just as 'public' is opposed to 'private'. What is common is not *only* what is one's own, nor is it what is *everyone's* without distinction. No-one among contemporary thinkers has seen these distinctions more clearly than Hannah Arendt. In her famous *The human condition* she writes that 'public' means what can be seen, what can be spoken of and discussed. 'Everything that appears in public [and] can be seen and heard by everybody'. 'Private', on the contrary, is what is concealed from view. 'Common', on the other hand', is 'the world itself, in so far as it is common to all of us and distinguished from our privately owned place in

14 See http://www.vatican.va/roman_curia/synod/documents/rc_synod_doc_20051022_message-synod_en.html (consulted on June 2017).

it'.[15] As such, 'common' is the place of what is not one's own, and hence the place of interpersonal relationships.

So who are the 'enemies' of the common good? On the one hand, those who behave as 'free riders', i.e. live at other peoples' expense; on the other hand, those who behave as pure altruists, and hence cancel out their own interests to benefit others. Neither type of behaviour enhances the common good, albeit for different reasons and with different consequences. Neither pure egoism nor pure altruism can – by themselves – make a human social order sustainable. So who are the *friends* of the common good? Those whose behaviour is driven by the principle of reciprocity, which means 'I freely give you something so that you can in turn give to others or perhaps to me, according to your abilities'. In contrast, the principle of exchange of equivalents states 'I give you something on condition that you give me something of equivalent value in return". So, whereas the principle of reciprocity – as Aristotle indicated – postulates proportionality, the principle of exchange postulates equivalence.[16]

No human life lived in common can last long and be a source of happiness, i.e. of full personal realisation, if everyone gives (in the manner of pure altruists or philanthropists) or if everyone claims the right to receive (in the manner of opportunists), or again if all intersubjective relationships are reduced to the pattern of exchange of equivalents. Cultural acceptance of the principle of reciprocity, and its political translation into practice, are the certain guarantees of harmonious coexistence and viability. This is the specific – although not the only – contribution that Catholic thinking can, and therefore must, make to the regeneration of the *civitas*. It is not difficult to understand this. The original structure of the principle of reciprocity is ternary (I, you, the third party), whereas that of the exchange of equivalents is binary (in a contract there is only an 'I' and a 'you'). And, as Paul Ricœur reminds us, it is the involvement of a third party in intersubjective relationships that creates society and keeps it alive.

The return of the 'common good' category

Why, in the last twenty years, has the common good discourse been re-emerging into the public debate after more than two centuries of silence?

15 Hannah ARENDT, *The human condition*, Chicago, The University of Chicago Press, 1958, 50, 52.

16 See David HOLLENBACH, *The common good*, Cambridge, Cambridge University Press, 2002.

Why is the shift from national economies to a global economy again making this discourse topical?

To answer these questions, we need to realise that since the first half of the nineteenth century the civil view of the economy has – as we have seen – vanished from both scientific research and the politico-cultural debate. The reasons for this have been many and varied, but I will confine myself to the two most relevant ones. On the one hand there is the spread within high European culture of the utilitarian philosophy of Jeremy Bentham, whose main work, published in 1789, took several decades to prevail in the economic discourse. It is through utilitarian morality rather than Protestant ethics – as many still believe – that the hyper-minimalist anthropology of *homo oeconomicus* took root in economics, and with it the methodology of social atomism. The following passage from Bentham is noted for its clarity and depth of meaning: 'The community is a fictitious body, composed of the individual persons who are considered as constituting as it were its members. The interest of the community then is, what? – the sum of the interests of the several members who compose it.'[17]

On the other hand, there is the full affirmation of industrial society in the wake of the industrial revolution. Industrial society is one that produces goods; the machine is all-pervasive, and the rhythms of life are mechanical. Energy largely replaces muscular strength and accounts for the huge increases in productivity which in turn accompany mass production. Energy and machines transform the nature of work: personal skills are broken down into elementary components. Hence the need for coordination and organisation. The result is a world in which people are seen as 'things' (for it is easier to coordinate 'things' than people), and in which people are separated from the roles they perform. Organisations, and above all businesses, deal with roles rather than people; and this happens not only within factories, but throughout society. This is the profound meaning of Fordism and Taylorism as a – successful – attempt to theorise this model of social order and put it into practice. The introduction of the 'assembly line' has its equivalent in the spread of consumerism, hence the schizophrenia that typifies 'modern times': on the one hand, people are exasperated by the loss of meaning of work (alienation due to the depersonalisation of the worker); on the other, by way of compensation, consumption becomes lavish. Marxist thinking and its political expressions during the twentieth

17 Jeremy BENTHAM, *An introduction to the principles of morals and legislation*, Oxford, Clarendon Press, 1998 (1789), I, IV.

century were used, with varying but modest success, to find escape routes from such a model of society.

The complex interweaving and collision of these two sets of reasons had a consequence that is important for the purposes of our discourse: the assertion, which still be seen in society, of two opposing conceptions of the market. One of these sees it as a 'necessary evil', i.e. an institution we cannot manage without, for it is a guarantee of economic progress, yet an 'evil' that we should protect ourselves from and hence keep under control. The other sees the market as the ideal place to solve the political problem – the liberal/individualist view, which holds that the 'logic' of the market must be able to spread, albeit with appropriate adjustments, to every realm of community life: the family, school, politics, even religious practices.

It is not difficult to identify the weak points in these two mirror-image conceptions. The former – brilliantly summed up in the aphorism 'The job of government is not to row, but to steer' – is based on the argument of the fight against inequality: only redistributive intervention by government can narrow the gap between individuals and between social groups. But this is not the current state of affairs. In advanced Western countries, inequality – which had decreased from 1945 onwards – has again increased shockingly over the last thirty years, despite massive government intervention in the economy. Of course, we know the reasons why this has happened – reasons that have to do with the transition to post-industrial society. Examples include the use of the new information and computer technologies in production processes, and the creation of global labour and capital markets; but we need to understand why equalising redistribution cannot be *solely* a task for government. The fact is that political stability is a goal which in the current model of democracy – Weber's and Schumpeter's elitist/competitive model – cannot be attained by measures to reduce inequality, but only by economic growth. The duration and reputation of democratic governments are determined far more by their ability to increase the level of wealth than by their ability to redistribute it equally among citizens – for the simple, though sad, reason that the 'poor' do not take part in the democratic game, and hence are not a class of 'stakeholders' than can have an impact on policy. So if we want to oppose the endemic increase in inequality, as a harbinger of serious threats to both peace and democracy, we must first intervene at the point when wealth is produced, and not just when it is redistributed.

What is wrong with the other conception of the market, today efficiently conveyed by the unchallenged idea that there is 'one best way', is its refusal to acknowledge that extending the market logic as far as possible will not increase everyone's well-being. In other words, the metaphor that 'a rising tide lifts all boats' is *not true*. The reasoning behind the metaphor is basically this: since citizens' well-being depends on economic prosperity, and since the latter is causally linked to market relationships, the true priority of government must be to create conditions in which market thinking can flourish unrestricted. So the more generous the welfare state is, the more it restricts economic growth, and the more it prevents the spread of well-being. Hence the notion of selective welfare, which will only be provided for those who cannot keep up in the market race. The rest – those that manage to remain within the virtuous circle of growth – will cope by themselves. Yet mere observation of the facts reveals the basic inconsistency of such thinking – namely that economic growth (i.e. sustained increase in wealth) and civil progress (i.e. increased freedom for individuals) no longer go hand in hand. Increases in welfare are no longer accompanied by increases in well-being; and reducing opportunities to include those who, for whatever reason, remain on the margins of the market, while giving nothing extra to those who are already within it, produces rationing of freedom which will always be detrimental to 'public happiness'.

These two conceptions of the market, which are so different in their philosophical assumptions and political consequences, have ended up producing – first and foremost at cultural level – a perhaps unexpected result: the assertion of an idea of the market that is contrary to the traditional notion of the civil economy. An idea that sees the market as an institution founded on a double standard: the *impersonal nature* of exchange relationships (the less I know about my counterpart the better for me, for it's easier to do business with people you don't know); the *entirely self-interested* motivations of those involved, so that 'moral feelings' such as affection, reciprocity, fraternity and so on play no significant part in the market. And so the steady and impressive expansion of market relationships over the past century and a half have ended up reinforcing the pessimistic interpretation of the character of human beings as theorised by Hobbes and Mandeville, who claimed that only the harsh laws of the market would succeed in taming their perverse impulses and anarchistic tendencies. This caricature of human nature has helped to lend credence to a twofold error: that the market sphere coincides with selfishness, a place in which, at best, everyone pursues his own individual interests and, symmetrically, that the government sphere coincides with solidarity, i.e. the pursuit of collective interests. It is on this basis that the well-known government/market dichotomy has been erected: a model in which government is identified with the public sphere, and the market with the private sphere.

At this point it is not difficult to understand the return of the notion of the common good to the contemporary cultural debate. Faced with the steady, and dismal, reduction of human relationships to the exchange of equivalent products, the contemporary human spirit rebels, and calls for a different story. The keyword that today expresses this call better than any other is 'fraternity', a word that already appeared in the form *fraternité* on the banner of the French revolution, but – for well-known reasons – was abandoned by the post-revolutionary order and eventually erased from our political and economic vocabulary. It was the Franciscan school of thinking that gave this term the meaning it has retained over time, both extending and going beyond the solidarity principle. Indeed, whereas solidarity is the principle of social organisation that allows the unequal to become equal, fraternity is the one that allows the equal to be diverse. Fraternity allows people who are equal in dignity and basic rights to express their life plan, or their charisma, in different ways. The periods behind us, the nineteenth and above all twentieth centuries, were marked by major battles, both cultural and political, in the name of solidarity, and this was a good thing – take the trade-union and civil-rights movements. The point is that solidarity does not suffice for a good society – for a society based merely on solidarity, but not on fraternity, is a society that everyone would attempt to get away from. The fact is that whereas a society based on fraternity is also one based on solidarity, the converse is not necessarily true.

Forgetting that a human society in which the sense of fraternity is extinguished and everything is reduced, on the one hand, to improving transactions based on the exchange of equivalents and, on the other, to increasing transfers by public welfare institutions is unsustainable makes clear why, despite the quality of the intellectual forces brought to bear, we have not yet found a credible solution to the great trade-off between efficiency and fairness. A society in which the fraternity principle disappears is not viable; in other words, a society in which the only motivations are 'giving to receive something in return' or 'giving because we have to' cannot make progress. This is why neither the liberal/individualist view of the world, in which (almost) everything is exchange, nor the government-centred view of society, in which (almost) everything is duty, is a reliable guide to getting our societies out of the doldrums they are now in.

Prospects for action, and a concluding note

How to help the market return to being what it was in the humanist period – an instrument for civilisation and a means of strengthening social ties – is the great challenge that faces us all today. That this challenge is a momentous one is above all confirmed by the following question: in the current context, dominated by capitalist-type market economies, can subjects whose *modus operandi* is inspired by the reciprocity principle succeed not only in emerging, but also in expanding?

What should make us think that the idea of bringing back the principle of the common good to the public sphere (not to be confused with the government sphere), and particularly the economic sphere, is not just a soothing utopia? Two factors, both of them verifiable. The first involves realising that the capitalist economy is based on a serious, pragmatic contradiction, not a logical one. To be sure, the capitalist economy is a market economy, in other words an institution based on the two basic principles of modernity: (1) freedom of action and enterprise, and (2) equality before the law. Yet at the same time the key institution of capitalism – the capitalist business – has continued to develop over the past three centuries on the principle of hierarchy. This has created a production system with a centralised structure to which a certain number of individuals voluntarily surrender in exchange for a price (wages), their work, which, once entered the firm, escapes the control of those who provided it.

We know well from economic history how this has happened, and we also know the remarkable economic progress that this institution has achieved. But the fact is that in the present transition – from modernity to postmodernity – more and more voices are being raised to point out the difficulty of reconciling the democratic principle and the capitalist principle. The main problem is the 'privatisation' of the public realm: capitalist businesses increasingly control the behaviour of individuals – more than half of living time is, spent at work – at the expense of the government or other agencies, above all the family. Notions such as freedom of choice, tolerance, equality before the law and participation, which developed and spread during the period of civil humanism and were then strengthened during the Enlightenment, as an antidote to the (almost) absolute power of the monarch, are being co-opted and suitably recalibrated by capitalist businesses to turn individuals, who are no longer in thrall, into purchasers of the goods and services they themselves produce.

The dycrasia here is that, if there are cogent reasons to see the greatest possible extension of the democratic principle as a good thing, we must then start to look at what happens *inside* businesses, rather than just to look at the relations between businesses interacting in the market. As Robert Dahl writes, 'if democracy is justified in governing the state, then it must also be justified in governing economic enterprises.'[18] A society in which the democratic principle is only applied in the political sphere can never be fully democratic. A good society does not force its members to make awkward dissociations between being democratic as citizens, but not democratic as workers or consumers.

The second consideration concerns the ever-increasing dissatisfaction with the way in which the principle of freedom is interpreted. As we know, there are three constitutive dimension of freedom: autonomy, immunity and capability. Autonomy means freedom of choice: we are not free if we are not in a position to choose. Immunity means the absence of coercion by any external agent; it is essentially the negative freedom (or 'freedom from') spoken of by Isaiah Berlin. Finally, capability, as posited by Amartya Sen, means our ability to choose, i.e. to achieve our goals, at least partly or to some extent. We are not free if we can never – or can only partly – put our own life plans into effect. Now, whereas the neo-liberal approach ensures the first and second dimensions of freedom at the expense of the third, the statist approach, whether in the mixed-economy version or the market socialism version, tends to promote the second and third dimensions at the expense of the first. Liberism is certainly able to act as a flywheel for change, but less able to deal with its negative consequences that are due to the high degree of asymmetry in time between distribution of the costs of change and that of its benefits. The costs are immediate and tend to fall on the segments of the population that are least equipped to cope with them; the benefits arise over time, and accrue to the more talented. As Joseph Schumpeter was one of the first to recognise, the creative destruction mechanism is not only the heart of the capitalist system – which destroys the 'old' to create the 'new', and creates the 'new' to destroy the 'old' – but also its Achilles' heel. On the other hand, although market socialism – in its many versions – assigns to government the task of dealing with the aforementioned asymmetries, it does not undermine the logic of the capitalist market; it merely restricts the area in which it can operate and take effect. The essence of the common good paradigm, in contrast, lies in attempting

18 Robert DAHL, *Democracy and its critics*, New Haven, Yale University Press, 57.

to maintain all three dimensions of freedom united. That is what makes it seem all the more worth investigating and working to implement.

In conclusion, a note on the philosophy of science. Of the three types of reason – theoretical, practical and technical – bequeathed to us by classical culture, economics properly belongs to practical reason. Yet over the centuries this discipline has always enjoyed a special relationship with theoretical reason. That is why the great economists of the past, whichever school of thought they belonged to, were also philosophers. The new element, especially over the last forty years, is that economics has ended up emphasising its link with technical reason, thereby severing its ancient link with theoretical reason, i.e. with knowledge. We can see the consequences. To be sure, the economic discourse has increased – considerably – its technical/analytical apparatus; but this seems incapable of dealing with reality. Take such crucial problems as the endemic, massive increase in social inequality, the scandal of hunger in a time of abundance, the outbreak of identity conflicts, the sustainability of the biosphere, the paradoxes of happiness, and many others.

It would be pointless – as well as irresponsible – to think of solving such problems by remaining on the technical level, although this is still necessary. The reason is that, at this point of transition, technology does not have much to offer the economic discourse, for although it is able to suggest answers it is unable to ask the right questions – above all the question of man. The reductionist path that economics took in the second half of the twentieth century ended up disarming critical thought, with consequences that are now plain to see. The belief that scientific rigour implied avoidance of personal traits, and that in order to be deemed scientific research must eschew all value judgements, ended up imposing libertarian individualism as a pre-analytical assumption which, as such, did not require any justification – even though we know that this itself is a value judgement, and a substantial one. Asserting that the good is whatever the individual deems to be such is the greatest of value judgements; but this does not absolve us from subjecting it to the test of theoretical reason.

There are two wrong ways – warns Pope Francis in *Evangelii Gaudium* (2013) – of facing up to these major challenges. One is to yield to the temptation to remain above reality through utopia; the other is to remain below reality through resignation. But if society is to be a match for today's challenges, it must avoid such pitfalls. It must not waver between the blithe optimism of those who see the historical process as a triumphant onward march of humanity towards its full realisation, and the despairing cynicism of those who believe, in Kafka's words, that 'there is a destination, but no way there'.[19]

Hence the need for a new message of hope. The certainties that technical and scientific progress offers us do not suffice. It has certainly increased, and will continue to increase, our ability to find the means of attaining all manner of goals. But although the problem of means now seems far less serious than it used to be, we cannot assume that the same will be true of the problem of ends – a problem that can be stated as 'What should I want?', rather than 'What should I do to obtain what I want?' Today man is afflicted by the need to choose his ends and not just his means. Hence the need for new hope: faced with a ever-stronger chain of means, people today seem unable to find any alternative to submitting or rebelling. Things were different when the chain of means was weaker. It is understandable that the have-nots will focus their hope on having: this is the "old hope". But it would be wrong to continue believing this today. Although it is true that it would be foolish to abandon the pursuit of means, it is even more true that the "new hope" must be focused on ends. What hoping means today is precisely this: not considering ourselves either as the mere result of processes that are beyond our control, or as a self-sufficient reality that does not need relationships with others.

19 Franz KAFKA, *The Zürau Aphorisms* (1931), Section 27.

Jean-Michel Bonvin

Defining the common good in terms of capabilities

This short paper sets out to tackle the question of the common good from the perspective of the capability approach developed by the philosopher and economist Amartya Sen. After presenting a definition of the term 'capabilities' and its specific features in comparison with other approaches to the common good, I will focus more specifically on the two components of capabilities: (1) the power to act, or real freedom as opposed to formal freedom, and (2) freedom of choice and the question of rationality or reason to value.[1] I will conclude by summing up the main ways in which such a conception contributes to the notion of the common good.

Definitions

Sen's capability approach focuses on the development of the real freedom to lead a life that we have reason to value. This approach is thus distinguished from conceptions of the common good that centre on increasing GDP or material wealth.[2] It is, moreover, the basis for the adoption of the human development index (HDI) in the 1990 s; this allowed health and education to be included alongside material wealth as components for measuring a given country's degree of development.[3] Increasing the common good is thus not just a matter of increasing GDP, which implies two differences from this perspective. On the one hand the common good is not just about accumulating material wealth or money; other dimensions must be considered. On the other, increasing overall wealth fails to answer the question of its distribution, which may lead to a definition of the common good that favours a minority at the expense of the majority. In contrast, the capability approach emphasises the many different dimensions that must be considered in promoting the common good (not just wealth, but also health, education, political participation and so on), as well as the need to

1 For a summary, see Jean-Michel BONVIN, Nicolas FARVAQUE, *Amartya Sen: une politique de la liberté*, Paris, Michalon, 2008.

2 Amartya SEN, *Development as freedom,* New York, Alfred Knopf, 1999.

3 Maroine BENDAOUD, 'Des travaux d'Amartya Sen à l'indice de développement humain', *Centre d'études sur l'intégration et la mondialisation*, April 2011 (consulted on 20 December 2016).

make each of these dimensions accessible to all, at least up to a minimum threshold.[4] In the absence of these two elements, it is only a truncated version of the common good that will be pursued – a doubly impoverished version in terms of its components and its target audience.

The capability approach also differs from utilitarian perspectives of well-being, which focus on maximising individual utility or pleasure and minimising individual disutility or pain.[5] In particular, such subjectivist approaches raise the problem of how to measure this utility: how, when faced with a dilemma or a conflict, do I decide that my utility is greater than my neighbour's, and how do I determine the exact value of these various utilities in order to calculate and compare them and arrive at the greatest possible sum, in accordance with Bentham's utilitarian precepts? If the sole measure of the utility or value of an action or good is the pleasure I derive from it, this implies that value or utility is ultimately based on a strictly subjectivist approach. Indeed, utilitarianism, with its propensity to define the common good as the sum total of individual goods, is a dead end, for the common good is more than just this. So we must look at how something 'common' emerges from the confrontation between individual conceptions; merely adding up individual utilities will not suffice. The capability approach instead invites us to see this confrontation between the various individual conceptions of the good through the prism of the notion of 'reason to value'.[6] It thus enables us to go beyond the contrast between a universal conception of the good (which is absolutist or dogmatic, insofar as it is imposed on the various protagonists) and a subjectivist conception of individual goods whose value cannot be compared (which is relativist, insofar as the sole unifying principle is the sum total of individual utilities) to arrive at a realistic, constructivist approach to the common good. We must now look at how such an approach can be achieved.

Real versus formal freedom

Real freedom to live a life that we have reason to value depends on a number of conditions that are carefully identified by Sen. First, we need a minimum basis of material resources. This entails effective access to goods and services, perhaps guaranteed by market players or, failing this, by sup-

4 Amartya SEN, *Inequality reexamined*, Oxford, Clarendon Press, 1992.

5 Amartya SEN, 'Equality of what?' *The Tanner lecture on human values*, Stanford University, 22 May 1979.

6 Amartya SEN, *The idea of justice*, London, Allen Lane, 2009.

plementary government action. If this basis is not guaranteed, we do not have real freedom, but formal freedom that may end up forcing us to accept conditions incompatible with human dignity in order to have access to this minimum basis of resources.[7] Imagine, for example, someone forced to work 16 to 18 hours a day for very low wages; such a view of access to resources would be clearly contrary to the capability approach. So it is not enough for resources to be accessible – they must also be accessible under conditions compatible with human dignity. Government action plays a key role here in dissuading market players from providing conditions worse than those guaranteed by the government; but this role must not replace that of market players, for it must remain supplementary in order to maintain people's dignity.

However, access to resources, which Sen thematises using the notion of 'entitlement',[8] is not sufficient. There must also be factors that allow the resources to be used in a way that the person has reason to value. Many parameters are involved here, and Sen groups them into three categories.[9] First, there are individual factors that depend on people's skills or abilities to use the resources properly. Having a bicycle will not develop your capabilities unless you know how to use it. The school system and education in general have a key part to play here. We are not just talking about providing effective access to resources, but about the skills to use them in a valuing manner – for the common good is not just a matter of material well-being, but also of 'agency', the power to act. In Sen's terms, this does not simply mean guaranteeing a minimum material standard of living, but enabling people to live lives that they have reason to value. This goal brings together the dimensions of well-being and agency.[10]

However, ability to act requires a favourable context in which it can be used. In other words, individual factors are not enough; account must also be taken of social and environmental factors, the other two categories identified by Sen. Having a bicycle and knowing how to ride it do not guarantee development of capability or real freedom to move about – the person must be authorised to use it (for example, riding a bicycle must not be considered inappropriate for certain groups of people), and the road infrastructure must allow this. If these conditions are not met, i.e. if the culture or

7 Amartya SEN, *Commodities and capabilities*, Amsterdam, North Holland, 1985.

8 Amartya SEN, *Poverty and famines*, Oxford, Oxford University Press, 1981.

9 See the categories suggested in BONVIN & FARVAQUE, op.cit., 2008.

10 Amartya SEN, 'Well-being, agency and freedom: the Dewey lectures', *Journal of Philosophy* 82/4 (1985), 169-221.

dominant values prohibit certain people from riding a bicycle, or if the area is not designed for cyclists (or is only accessible on payment of a large fee), having a bicycle and knowing how to ride it will mean nothing in terms of capability development. Ultimately, then, it is the whole configuration that matters: having resources, the capacity or skill to use them, and a suitable context that provides real opportunities to do so. What we have here is thus a configurational approach[11] in which promotion of the common good involves giving all the members of society factors that allow capability development: guaranteeing everyone access to appropriate resources and the ability to use them, in a context that allows everyone to do so.

As regards agency, the common good requires extensive government action; but, as we have seen in connection with resources, Sen believes this action should remain supplementary. Collective responsibility, that of the central government or the local authorities, should not replace individual responsibility, but should instead create conditions for individual responsibility and, when these are met, allow it to be exercised. Sen is quite clear about this: without real freedom, i.e. without capability, individual responsibility cannot be exercised. [12] So the government has to ensure that access to capabilities is guaranteed – failing which the conditions for individual responsibility are not met, and it would be absurd to ascribe behaviour that is perceived as irresponsible to individuals' ill-will. Again, the government is not the sole guarantor of capabilities, but plays a supplementary part, insofar as action by the market and civil society is predominant. What Sen thus recommends is a 'welfare mix', rather than nationalisation of the economy and other sectors of society. To be sure, the harmonious development of society on behalf of all requires government action; but this must support, rather than stifle, initiatives by other players. Yet, as Father Lacordaire stated, the weak are oppressed by unrestrained freedom and liberated by the law. It is therefore important to take a positive view of government action, without demonising the market. In Sen's view the government does not replace the market, but lays the necessary foundations for its operation on behalf of the common good and social cohesion – something the market can never guarantee if left to its own devices, for the market seeks to maximise wealth, thereby penalising those who do the least to maximise

11 Jean-Michel BONVIN, "Capacités et démocratie", *Raisons pratiques* 18 (2008), 237-261.
12 Amartya SEN, *Development as freedom*, 13-18.

it.[13] In contrast, capability development is based on a multidimensional conception of the common good that includes not just economic wealth, but all the factors that people have reason to value. Civil society and the government are better placed to take account of these various dimensions, and hence it is through joint action by the market, civil society and the government that this plural conception of the common good can best be achieved.[14]

Since Sen's approach no doubt seems very idealistic, it is important to indicate the spirit in which he formulates it. To him, this is not some transcendental perspective that seeks to impose an inaccessible ideal or to judge reality in this light. On the contrary, Sen takes as his departure the world as it is, assesses it in terms of resources and individual, social and environmental conversion factors, and suggests avenues for reform that could favour the most harmonious and fairest development of capabilities for all.[15] The point is not to advocate an illusory equality, but to reduce inequalities in capabilities so that the pursuit of the common good can benefit all without exception. It is thus presented as a resolutely realistic, reformist perspective: the goal is not to blame reality for failing to meet an inaccessible ideal, but to change it so that it will come as close to this ideal as possible.[16]

Freedom of choice and reason to value

However, capability development is not just about being able to act. If it were nothing more than that, it could become a kind of glorification of individual action, implying that we should all be able to live the life we choose. This could reduce the common good to the concomitant pursuit of individual selfishness, with everyone equally equipped to do so thanks to the availability of appropriate resources and conversion factors. This is not Sen's position, as we can see from his conception of real freedom of choice and its intrinsic link to the question of rationality.[17] The goal is to increase

13 Some sociologists such as Robert Castel describe them as 'supernumerary' or 'of no use to the world' in the context of neoliberal societies that focus on maximising wealth. See Robert CASTEL, *Les métamorphoses de la question sociale*, Paris, Fayard, 1995.

14 Jean DRÈZE & Amartya SEN, *India, development and participation*, Oxford, Oxford University Press, 2002.

15 Amartya SEN, *The idea of justice*, 31-51.

16 Amartya SEN, 'What do we want from a theory of justice?', *The Journal of Philosophy* CIII/5 (2006), 215-238.

17 Amartya SEN, *Rationality and freedom*, Cambridge MA, Harvard University Press, 2002.

real freedom to lead not the life we choose, but the one we have reason to value. This reference to the notion of rationality is crucial to Sen's perspective. It is the basis for the constructivist dimension of his conception of the common good: if the common good is not a pre-existent factor, but has to be built through confrontation between members of society and their conceptions of what it means, we must determine the conditions in which it can be suitably built.[18] To Sen, this involves the notion of 'reason to value' which lays down the rules for a fruitful confrontation between individual and collective rationalities.

First let me point out the incompleteness of Sen's notion of rationality. Its content, i.e. what should be considered rational or irrational, is not predetermined, but emerges (at least partly) during the public discussion or debate.[19] It is in this sense that the notion of undecidability should be understood: what is rational cannot be decided ahead of the public debate. On the contrary, it is during such a debate that what is rational or irrational will gradually become clear. The incompleteness of rationality, in the sense that the notion is not fully defined in advance, is thus a precondition for a fruitful public debate. In contrast, if everything is decided in advance, there is nothing to discuss – rather than build the common good together, it is simply a matter of convincing the undecided that a pre-existing conception is well founded. Incompleteness, which some may see as a kind of excessive weakness or lack of firmness, is thus the essential basis for a constructivist conception of the common good.[20] This is a crucial point, for it implies recognising individual reasons to value – in other words, it prevents collective rationality from simply being imposed on individual rationalities, without any public debate. We are not dealing with a predetermined notion of the common good that is to be inculcated into members of society, but a definition that is to be built by integrating all the individual rationalities. This first point thus shows the difference between the capability perspective and any paternalistic or dogmatic notion of the common good: dominant conceptions of the common good are likewise submitted to public debate, and hence are liable to be revised. Again, if we stop at this point, we may lapse into a kind of subjectivist relativism in which we could all lead the life we choose. The reference to rationality helps us out of this rut.

18 For the importance of the constructive dimension of democracy, see Amartya SEN, 'Democracy as a universal value', *The Journal of Democracy* 10/3 (1999), 3-17.

19 Amartya SEN, *The idea of justice*, 338-354.

20 Amartya SEN, *Rationality and freedom*, Cambridge MA, Harvard University Press, 2002.

Once again, the capability approach does not emphasise the need to let us all live the life we choose, but the one we have reason to value. In other words, individual choices and preferences must be rational or reasonable, which in Sen's view means they must be submitted to public debate. Indeed, we should not take account of, and support the achievement of, *all* individual preferences, but only those that successfully pass the test of public debate. Here we may refer to classic debates on costly or expensive preferences[21] that should not be supported by government action – thus the government does not have to enable all the members of a community to fly to the moon or go surfing at Malibu. Here the question of the resources available to government is crucial: the funds needed to support individual preferences being limited, they must be used for reasonable preferences (rather than expensive whims) and also fairly, so that everyone is able to achieve these reasonable preferences. Another no less classic example concerns adaptive preferences,[22] whereby people adjust their aspirations upwards or downwards according to the setting they find themselves in. In some cases this leads them to assume 'luxury' preferences, for these are the dominant social norm in the environment concerned; according to the aforementioned logic, the government or local authorities are not then bound to support the achievement of such preferences. In other cases, which are more worrying in terms of recognition of human dignity, individuals are led to reduce the level of their aspirations in accordance with a supposed principle of reality. This may thus cause them to accept very arduous working conditions, for having a job, even a poor-quality one, seems necessary to ensure survival, or again to put up with ill-treatment, since this seems 'normal' in their living environment (Nussbaum mentions the example of battered women in India, where women resign themselves to their fate since in their cultural environment it is apparently not seen as a problem). Such cases reveal a deficit in the ability to aspire or plan ahead[23] – in other words, the living conditions to which people are reduced prevent them from planning futures that they value or developing aspirations that allow them to flourish. The notion of 'reason to value' is crucial in order to deconstruct or submit for debate such adaptive preferences; it enables us to identify the extent to

21 John Rawls, *Political liberalism*, New York, Columbia University Press, 1993.

22 Jon Elster, *Sour grapes: studies in the subversion of rationality*, Cambridge, Cambridge University Press, 1985; Martha Nussbaum, *Women and human development: the capabilities approach*. Cambridge, Cambridge University Press, 2000.

23 Arjun Appadurai, 'The capacity to aspire: culture and the terms of recognition', in Vijayendra Rao & Michael Walton (eds), *Culture and public action*, Palo Alto, Stanford University Press, 59-84.

which people's situations may be considered of value, and/or the extent to which circumstances make people resign themselves to a fate they do not value.

As we can see, the notion of 'reason to value' is crucial in Sen's approach; not only does it allow social and collective norms to be debated, and their reasonableness and value to all the members of the community to be questioned, but it also submits individual preferences to the test of public debate. If they are unreasonable, either because they are too high (and hence too costly to the community) or because they are too limited to meet the requirements of human dignity, there is no reason to value them, and so no reason for the government to support them. In the former case (expensive preferences), they can only be pursued independently under individual responsibility, without help from the community; in the latter (preferences adjusted downwards), the government must refuse to tolerate the circumstances that produce this downward adjustment of individual aspirations, and hence provide appropriate social and environmental conversion factors that will enable the people concerned to achieve preferences that they really have reason to value. From this perspective, the common good involves giving us all the means to pursue the aspirations we have reason to value, i.e. those that seem reasonable and compatible with human dignity following a public debate.

Rationality (or rather 'reasonableness') is central to the conception of the common good suggested by the capability approach. This notion of rationality is not just an instrumental conception that emphasises the pursuit of the most efficient means. Reducing it to this dimension would mean seeing people as 'rational fools'[24] who cannot query the relevance of their goals, but can do no more than seek the most appropriate means of achieving them. Thus, taking the example given by Sen,[25] someone who wants to chop off his finger should be given the sharpest knife so that he can achieve his goal as efficiently as possible. Sen does not see rationality in such instrumental terms; instead, he insists that the *purpose* of the action should also be rationally analysed. Indeed, according to the capability approach, *homo economicus* – the anthropological translation of the view conveyed by instrumental rationality – is a rational fool. This point is crucial, for it implies that rational analysis covers not only the economic aspects based on cost/benefit calculation, but also other dimensions such as the relevance of goals, human development, social justice and so on, that all

24 Amartya SEN, 'Rational fools', *Philosophy & Public Affairs* 6/4 (1977), 317-344.

25 Amartya SEN, *Rationality and freedom*, Cambridge MA, Harvard University Press, 2002.

underpin a broader conception of the common good than the truncated version proposed by utilitarianism.

It is a radically constructivist version of the common good that is suggested here. The result is not predetermined, but emerges in the course of public debate. Indeed, this debate is bound to continue, in the endless quest for the common good. The democratic nature of the debate is essential, for it enables all individual rationalities (i.e. every individual's reasons to value) to be taken into account when defining the common good. Failing this, the absence of certain individuals could lead to the dominant conceptions, those most strongly represented in the public debate, being imposed on them, to their cost. In the approach proposed by Sen, there is no insurmountable conflict between individual and collective rationalities – only the (difficult) pursuit of their combination in a definition of the common good that is reasonable and compatible with all the community members' human dignity and reason to value.

Conclusion

The capability approach lays the foundations for a both realistic and constructivist approach to the common good. On the one hand, it reveals the preconditions for a common good that can benefit us all, rather than just a privileged minority, in terms of resources and the capability of using them for purposes that can be valued. The role of government is seen as supplementary to the action of the market and civil society, from a reformist and pragmatic point of view. At the same time, it suggests a path towards a constructivist conception of the common good that creates the conditions for a fruitful coexistence between individual and collective rationalities. The notion of 'reason to value' is proposed here in order to avoid the pitfalls of paternalism (in which the community imposes its view) and relativist subjectivism (in which individual preferences flourish at the expense of the community, and hence the common good). These two aspects – promotion of everyone's ability to act, and recognition of freedom of choice as long as it is reasonable and can be justified in public debate – are designed to be complementary: the common good is thus seen as consubstantial with people's capability development, i.e both their ability to act and their reasonable freedom of choice.

The common good: Still pertinent today? Theological and political philosophy

Mathias Nebel

Searching for the common good

Introduction

The notion of the common good has been seen by political philosophers as obsolete, superfluous and potentially dangerous. The post-war years saw its rapid abandonment in political discourse, and the Catholic Church was almost alone in continuing to use the concept as though it were still relevant. Yet the eclipse of the common good has only been temporary. Since the 1990 s we have seen the term being re-used in practical contexts such as cultural rights (artistic heritage as the common good of a people), the environment (the water and climate as global common good) or development (governance should aim at the common good). However, such revivals have not yet undermined political philosophers' criticisms of the notion – which this paper sets out to rehabilitate as one of the key categories of public and political action.

It will do so in two stages. The first part will respond to the criticism of the notion of the common good – indeed, its outright rejection – by liberal political philosophers in the 1960 s as superfluous, sectarian and potentially totalitarian towards minorities that did not share a same understanding of what the common good could mean. The second part will offer a reinterpretation of the notion based on a political philosophy of action. This updating will shed light on the essential, fruitful nature of the notion following the post-modern erosion of Enlightenment philosophy, especially as regards the limitations of political liberalism.

Part 1: Why the notion was rejected

1. *The operational need for the common good*

The historical reasons for the eclipse of the common good in the twentieth century are many and complex, and cannot all be stated here[1]. They were

1 Tim GORRINGE, *The common good and the global emergency*, Cambridge, Cambridge University Press, 2014, 21-26; David HOLLENBACH, *The common good and Christian ethics*, Cambridge, Cambridge University Press, 2002, 3-31.

part of a more general movement by Enlightenment thinkers to secularise theological principles while thinking the newly created state; a movement that saw, for example, 'the common good' and 'hope' replaced by 'the general interest' and 'progress'. Among the reasons for the eclipse of the common good, three – while very different in nature – can be single out. Between them they led to the almost total abandonment of the notion after 1945. The first is the National Socialist use of the notion of *Gemeinwohl* ('commonweal', or 'common good') and its fierce rejection after the war as implicitly totalitarian;[2] the second is a progressive oversight of the complex role the notion played up to the eighteenth century;[3] and the third is the fierce rejection of the concept by liberal political philosophers since the sixties.[4]

These three mutually reinforcing factors sealed its fate in the twentieth century. From the 1960 s onwards the notion was flung into the mass grave of history in the firm conviction that it would never rise from the dead. Never again would it infect modern society with obsolete, dangerous dreams that were a direct threat to its plurality and its respect for minorities.

This modern anathema – like all anathemas – was suspect. With hindsight it may be wondered whether its unanimous adoption within a matter of years was due to the quality of the arguments or that of the post-war sociopolitical consensus that emerged in Europe and the United States, and is now disintegrating: (a) a rejection of totalitarianism, (b) the rule of equality stated in terms of civil and political freedoms, (c) the self-evident nature of the state, and (d) rational cosmopolitanism in both the political (UN) and economic (globalisation) spheres. The reasons for this rejection – whatever they may originally have been – were soon forgotten in this supposedly self-evident consensus.

2 Mary Key, 'Personal dignity and the common good', in Kenneth Grasso, Gerard Bradley, Robert Hunt (eds), *Catholicism, liberalism and communitarianism*, Lanham, Roman and Littlefield, 1995, 173-195.

3 To grasp the full complexity and fluidity of the notion during the scholastic period alone, see Matthew Kempshall, *The common good in late medieval political thought*, Oxford, Oxford University Press, 1999, and Peter Hibst, *Utilitas Publica – Gemeiner Nutz – Gemeinwohl*, Frankfurt, Peter Lang, 1991. A reading of ancient texts reveals the full extent of our present-day preconceptions, which have confined the contemporary debate within the narrow limits of liberal and democratic orthodoxy. The full relationship between truth and power is revealed here. Cf. Michel Foucault, *Discipline and punish*, New York, Pantheon Books, 1977.

4 John Rawls, *Political liberalism*, New York, Columbia University Press, 201-206.

This makes the present revival of the notion all the more surprising. How, after such condemnation, can we explain today's re-use of the notion? The main reason is that the problem has shifted.[5] The notion has not re-emerged in the expected place, or in its earlier form. Its revival seems closely linked to *public action*, i.e. the need for governments to set themselves public policy goals that identify specific 'good we have in common'. So it is a *pragmatic* revival, normally linked to the preservation or creation of a 'public good', a 'common benefit' whose value is essentially intangible, such as health, education, enjoyment of a cultural heritage, well-being or the environment. Indeed, once we have to set pragmatic priorities for public action, once we have to define government goals, we return to the classic exercise of determining specific common goods, i.e. whatever aim and action we share in common. This is remarkably evident when the World Bank, confronted with governments' mismanagement, attempts to define governance as the exercise of political power for the common good.[6]

This revival is not only welcome, but also problematic: *welcome* because it proves the practical need for such a notion (the common good cannot be reduced to interest or utility), but *problematic* because these separate revivals lack an overall coherence that would link each of these particular 'common goods' to the overall common good. In other words, the dynamic *coalescence of common goods into a shared striving for the common good* is lacking. Just as problematic is the fact that these 'common goods' are no longer usually perceived as moral goods, i.e. as goods that express human freedom and dignity, but as instrumental issues of power and discipline designed to *generate a particular social order* (radical heteronomy, social normalisation).[7]

It is therefore not surprising that this revival has been accompanied since the turn of the twenty-first century by a cautious resumption of studies on the notion of the common good in the field of political science or ethics. Here we may quote works by Christian Blum (2015), Patrick Riordan (2014; 2008; 1996), Hans Sluga (2014), Axel Kahn (2013), Tim Gorringe (2014), Dennis McCann and Patrick Miller (2005), David Hollenbach (2002) or the

5 See Christian BLUM, *Die Bestimmung des Gemeinwohls*, Berlin, De Gruyter, 2015, 7-9; David HOLLENBACH, *The common good*, 3-16.

6 WORLD BANK, 2004. Definition of governance: 'We define governance as the traditions and institutions by which authority in a country is exercised for the common good.'

7 Michel FOUCAULT, *Security, territory, population*, New York, Palgrave Mcmillan, 2009.

four volumes edited by Herfried Munkler and Harald Bluhm (2001-2002).[8] Most of these works revive the debate with Rawls and point to the limitations of political liberalism. Yet the concept of the common good that they propose in its place still lacks coherence and acumen. Although a revival of the notion of the common good must entails a critical appraisal of post-modernity and secularity, these two features of the present-day West cannot be naïvely seen as the end of humanity's political history. Both the post-modernity and secularity of our society are rather to be understood as an advanced state of *deconstruction* of the Enlightenment than a new model. It will be argued below that the notion of the common good – as a political goal – may allow a new synthesis and revive collective hopes. A common good approach can lend meaning to a political project that goes beyond the now too narrow one based on the sovereignty of nation states.

2. *Liberal criticism and its inconsistencies*

2.1 The totalitarian nature of the notion of the common good and the retreat on the question of justice

When John Rawls published *A theory of justice* in 1971, he probably did not imagine that his work would seal the fate of the common good in political philosophy. Yet this was one of its effects. Like so many others I will therefore focus my criticism on Rawls's liberal conception of justice[9]. In *A theory of justice*, and even more clearly in *Political liberalism* (1993), he developed the idea that the just mattered more than the various – and, in his view, incommensurable – 'comprehensive' conceptions of the good. Pluralism in society was such, in Rawls opinion, that every comprehensive view of the

8 Christian BLUM, *Die Bestimmung des Gemeinwohls,* 2015; HANS SLUGA, *Politics and the search for the common good*, Cambridge, Cambridge University Press, 2014; Axel KAHN, *L'homme, le libéralisme et le bien commun*, Paris, Stock, 2013; TIM GORRINGE, *The common good and the global emergency*, Cambridge, Cambridge University Press, 2014; Dennis MCCANN & Patrick MILLER, *In search of the common good*, New York, Clark International, 2005; David HOLLENBACH, *The common good*, 2002; Patrick RIORDAN, *Global Ethics and Global Common Goods*, London, Bloomsbury Academic, 2014; *A grammar of the common good*, London, Continuum, 2008; *A politics of the common good*, Dublin, Institute of Public Administration Press, 1996; Herfried MUNKLER and Harald BLUHM (Ed.), *Gemeinwohl und Gemeinsinn*, Band 1-4, Berlin, Akademie Verlag, 2001-2002.

9 I owe much of the following critique to Rawls understanding of justice to Roberto ALEJANDRO, *The Limits of Rawlsian Justice*, Baltimore-London, John Hopkins University Press, 1998.

political good could not be reduced to the others, and was inevitably conflictual if it had to be applied to society as a whole. According to Rawls, a comprehensive view of the good as a political form of society was necessarily 'sectarian', and a constant threat to all the minorities that did not share it. Yet even if they were incommensurable, these comprehensive conceptions of the good had some features in common. This was Rawls's great intuition in *A theory of justice.* It should be possible to envision the form of a society based on these common features – fairness and justice.

Using a conception of the good as rationality, Rawls went on to state that a partial agreement on a narrow view of the *social good as justice* could guarantee all citizens the pursuit of their own conception of the good life. His *theory of justice* thus developed the nature and main features of the consensus or social contract that, according to Rawls, legitimised liberal democracy. The two principles of justice that he formulated are well known: a strict *equality* of civil and political rights; a *distribution* of opportunities that respect equal rights but creates equal opportunities (distribution of, and access to, primary goods according to a complex equality). Regarding the common good, his argument was simple. This ancient category was incompatible with a liberal theory of justice. It must be abandoned as a political category in favour of that of justice: only equal rights within republican institutions allowed for a mutual tolerance and the respect of the different conceptions of the good.

Rawls's position has come in for a great deal of criticism, particularly regarding his a-priori exclusion of comprehensive views of the good from the agreement on justice. David Hollenbach's *The common good* points out the limitations of this liberal view of society[10], whose conservatism is only now fully apparent[11]. First, the conditions of justice stated behind the 'veil of ignorance' basically reflected an idealised view of the United States. Modern attempts to replicate the model in the former Soviet Union, Africa or the Middle East have not been successful. It seems impossible to build liberal democracy on a voluntarist basis.[12] Second, Hollenbach points out that Rawls's principles of justice cannot resolve situations of structural injustice.[13] His criticism is above all practical rather than theoretical. In the

10 See HOLLENBACH, *The common good*, 32 ff.

11 Cf. ALEJANDRO, *The Limits of Rawlsian Justice*, 155-163; 178-180.

12 Drawing up a constitution, establishing the rule of law and giving a nation democratic institutions cannot by themselves create the liberal society imagined by Rawls. Two recent examples are Afghanistan and Iraq.

13 HOLLENBACH, *The common good*, 34-41.

United States, the country that has inspired the Rawlsian fiction, political liberalism has failed to integrate indigenous peoples or give the Afro-American population equal opportunities. Third, says Hollenbach, a liberal view of justice seems incapable of responding to new, transnational challenges such as climate change, globalisation, political Islamism or mass migration[14]. The Rawlsian principles of justice are not sufficient to drive the common fate of humanity.[15] Although political liberalism is able to manage abundance, it is unable to govern in times of adversity or profound social transformation that goes beyond the nation state[16]. According to Sluga, a renewed and pluralistic conception of the common good is required to shape a common future in the present times of crisis and social transformation.[17]

2.2 Rawls's use of the notion of the common good

I want to review with greater depth here the intuition at the heart of the last of Hollenbach's remarks. Is it true that our inability to conceive of a common future is due to the rejection of the political relevance of comprehensive conceptions of the good, or the common good?

Few commentators have noted it, but although Rawls does not use the term 'the common good' he quite deliberately refers to some of its most classic features. Thus, when raising the question of the 'good of political society',[18] he calls it 'the good that citizens realise as persons and as a corporate body in maintaining a just constitutional regime and in conducting their affairs'.[19] A society based on the pact of justice - i.e a 'well-ordered' society in Rawls's terms - is good both for each individuals and for the society as a whole. He thus recalls the central intuition of the common good as stated in Aristotle's *Nicomachean ethics* : a real coincidence between the good of the individual and the good of the community. And he does so in the very terms of the scholastic debate: the dialectic between the part and the whole, the priority of the whole over the part, the good of order, etc. Rawls put forward two arguments:

14 Ibid, 51-56. See also RIORDAN, *Global Ethics and Global Common Goods*, 113-130.

15 *Ibid.*, 56-61.

16 ALEJANDRO, *The limits of Ralwsian Justice*, 172-177.

17 SLUGA, *Politics and the Search for the Common Good*, 89-91, 102-111.

18 RAWLS, *Political Liberalism.* New York, Columbia University Press, 1993, 201.

19 *Ibid.*, 201.

(a) If a well-ordered society is also meant to provide the good of individuals it is: a) because it allows 'the exercise of the two moral powers [reason and will]' to each individuals,[20] and b) because '(...) it secures for them the good of justice and the social bases of their mutual self-respect'.[21] By guaranteeing equal rights and opportunities, liberal society enables everyone to meet their basic needs, thereby allowing their good.
(b) Well-ordered society is also good for society as a whole, for it is the result of cooperation by the greatest number for an ultimate purpose: 'For whenever there is a shared final end, an end that requires the cooperation of many to achieve, the good realized is social (...)'.[22] In this sense, the existence and operation of just and lasting democratic institutions '(...) is a great social good and appreciated as such'.[23]

This is thus an utterly classic use of the category of the common good, yet essentially reduced to the *goods of order* (security, the rule of law, the social basis for self-respect), and fleshed out by matching *civil virtues* (tolerance, fairness, justice). However, it categorically excludes the question of the good life or the overall purpose of politics. This particular interpretation of the common good is by no means original,[24] but Rawls's theoretical elaboration deprives it of its dynamism, that is, its ability to govern a rapidly changing society.

Indeed, Rawls turned the concept on its head. What belonged to the *order of ends* (to the common good as the horizon to which we aim) was presented as corresponding to the *order of origin* of politics (the common good as a precondition for the existence of politics). In other words, the end goal of politics was postulated as already existing at its very beginning, using a trick of argument: the myth of the social contract. Although neither Rousseau nor Rawls never believed the myth to be real, its character as a myth describing the origins of society had a number of important consequences – one of which was the abandonment of the category of the common good.

20 *Ibid.* 202-203.
21 *Ibid.*, 203.
22 *Ibid.*, 204.
23 *Ibid.*, 204.
24 It can be traced back to Marsilius of Padua's *Defensor Pacis*. See KEMPSHALL, *The common good in late medieval political thought*, 354-359.

2.3 The contractualist inversion of eschatology and protology

One of the most striking features of contractualism in political philosophy is the inversion of eschatology and protology. In other words, a supposedly metaphysical doctrine of ends is unblinkingly replaced by a supposedly formal and rational doctrine of origins. It is in fact an inversion regarding the sources of social normativity and the legitimacy of government (the political counterpart of the Kantian inversion of the origin of moral obligation). Normativity reaches present society not *from* the future (the reign of ends), but proceed from the origin, *from* a myth sited at the beginning, which authorises society and legitimises government (order and power).[25]

For the social contract imagined by Rousseau and adopted by Rawls are but myth, i.e. a mythical account of the origins of society that serve to legitimise the state and a concept of justice. Thus the 'original position' constructed by Rawls in an immemorial, imaginary time is designed to legitimise a particular society (the United States, from a liberal perspective) and the operation of a particular state (the legitimacy of American political institutions)[26]. From a pragmatic point of view, the whole Rawlsian construction is no more than a particularly, and ultimately partisan formulation of the common good, one that is historically marked by a specific context and could not lay claim to universality. Far from being just a minimum, cosmopolitan agreement on what was just, political liberalism protected and imposed a comprehensive conception of the political good, or, if you will, a particular, and limited, view of the common good.[27]

This paradox contradicted one of the essential tenets of the Rawlsian position: the claim to allow the private pursuit of the good to *all people* within a just set of rights and institutions. This wish to include every member of society – to seek universality – can be seen then as a meta-narrative discourse. One that disguises a particular political claim and ultimately prevents all other views of the common good from emerging on the

25 It is all too easily forgotten to what extent social contract theories were originally instruments in the struggle against the various monarchist regimes. In the field of thought they serve to justify a new order and a new power. Hans LINDAHL, 'The paradox of constituent power: the ambiguous self-constitution of the European Union', *Ratio Juris* 20 (2007), 485-505.

26 'The liberal argument seems to suggest that since its principles were articulated and arrived through a rational process they do not need to be subject to any further evaluation. Rawlsian justice is meant for a society conceived in perpetuity'. ALEJANDRO, *The Limits of Rawlsian Justice*, 11-12.

27 Ibid., 10-11.

political scene[28]. Rousseau's genius was to shift this view of the good from the realm of ends to that of origins – to make out of it a mythical account of the origins of society.

This inversion between eschatology and protology has several advantages:

a) It posited this partial, and ultimately limited, conception of the common good as a condition for the existence of all other comprehensive conceptions of the good – i.e. the criterion whereby their democratic validity and social legitimacy (a conception of the good that satisfied the criterion of the just as understood by the liberal state) would be judged.
b) It resolved in a mythological manner – by positing a rational dialogue behind the veil of ignorance – the conflictual nature of this liberal view of the common good. It disguised questions of power and its conflict with other views of society. The rational discussion in the original position concealed the use of force and all the barbaric violence that had historically marked the birth of the modern state. This masked violence, sublimated in the mythological rational consensus, is a lie and a delusion[29]. Neither unity nor social and political life are *only* rational.
c) By no longer presenting the common good as a purpose to be achieved, but as the precondition for the existence of a just and democratic society, Rawls assumed it to be *already* operating, *already* achieved. Government thus only had to *guarantee* the fair distribution of, and access to, primary goods, and everyone could rationally claim *their rights* on the grounds that the consensus on what was just was normatively prior to their own particular situation. In so doing, Rawls made this *liberal common good* static and unalterable.[30] Without realising it, he emasculated all political life by reducing it to little more than the instrumental management of state institutions in order to ensure an ever more successful achievement of the private good of individuals and groups (reducing the political function to the legislative function). But any challenge to liberal social structures was eliminated from the debate. That is why this model is ultimately conservative. It presupposes an eternal and impossible return to the lost paradise of a mythical equality. The social system is frozen in its essential structures and cannot evolve, but only periodically

28 'If there is a feature of liberal order worth discussing as a political problema, it is the tendency to call reason to scrutinize critically its opponents' claims while putting the core of its own principles beyond rational crutiny'. Ibid. 11.

29 See John MILBANK, *Theology and social theory*, Oxford, Blackwell, 2005, 278 ff.

30 Cf. ALEJANDRO, *The Limits of Rawlsian Justice*, 10-18.

> go into reverse (involution). In other words, such social model can't adjust to new circumstances by moving forwards, in social creativity, but only toward the past, moving backwards and withdrawing towards the origin.

This is quite some claim. It must therefore be applied more precisely to Rawls's work in order to justify it.

2.4 A critical review of Rawls's use of the 'political good'

Rawls posit a priority of justice over the comprehensive ideas of the good in the public square. This is not to say that he rejects any notion of the good in politics, or the moral legitimacy of the different comprehensive notions of the good. On the contrary, he grounds his theory of justice on more than a few meanings of the good in politics: a) The good as rationality; b) Primary goods; c) The acceptability of comprehensive conceptions of the good; d) Political virtues; e) The idea of the good in well-ordered political society. [31] I will take a closer look at the three first points to see if our hypothesis can be sustained.

a. The good as rationality. Rawls understands the rationality of public space – the *logos* that constitutes and drives it – as the most fundamental good in the political sphere: the good founding a political community as such. This shared rationality is that of the agents behind the veil of ignorance and hence, to Rawls, also entails the consensus on the just (two principles of justice). This consensus on the just is thus a good in itself – more specifically, it represents the culmination or accomplishment of a conception of the political good as rationality. In embodying this good of rationality in politics it becomes prior to all other conceptions of the political good (which are deemed implicitly as irrational – ultimately unjust – if they do not subscribe to the agreement on justice). Hence Rawls's need to rationally exclude all other forms of the political good while still discussing under the veil of ignorance. And this in turn is only possible if the question of the origins of power is omitted from the discussion.[32] Now this is precisely what is reached throught the *a-historical* and *protological* nature of the consensus reached under the veil of ignorance. It is in this sense that the whole Rawlsian's construction is ultimately a myth constructed to free political liber-

31 Rawls, *Political liberalism*, 173-211.

32 Hans Lindahl, *Fault lines of globalisation: legal order and the politics of a-legality*, Oxford, Oxford University Press, 2013, 156-183.

alism from power plays and make it morally prior to all other conceptions of the good in politics.

b. Primary goods. Primary goods gave shape to the agreement on justice, and formed what Rawls called the 'basic structure' of society. Among these primary goods there were some that ensured 'equality of basic freedoms', and others that were needed in order to ensure 'fair equality of opportunities'.[33] Accessible to all as a condition for the agreement on justice, these primary goods were guaranteed by the state. This meant that the basis and purpose of the operation of public and political institutions was the fair distribution of these primary goods. They would also serve as a yardstick for judging the private pursuit of the good as socially 'acceptable'. Specifically, these primary goods served as standards for citizens' desires and aspirations in the public realm, for they were assumed to have been accepted in the original position (non-negotiable standards). The priority over political life and the non-negotiability of these public standards were legitimised by recourse to the protological myth and its formal rationality. In other words, it meant that the timeframe of consensus had priority over the timeframe of political existence (primacy of mythical time over real time). The only option left for historical citizens was to accept the primary goods; this acceptance was deemed unanimous and total because the consensus was rational; and public force would be used if this acceptance were lacking. All the primary goods in fact formed the specific, material content of the particular view of the common good promoted by the agreement on justice. The difficulty lay in its protological nature. Fixed once and for all, the content of the consensus was no longer dynamic. Its implicit consequences could be displayed, enriched and refined, but it could not be changed.[34] It thus lacked the political plasticity necessary for political action; it had no internal structure that provided enough creativity for it to move beyond its own historical basis. It lacked universality. To put this another way, it sanctified a particular time and political regime, and thus lost its fundamental ability to recreate. Rawls's political liberalism does not look forwards, but

33 'The basic list of primary goods (…) has five headings as follows : a) basic rights and liberties, also given by a list ; b) freedom of movement and free choice of occupation against a background of diverse opportunities ; c) power and prerogatives of offices and positions of responsibility in the political and economic institutions of the basic structure ; d) income and wealth ; and finally, e) the social bases of self-respect.' Rawls, *Political Liberalism*, 181.

34 Whatever Habermas's discursive ethics may claim. Debate in a liberal democracy has its limits: institutions and valuescan be questioned theoretically but challenged practically. There is no real possibility to escape the liberal ethos..

backwards. It does not seek novelty. It sought to guarantee primary goods – forever stolen and violated in real historical circumstances – by a return to the lost paradise of original equality. It sanctifies a mythological equality.[35]

c. Acceptability of comprehensive versions of the good. This allows us to move on to one of the most controversial areas of Rawls's theory: the irreducible plurality of comprehensive views of the good in politics. The insurmountable conflict was theoretically resolved by Rawls by returning to a narrow definition of the good in politics, reduced to the sole idea of the just (excluding any comprehensive view of the good from the political field). This meant that the state and its institutions must not favour any particular view of the comprehensive good, but confine themselves to an instrumental role: that of ensuring equal treatment for all. Only at private level could the plurality of views of the good operate freely. The state's procedural neutrality would therefore favour the values of equality, impartiality and tolerance when settling conflicts. However – and this was crucial – political liberalism could not be completely neutral. Rawls admitted that in the long term it excluded certain comprehensive views and favoured others. Yet, he said, this non-neutrality was not due to the state and its arbitration, but to the very content of the agreement on justice. In other words, what was involved here was the historical unfolding of the normative content of primary goods. The rationality of the good was therefore imposed gradually, through its own dynamics, on the historical forms that contradicted it.[36] Rawls's answer on this particular point was important for our perspective, for it marked its culmination. It was here that he rejected the common good as the ultimate value in politics: the state was not ordered to the common good, and simply had an instrumental value as the guardian and promoter of the equality of basic freedoms and equal opportunities (the irreducible plurality of comprehensive views of the good in politics; the rational unity of agents through

35 The use of religious terms is relevant here, for, as with Solon, what we have here is an almost religious adherence to the idea of *demos*, *polis* and *epikeia*.

36 The dependence on the Enlightenment ideal is obvious here, as is the assumption that all opposition was obscurantist and irrational. Perhaps more relevant here is that this question of the influence of the agreement on justice, which Rawls belatedly acknowledged, reintroduced a teleological element – which he hastened to neutralise by saying that the influence of this historical non-neutrality was not due to power, but to reason (for the agreement was rational).

civil citizenship).[37] The procedurally neutral state should not favour any of the comprehensive views of the good, i.e. it should not adopt any of them, and should only promote equality of treatment among them. With regard to the reign of ultimate purposes, said Rawls, the state could only be strictly neutral and could 'only' promote the instrumental value of the agreement on justice. That was why any acknowledgement of the common good as a purpose of the state would be 'sectarian', a threat to minorities who did not share that view, and ultimately an intolerable violation of basic freedoms and a serious failure to respect the equality of treatment to which all were entitled.

In the light of my analysis, however, such a criticism of the teleological notion of the common good no longer holds up. Ironically, it even becomes self-criticism, for it was Rawls's inversion in time of the *eschaton* and the *proton*, of *eschatological accomplishment* and *protological ideal*, that enabled him to present a very unusual interpretation of the common good as the precondition for the existence of any just society. It was this reversal that legitimised and universalised the exclusion of all other conceptions of the common good from the field of politics and their relegation to the private sphere. By conceding that a liberal society and state ended up influencing – i.e. adapting – citizens' values and desires in their own image, Rawls thus revealed the extent to which the good pursued by a liberal society and state was sectarian and potentially totalitarian. Placed at the origin, and politically non-negotiable, the agreement on justice allowed no debate, and hence would have been historically recognised as a totalitarian view of the good in politics if care had not been taken to shift the narrative onto the mythological level. As a mere guardian of the agreement, the state was the sole instrument of this view (monopoly on force). It made sure not to let any other social institution challenge the agreement on justice. Finally, plurality, seemingly the basic fact on which the theory of justice was constructed, was finally confined to the private sphere, leaving a perfectly uniform political field dominated by the liberal view of the good in politics (with the nation state assumed to be a historical given).

So the liberal arguments against the common good are neither acceptable nor legitimate. On the contrary, it must be clearly stated today that Rawlsian political liberalism leads to social paralysis and political exhaustion

37 'As a form of political liberalism, justice as fairness is said to regard political institutions as purely instrumental to individual or associational ends, as the institutions of what we may call a "private society". As such, political society itself is not a good at all, but at best a means to individual or associational good'. Rawls, *Political liberalism*, 201.

– for equality, rights and tolerance alone cannot resolve the new social issues we are facing in the present world.

2.5 The usefulness of the social contract myths

The foregoing criticism goes far beyond Rawls, and concerns all the social contract theorists. Whether Rousseau, Locke or Hobbes, they all refer to an 'original myth' – not naïvely of course, in the sense that the myth might have been historically real, but as a narrative that explains, and hence authorises, a particular *social fact* as though it were universal.[38] Social contract philosophies pursue two goals: (a) equal rights and freedoms for all, and (b) the state's monopoly on force and coercion (a twofold legitimisation powerfully summed up by the French term *Etat de droit*, that is 'rule of law').

As mentioned earlier, the point is that these are *protological* myths (unlike other *eschatological* political myths such as Marxian communism). The questions of the *purpose* and *form* of society are *decisively resolved* through the narrative of the supposed origins (central institutions, corpus of rights). Cru-

38 I wish to emphasise this point, for it is very important. There is a tendency to see myth as a mere rhetorical instrument whose real importance lies in the formal and rational justification of the social and political facts that it allows. The a-temporality of the rhetorical form is that of reason, and the fact that the social contract narrative is placed at the origin supposedly only reflects the theory that politics is born of reason. Yet I do not believe that myth is merely a rhetorical mean. On the contrary, I believe that myth, in its evocative power and the coherence of its inherent meaning, is convincing in itself. It is as important in what it explains as in what it chooses to exclude. Historically all social contract philosophies were developed as criticisms of a social order, i.e. as alternatives to a pre-existing balance of power. They sought to impose themselves in a context that was unfavourable to them. Use of the origin (beginning) narrative, use of myths was then a way to sublimate political weakness and lend the proposition ethical superiority. Yet myths did not gain support because of their rationality, but because their narrative was coherent in meaning. It was this meaning that gained support, because of its credibility, its ability to 'make sense' of existence, particularly social and political existence. In other words, the social contract myths were supported just as religious faith was. People believed in the social contract just as they believed in God. But once the myth ceased to be relevant, once its credibility was contradicted by the tensions it had concealed, its use became problematic. Why focus in such detail on a solely rational origin of the public fact? Why base the social fact on reason rather than action, on *logos* rather than *praxis*? Why reduce the public space to equality, rights and tolerance? Why exclude from it a broader view of human good? Why assume an irreducible conflict between individual interests? Why have such naïve trust in the state? These are the main questions raised by SLUGA in *Searching for the common good*, 89-113.

cially, this resolution can no longer be challenged later, for the myth legitimises a social fact. Three assumptions are thus made:

a) *There is an irretrievable conflict* between different and diverging private interests (the state of nature is one of conflict). These myths are part of what Milbank has called an 'ontology of violence'.[39]
b) *The conflict between private interests is resolved by the imposition to all citizens of the state's coercive power* – an imposition that is assumed to be agreed, with freedoms surrendered for the benefit of the state. This is in fact the notion of the social contract, whereby the state is granted a monopoly on force provided it respects and guarantees equal rights for all (the rule of law).
c) *The state is the sole embodiment of the general interest, of which law is the maximum expression.* Law is the framework and the limit of the state's will and power.

As a result of these three mythological assumptions:

a) The social good can be defined as consisting of the *equality of rights* and *the existence of the state.*
b) The definition of the social good is made inaccessible, protected against any later redefinition by the value of the timeless original myth.

And so the question of the good, and especially the common good, can be deemed irrelevant to the democratic political debate, and even a threat to plurality. Behind the cloak of the mythological meta-narrative, social contract philosophers could in fact cling to a casi-totalitarian notion of the social good, historically linked to the fact of state power that had to be created and justified. And this conception of the social good is not posited as a future ideal to be achieved, but as an *original fact* from which historical achievements of this social good derives. As we have seen, any detachment or malfunction is then resolved by a return to the source, to the origin, to the myth. This is why these myths, once achieved, lead to frozen societies with no future, or rather a society whose future is a constant return to a mythological past – as witness the current erosion of these myths, which are struggling to generate the same support as after the second World War, the ideological shifts toward equality and tolerance that have become the core values in public space, and the corollary rise of populism which blunts the division between right and left.

39 See John MILBANK, *Theology and social theory*, 278 ff.

I therefore believe it is essential to get rid of the social contract myths. Neither justice, nor democracy, nor virtue, nor law, nor freedom, nor dignity need this mythology in order to exist. The notion of the common good seems far more convincing, far more realistic and far more liberating than these mythical narratives of an imaginary social contract. Why? Because the common good is essentially a forward-looking concept – a generator of a future, a shared common future.

Part 2: The fundamentals of a reinterpretation of the notion of the common good

The criticism so far cannot merely deconstruct liberal arguments and point out their limitations. If it is to be constructive, it must also provide responses and offer a credible reinterpretation of the notion of the common good. What follows is intended to reinforce the statement made at the end of the previous part. The notion of the common good is essentially linked to the category of action; it is creative, capable of novelty, and inclusive; it takes account not only of law and justice, but also of the purpose of the good life in politics. How? This is what this second part will set out to show.

This will be done in two stages. The first section will lay the foundations for a reinterpretation of the common good. The second will consider the purpose of the common good both in its dynamics and in its structure and content.

1. The common good belongs to the sphere of action

1.1 The notion of the common good is implicit in all public action

The intuition that forms the basis for what follows is a simple one. The common good is not primarily a metaphysical concept – it is an ethical principle, a principle that governs public action and remains implicit in all action undertaken in the public realm. It is not primarily a question about the good in itself, or about the hierarchy in human goods, or about orders of priority between the whole and the part. It is not primarily a comprehensive view of the good – a complex, splendid architecture in which each part fits into the whole, as in a cathedral. The common good is based on the logic of common action and cooperation.

The essential input from scholastics regarding the common good was metaphysical.[40] The main focus was then on the quality of the 'good' in the term 'common good'. But in the order of action the crucial question regarding the common good to be achieved is that of the 'common' generated by our interaction.[41] How a community gathers round a goal, and arises from the pursuit of that goal, is the primary aspect of the common good.

That is why the question of the common good is far more prosaic and specific than is usually thought, for it is implicit in all common action. As soon as it is *wanted*, common action carries a hope, the hope of a common good; and as soon as it is *conceived of*, it reveals the structure of a dynamic, the dynamic of the common good.[42] The issue of the common good can be extended to all public or political action, for it is its principle and its driving force.

Of course, this assertion can be deemed to conflict with warfare, the constant wish throughout history to appropriate other people's goods by force, subterfuge or lies. It seems almost laughable to claim that the basis of public action is that of the common good, for experience seems to show that private interests and power plays are the *true* basis for politics. This is an old argument. Machiavelli framed it in a treaty; Ludwig von Rochau gave it a name: *Realpolitik*. Yet it is not the only reasonable, prudent option, nor does it reflect the whole experience of politics.[43]

Maintaining that the common good is based on action means asserting that it can only be grasped and understood *through action*. If the common good is a normative concept, it is so dynamically, as a duty to act and a horizon for action. For in action, as Blondel once remarked,[44] there is something like a Kantian categorical imperative.[45] There is a need to act. There is a duty to act. And since antiquity this duty in the public and political realm has been given a name, has been framed through a concept: the common good.

40 Kempshall, *The common good in late medieval political thought*, 76-101.

41 Hannah Arendt, *The human condition*, Chicago, Chicago University Press, 1958, 50 ff.

42 Mathias Nebel, 'El bien común teológico: ensayo sistemático', *Revista Iberoamericana de Teología* 1 (2006), 7-32.

43 Public action has never only been conflict, subterfuge and lies. On the contrary, a lasting community on a human scale – one that is able to welcome, recognise and protect fragile human dignity – cannot be constructed on conflict, subterfuge and lies.

44 Marc Blondel, *L'action*, Paris, Alcan, 1893, 326.

45 Mathias Nebel, 'Action de Dieu et actions de l'homme', *Transversalité* 128 (2013/4), 151-163.

1.2 The need to act in common, and the community created by common action

Once there is a mass, however amorphous, it tends to organise itself on the basis of a shared history, common needs or the effect of primary forms of human solidarity. Certain goods emerge spontaneously as being useful to all, appreciated by all. Producing such goods, organising their distribution and obtaining them – this is what will organise the mass, this is what forms the basis of society, this is what makes a mass of individuals gradually create a common way of life, shared institutions and a culture whose social goods are moulds for collective habitus.[46]

This is not some theory, but an empirical fact. It can be seen whenever war, poverty or misfortune forces a whole population to flee. What makes the rationality of everyday life – family, work, friends – is now lost. War or poverty have destroyed the former structure of society, and its culture, standards and institutions no longer operate. In fleeing imminent danger, refugees are now simply a mass of individuals united by misfortune, the hope of a refuge and the desperate urge to survive. And it is these common features that generate the embryos of society: on the road you have to keep eating, find water and shelter for the night, plan the next day's journey. The importance of these primary goods is the basis for *collaboration*. People work together to meet these needs. They organise themselves in order to obtain these goods together, because it is easier to obtain them together.[47] It is this shared action, this common organisation to obtain a social good that describes the notion of the common good.

The notion of the common good is linked to these actions that create a community. It is related to these common needs, shared goals and primordial forms of care and solidarity that tend to unite us. Wherever there is a community, the question of the common good arises. What are our

46 As expressed by Bourdieu: '… The habitus is the product of the work of inculcation and appropriation necessary in order for those products of history ... to reproduce themselves more or less completely, in the form of durable dispositions, in the organisms (which one can, if one wishes, call individuals) lastingly subjected to the same conditioning, and hence placed in the same material conditions of existence.' Pierre BOURDIEU, *Outline of a theory of practice*, Cambridge, Cambridge University Press, 1977, 85.

47 Similarly, archaeologists distinguish the advent of first great Mesopotamian civilisations by their major agricultural works, their creation of law, their ability to make military plans and their development of trade. All these features point to the importance of agricultural production, law, trade and security as specific social goods. Cf. Elinor OSTROM, *Governing the Commons*, 88-102.

common needs? What goods do we need? What shared benefits may we get by seeking together a specific goal? The question of the common good is specific; it is pragmatic.

It arises again and again in every community or society because of the innumerable interactions that take place in it and that must be continued, recast or abandoned. None of these interactions is spontaneous or natural. On the contrary, they are fragile. And so the question of the common good keeps returning to the forefront, as a question that requires decisions to be made. These interactions must be governed; society needs political governance. It is here that the question of the common good is linked to practice, to public action.

1.3 The elements of common action

What are the elements of common action? With Mounier and Ricœur we can distinguish the following elements: the *subject* of the action, the *object* of the action and the *stage* on which the action unfolds.[48] The subject is of course the 'who' that performs the action (in this case a collective subject), a group of people sharing a common intentionality and linked together in pursuing the object of the action. The object describes the purpose of an action, the goal it aims at and gradually achieves, while the stage is the social environment 'enabling' the action and where it 'makes sense'.[49]

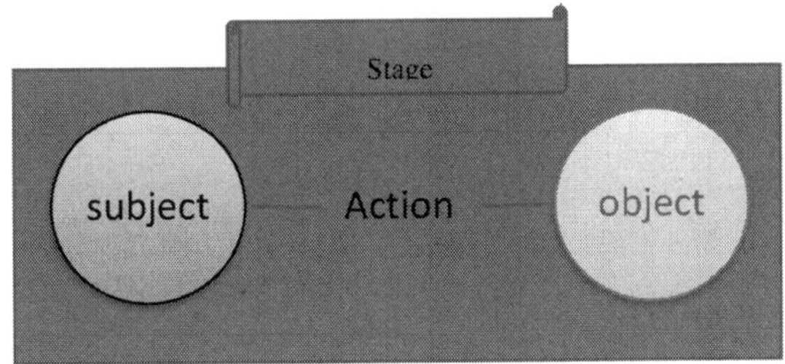

The action is what is keeping the subject and the object together on the stage,[50] the specific form through which the subject appears on the stage – the only and unique way it exists in this environment. What appears on the

48 Emmanuel Mounier, *Le personnalisme*, Paris, Presses Universitaires de France, 1949, 15-29. Paul Ricœur, *Soi-même comme un autre*, Paris, Seuil, 1990, 86-89, 109-110, 167-179.

49 Paul Ricœur, *Du texte à l'action*, Paris, Seuil, 1986, 168-175, 184-197.

50 *Ibid.*, 193.

stage is not the subject 'in itself', but an 'acting subject'.[51] Similarly, the way the goal of an action is 'present' on the scene is mainly through the very action achieving it.[52] It is present on the stage as an 'object being realized'. Finally there is the 'world of the action'[53], i.e. the social space whose coherence and rationality depend on this action. The action is thus never a mere machine that mechanically achieves the intended object of the action, but the main way in which both the subject and the object exist on the stage.[54] It is in the form of a dynamic that we - as acting subject - appear on the stage. The previous diagram could thus just as well be drawn like this:

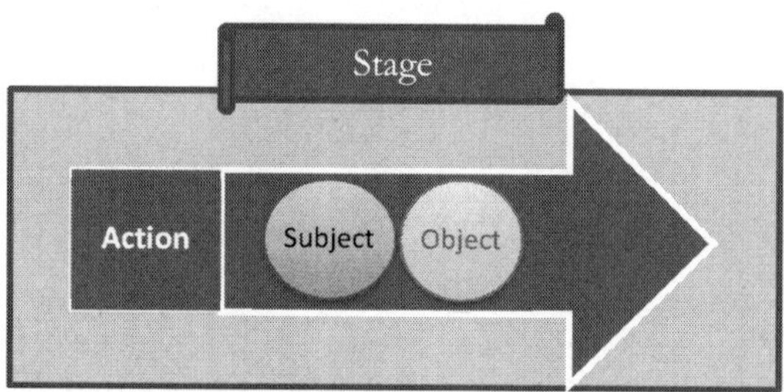

On the stage, the subject is never neutral. It is informed by the stage. The subject of a common action is always a situated subject, regulated by the stage in its language, in the shared rationality used by the group's members and in the cultural assumptions that feed it. As Walzer indicated, there are no pure, timeless or a-cultural subjects.[55] It is on a distinctive stage that both the 'acting subject' and the 'achieved object' will acquire a specific meaning and be appreciated as having a value and representing a good.[56]

51 This recalls the Arendtian conception of action as the vehicle of thought and the place where interiority is revealed to others – action that constructs the common artefact, action that constitutes the common world. See ARENDT, *The human condition*, 73-78, 175-188.

52 *Ibid.*, 175-176. The object's independence and otherness in contrast to the subject only apply to material objects. Most objects involved in a common action are immaterial: education, peace, stability. Although they have a material dimension, these goods are essentially common meanings that are inseparable from the subject that carries them out and the community to which they have meaning. It is in the action that creates it that the object will then be chiefly present on the stage – as an object being created.

53 RICŒUR, *Du texte à l'action*, 168-172.

54 RICŒUR, *Soi-même comme un autre*, 86-92.

55 Michael WALZER, *Spheres of justice*, Oxford, Blackwell, 1985, 6-10.

56 Alasdair MCINTYRE, *After virtue*, Notre Dame, IN, University of Notre Dame Press, 1984, 206-210.

What strikes then is is the great fragility of action, its impermanence.[57] Action must constantly renew itself in order to endure. It must constantly retrieve its intention and reinvent itself in response to face unforeseen events, while making sure to maintain the commitment of the people involved in it. The miracle of action is that it exists! Its main hazard is that it may lose its dynamism and be dispersed. Action is maintained as a tension – an in-tention to achieve something – that is constantly threatened by the fragility of human commitment, the tribulations of time and people's assent.

This perspective affects the way we perceive subjects. The main question is then how the subject may sustain itself. How can the subject's intention and commitment be maintained during the action, in the long term? We are talking here about the subject's unity and permanence while acting.[58] Similarly, this perspective changes the way in which the object of the action is perceived. The main question is then how to maintain the unity of the object pursued by the action while the action is taking place.

I will therefore study the notion of the common good by transposing the question from the metaphysical level to the ethical level of public action – in the hope that this will re-emphasise the practical dimension of the notion of the common good.

2. *The vocabulary of the common good*

The notion of the common good is an old one, and its lexical field is broad. Down the ages, and through translations, many terms have been added to the field, either to establish distinctions that were deemed necessary or to express specific aspects.[59] It seems impossible to speak of the common good without using a broader vocabulary. The use of the same term by different writers should therefore always be treated with caution. More often than is realised, the notion may be understood in quite different ways, and this article may be no exception. I will therefore explain the vocabulary used.

57 Arendt, *The human condition*, 188-191.

58 This, of course, is the essence of Ricœur's thinking on his notion of narrative identity. Ricœur, *Soi-même comme un autre*, 167 ff.

59 We now have a series of modern studies on this history: Hibst, *Utilitas Publica – Gemeiner Nutz – Gemeinwohl*, 1991, Jehne, Lundgreen (eds), *Gemeinsinn und Gemeinwohl in der römischen Antike*, Stuttgart, Steiner, 2013, and Kempshall, *The common good in late medieval political thought*, 1999.

2.1 The social good and the shared value of the common benefit

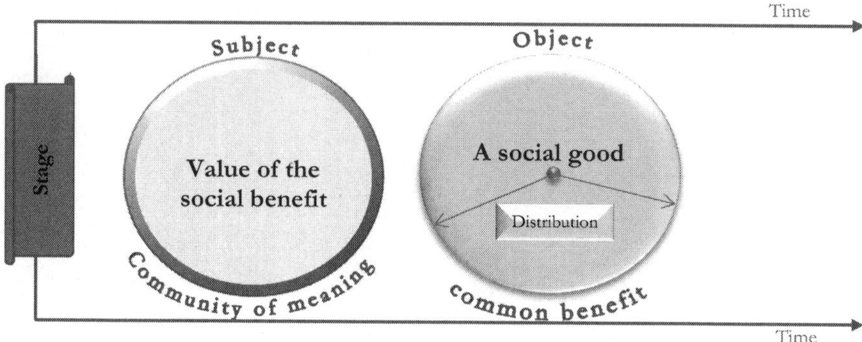

Every interaction has a certain object and gradually achieves it, unless the interaction is in vain. I will call this goal of the interaction, the object it creates and maintains, the '*social good*'. As we have seen, it is not just the resultant of an interaction, but is immanent to the interaction itself. The term 'good' is not used here in an explicitly moral sense; it simply means that the community of people that create it agree to assign it a value. This social good has a certain utility, whose distribution creates a '*common benefit*' that is shared among the community.

The relationship between involvement in the interaction and sharing in the common benefit is one of the main features of the common good. Yet the criterion for distributing the benefit is not necessarily equality, even complex equality. For instance, someone may be illiterate and still be involved in the collective effort to build a school in the village and pay a teacher so that the children can be given an education. What is shared is the valuation of the common benefit in itself. The community gathered around a social good is therefore more than just a community of interests. It is not necessarily united, as social contract theories would have us believe, by a correlation of individual interests. That is why the people who create the social good are not always, or necessarily, the same as those who benefit from it. The benefiting community may be larger, or smaller, than the creating one.

This is not to say that the common benefit need not be distributed fairly. When the hoped-for benefit is unduly diverted or appropriated by a person or group, people's anger and indignation are a reaction based on their sense of fairness. However, what is claimed is not necessarily one's own share, but respect for the meaning of the social good in itself, i.e. for the value assigned to it by the community. It is the common nature of the benefit, linked to the shared recognition of its value that is negated by undue appropriation. Back to the previous example. If a local shopkeeper offers to rent an 'unoccupied part' of the classrooms as a storehouse for his goods, then takes advantage of this agreement to gradually turn the whole school into a storehouse, forcing the teacher to give his lessons out in the playground, the community of people that have built the school and pay the teacher will have been swindled out of their social good. They will feel robbed of the common benefit created by their interaction – and that is unfair! Not primarily because they are denied their 'due', but rather because there is a conflict with the meaning of the social good – the shared valuation of the social good. They will say 'We didn't build a school for it to be used as a storehouse!' It is the meaning of the social good – the school, and the children's education – that is diverted and then negated by the shopkeeper's action. Being well aware of this, the shopkeeper will take good care to avoid claiming that the building is not a school, but will argue speciously that 'he has a fully legal contract', that the 'children can be taught in the open air anyway during the dry season', or even that the whole thing is a 'temporary', an emergency measure and that he will soon stop using the premises. He will never say 'The building isn't a school any longer – it's my storehouse.' But that is what he really means.

So the social good can't be detached from a 'communality of meaning'[60]. What this neologism means is that the social good does not only exists materially – in the school's walls, the tables and the chairs – but also as a meaning shared by the people involved in the interaction. The community gathered around the meaning of this social good make it exist as such, and impose this meaning on anyone that seeks to misuse it. An immanent feature of every social good is therefore a community to whom it has a particular, normative meaning. This is what the population blames the shopkeeper for, and it is this meaning that the shopkeeper knows he has violated. And thus the people of the village will reject the shopkeeper's specious arguments 'in the name of the common good'.

60 Cf. Riordan proposes to understand the 'common sense' associated to a common good as one of its crucial elements. See Patrick RIORDAN, *Global Ethics and Global Common Good*, 83-96.

2.2 The good of order and the common rationality it creates

When a number of people want to get something done, they organise themselves. No-one can do everything. The good we want to achieve together, the object of the interaction, will have to be planned. If we want to build a school, we need a site, plans and funding; we have to persuade the families and children, find a teacher and agree on the school timetable. We must organise ourselves. The interaction that creates the social good therefore also implies organisation, a 'good of order' that is immanent to the social good.

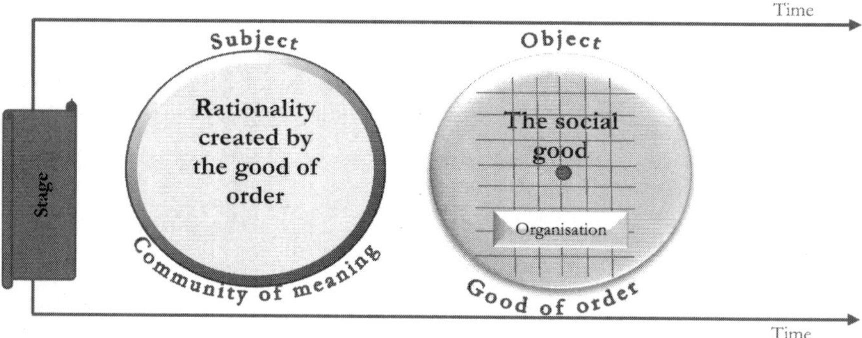

A community is ordered – organised – so that it can produce the social goods to which it assigns value. This organisation of interaction generally involves determining the overall good, each person's role and responsibilities in the interaction, and the rules that will govern our cooperation. The fact, then, is that the 'communality of meaning' is always accompanied by a specific order, by an organisation of the community. One person is responsible for finding and purchasing the future site, another draws up the plans of the school, those who are masons will supervise the volunteers who are to build it, and someone else will look for a teacher. Any interaction that seeks to produce a social good efficiently will necessarily produce a social order (ever more so when an interaction increases in complexity). This 'good of order' designates the organisation of the community so that it can realise and maintain a common benefit.

The good of order derives its *raison d'être*, its value, from the object of the interaction, the social good it seeks to achieve. It therefore has an instrumental value and its quality may be judged by: (a) its coherence with the meaning of the social good ; (b) whether the good is achieved effectively and efficiently.

Finally, by the 'subject' we describe the community that shares a same understanding of the social good. Each and every member of this group will have internalised the 'good of order' as the 'common rationality' of their interaction. For any given organisation defines a set of standard behaviours that are *rational* in this specific context. Two chess players, for example, are bound by the rules of the game and the moves that can be made by the various pieces. They analyse their opponent's strategy and devise their own on the basis of these rules. The rationality of each move on the chessboard depends thus on the logic of the game. The more the players have internalised this rationality, the more they will manage to get into the game and predict their opponent's next moves. It is the logic of the game that explains the opponents' strategies. However, just like the good of order, the value of this rationality is instrumental. It will be judged by its coherence with the social good and its ability to achieve it efficiently.

2.3 The specific common good

Together, the 'social good' (communality of meaning), the 'common benefit' (shared valuation) and the 'good of order' (common rationality) form what I will call a specific common good (the communality of a common good). The common good created by an interaction is made up of these three features: the 'social good', the 'common benefit' and the 'good of order'. Correspondingly, the common good will be in the subject a 'shared valuation', a 'common rationality' and a 'communality of the common good'.

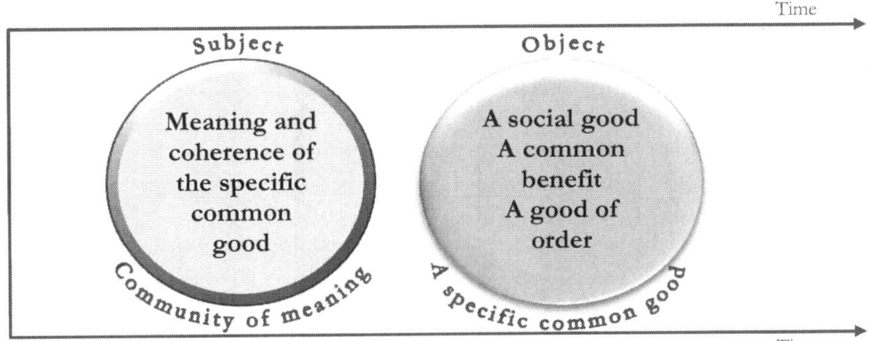

It is now time to bring together what I have divided up for the sake of clarity. The subject and the object are held together in the dynamic of the action. The common good cannot be reduced to its objective dimension (the social conditions necessary for the full development of the person), but nor can it be reduced to its purely subjective dimension (a communality of meaning and habitus). The common good is a constant dynamic: that of a community that creates a social good according to a fragile, unstable equilibrium – that of action – and *within* a communality of meaning.

For the common good is a dynamic whereby a community exists and in which it asserts itself. It is a particular community, as specific as the social good and the hoped-for common benefit. Among the people of the village, it is those who wanted to create the school and organised themselves to do so. Of course, it is also the children who attend the school; and it is also all those in the village who support the project and consider that it is important for the children to have access to education. This community is very specific. It enables the social good to exist and be maintained. Yet, although it is specific, its boundaries are hard to draw. At the centre there will be a number of people who are clearly part of it: the parents, the teacher, the children. Further away, there will be those who helped to build the school and whose tasks in the project are now over; and even further away, the broad circle of those who support and approve of the project without benefiting from it or being actively involved in it. It is clear that the boundaries of this community are essentially the boundaries of the communality of meaning, the positive meaning that the population assigns to the creation of this specific social good. In contrast, those who are not part of this community are those who do not share this conception, and whose actions conflict with the coherence of the common meaning – such as the shopkeeper.

Seeing the common good as a dynamic also means that none of its historical realization can be considered as settled once and for ever. The common good must be constantly reinvented over time to be maintained. It is an interaction, and no interaction is spontaneous – it is the result of a certain communality of meaning and continuity of will. A specific common good will therefore have to be readopted and reinvented by each generation if it is not to be lost and disappear – which also effectively means that the community of the common good is not itself natural, but the result of the real sharing of the communality of meaning. This is something that can be lost. Over time, the village in our story may become a smart suburb of a nearby city, whose children attend private schools. The village school, and what it once meant to the original population, will then gradually lose its meaning.

2.4 The common good as a nexus of relationships between specific common goods: the universal common good (the horizon of the common good)

It goes without saying that every society is built on an often very broad set of common goods that only partially overlap. There is a whole series of relationships between these specific common goods. Most of them are complementary, superimposed and mutually reinforcing. This is not to say that all these specific common goods are uniform or equally important. There are tensions, or sometimes even contradictions, between them that make it hard for them to coexist within the same society. I will use the expression '*nexus of the common good*'[61] to express the real relationships between these various specific common goods in a given society.

This nexus does not appear of its own accord, as a kind of spontaneous self-organisation of society.[62] On the one hand it is the result of a shared history – centuries of common experience that have gradually brought various social goods together and created a hierarchy among them – and on the other the constant efforts of the present generation to reframe and to some extent reinvent it. This is a shared responsibility, a political effort *par excellence*. The nexus of the common good is the result of exercising this political responsibility. That is why it varies considerably in quality, with substantial gradations. Its quality will partly depend on this shared history, and partly on the present generation's commitment and wisdom.

This commitment takes usually the form of a specific interaction seen as a particularly important social good: the one providing political governance to the 'nexus of the common good'. It is political power itself that is here valued and constructed as a common good, though one which is of crucial importance to any society. Indeed, the task set to these governing bodies is to pursue an ever richer, deeper and more universal common good. Theirs is the task to work out a real conjunction between the many specific common goods existing in the society, so that their nexus may be more human (coherence, hierarchy, resolution of conflict).

61 Rather than the terms 'network' or 'web' – now overused because of the Internet and globalisation – I prefer the Latin term 'nexus', which means 'relationship, intertwining or linkage of causes, connection, bond', a term linked in Roman law to that of responsibility or duty. It is derived from the verb *nectere*, which means 'to tie together, to unite, to link'.

62 As suggested in Nicklas LUHNMANN, *Soziale Systeme: Grundriss einer allgemeinen Theorie*, Frankfurt, Suhrkamp, 1984, 15 ff.

A frequent error is to believe that the nexus of the common good is a given, a natural state of affair. On the contrary, it changes constantly and turns out to be fragile. Its humanity is the result of age-old wisdom about what is more and what is less human in the organisation of society. Sometimes it is also the age-old result of collective blindness to, and tolerance of, structural injustices. That is why its political governance needs more than mere legislators and judges to determine what is just. It needs politicians who can assign a value to the coherence between the many specific common goods, understand their limitations and the tensions that both separate and unite them – in other words, politician that endeavour to judge the moral quality of the nexus. This essential exercise largely depends on the horizon of the universal common good.

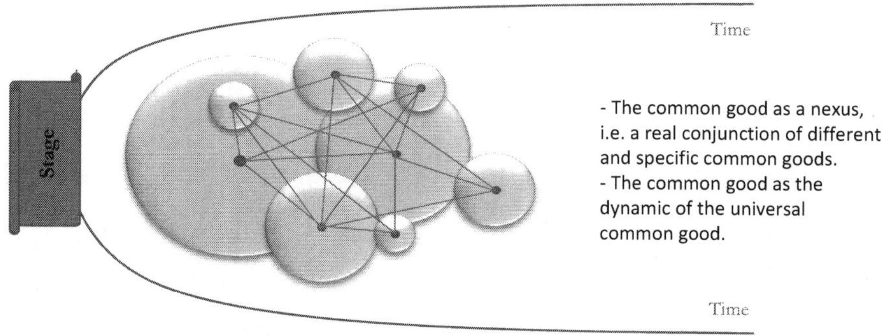

It is also important to underline that the nexus of the common good is what lends societal coherence to the communality of meaning. It is what binds a community or a culture, and gives it identity and unity – a fragile and dynamic identity, to be sure, but an identity nonetheless. Perhaps even more important, from its quality will derive its stability and resilience. The richer and more coherent the nexus is, the better it will be able to withstand shocks and reinvent itself. The poorer and more superficial it is, the more blindly it will focus on its identity, and the more likely it is to be destroyed when confronted with a different social ethos.

Using this vocabulary, the remainder of this paper will attempt to explain the specific features of this nexus and its dynamic tendency towards an ever more real creation of the universal common good.

3. *Aiming at the common good in politics*

3.1 The Living together bears the hope of a conjunction between the personal good and the good of the community – it shelters the liberating power of a transcendent hope.

Human freedom becomes part of being through action.[63] Freedom of thought – this utterly internal freedom – only becomes real to the extent that it is expressed historically and marks its human environment with its novelty.[64] Freedom that rejects action is freedom that rejects itself. To Arendt, freedom only achieves the radical novelty it carries insofar as it engages in action. Action is thus the place where human freedom is actualized and achieves itself.

That is why, to Arendt, political society results from action.[65] It is born of shared action, free interaction between human beings. It is not the total sum of human actions, but the interplay of these actions as they produce an environment, a sphere in which each action is not only recognised as achieving an utility, but as the revelation of a thought and a freedom (*novum*). What she calls politics is thus the only space in which a human action is recognised as human through its involvement in social interaction. Politics is the space in which an agent's action is recognised as human, the space in which the various agents' inputs construct a common world whose primary feature is humanity (accepting the fragility of humanity, making it possible, deepening it and continuing it). In Arendt, this recognition does not initially assume the form of law (which remains formal). It is only real where an interaction operates and develops it.[66] Thus the humanity of society is not so much to be sought in the various meta-discourses that sup-

63 Arendt, *The human condition*, 175-176.

64 *Ibid.*, 177.

65 *Ibid.*, 199.

66 *Ibid.*, 230-235.

posedly legitimise it,[67] but in the very specific way that interactions operate and favour this recognition of humanity.

The paradox of society is that, being born of possible cooperation between freedoms, born of deliberate interactions, it is constantly *undone* by the conflicts that undermine it. Conflict and violence are so co-extensive with society that they may be considered as the primary evidence of political philosophy. This is the whole Augustinian current of thinking, which sees in the power of political authority the necessary remedy for the violence that original sin induces in social relationships.[68] It is on this scepticism that British philosophers, at the dawn of the modern age, based their view of the need for state power. As Hobbes saw it, the natural and insurmountable conflict of private interests required state power and the priority of the general interest over private interest to ensure that a minimal threshold of peace and justice could reign.[69] And yet the vitality of society and its constant historical reinvention bore witness to the priority of *the hope of a possible and real conjunction between the personal good and the good of the community*. At the heart of society is the invincible *hope of the common good*. The will to live-together is hosting in its core a hope[70]: the hope that one's own good can be reconciled with that of other people.[71]

This by no means denies the conflict inherent to social relationships; but it does not posit it as a state of nature (warfare and violence) against which the sovereign's power imposes a state of culture (peace and law).[72] An anthropology of the common good states that, even though conflict exists, it is no more 'natural' or 'original', or even more dominant, than the hope of the common good. However, this conflict in social relationships, the frequent incompatibility between the private good and the good of the community will be one of the specific features of the common good. To desire and aim at the common good will always be marked by conflict; and this is why the *hope* of the common good must be backed by a *will* for the common good in order for it to be achieved. It is also why the historical

67 *Ibid.*, 294 ff. Although Arendt does not use the term 'meta-discourse', she lays the groundwork for analyses such as Foucault's on the relationship between truth and power.

68 Etienne GILSON, *Les métamorphoses de la cité de Dieu*, Paris, Vrin, 2005 (1954), 47-80.

69 Thomas HOBBES, *Leviathan*, 1651, Chapter XVII.

70 Paul RICOEUR," Pouvoir et violence ", in *Lectures 1 : Autour du politique*, Paris, 1991, 21-42;

71 See Mathias NEBEL, 'Espérance et bien commun', in Anto GAVRIC, Grzegorz W. SIENKIEWICZ (eds), *Etat et bien commun*, Berne, Peter Lang, 2007, 217-232.

72 Jean-Jacques ROUSSEAU, *Le contrat social*, 1762 (published in English as *The social contract* in 1782), Book I, Chapters III, VI and VIII.

achievement of the common good will never be total or complete. Always specific, the *will* for the common good will also be specific and limited in time and space. And hence – because it excludes from the achieved good those that are on its boundaries – any achievement of the common good will always be partial and will always entail a potential conflict that is linked to its very limitations. The common good is thus a *dialectical* concept[73] whose horizon is *the hope of a future humanity in which each person's good would finally coincide with the good of all.*[74] This is why the hope of the common good is ultimately based on a transcendent hope: that of an *eschaton* of human history in which the good of the whole of humanity would coincide with that of each of its members. The hope of the common good thus depends on the *faith* in the eschatological advent of a reconciled humanity.[75]

In other words, wanting to live together is not just a matter of wanting to survive, but of wanting to live well – as a possible and real purpose, not a utopian one.[76] The good life – *the hope of a future humanity in which each person's good would finally coincide with the good of all* – is the horizon founding the aspiration to the common good. Without this hope, the conflicts that mark the pursuit of the common good could no longer be seen as the movements of an ascending dialectic, but on the contrary as evidence that its pursuit is irrational. The obstacles to the broadening of the common good would then finally exhaust the hope that drives political action;[77] for, once the dialectical pendulum is broken, the hope that dwells in wanting to live together will seem little more than a naïve illusion or a theological relic from which we should be 'brave' enough to break free. 'Political realism' – cynical rather than empirical – then withdraws to a minimum: limiting conflicts, preserving public order and peace, maintaining the rule of law. Yet the hope of the common good is constantly reborn, over and over again, and no historical failure seems able to destroy it. Life in society never comes to a halt! Though defeated, conquered and bruised, it is always reborn. The hope that drives social action is invincible – and this is the paradox! The common good is not just hope; it is the eschatological

73 Fessard, in particular, recognised a dialectic dynamic in the purpose of the universal good in his Hegelian reinterpretation of the common good. See Gaston FESSARD, *Autorité et bien commun*, 96-98.

74 ARENDT, *The human condition*, 305-308.

75 The introduction of this historical tension into the notion of the common good is specifically Christian. See HIBST, *Utilitas Publica,* 144-157.

76 Paul RICŒUR, 'De la morale à l'éthique et aux éthiques', in *Le juste II*, Paris, Esprit, 2001, 55-67.

77 This lies at the root of today's disenchantment with the European project.

horizon onto which all political action is projected. Hope is inchoate in action, and immanent in hope is a metaphysical – not religious – hope.[78] A reinterpretation of the common good must therefore, in my view, account for this paradox that forms the dynamic of politics.

4. *Aiming at the common good as the dialectic of politics*

I have identified the elements of the common good, and mentioned the hope that dwells in its pursuit; but I have not yet specified the content of this hope. This final section will attempt to do so.

4.1 The conjunction of the good of the individual and the good of the community

Historically, the concept of the common good refers to a relationship – the relationship between *the good of an individual* and *the wider community he belongs to*. So it is not a particular good that is fixed and determined once and for all, but the *dynamic coincidence of two or more goods* that will fluctuate over time.[79]

It is interaction that combines these two goods, for every interaction is simply the organised collaboration between different freedoms, united around the achievement of a given social good. It is people who coincide in the intention and creation of a social good; it is people who share a common benefit and a certain practical rationality derived from the good of order. So their own good is involved in this collaboration. The social good that they produce together is thus both the good of all and the good of each of them.

78 'Torn between what I do without wanting to and what I want to do without doing it, I am always as it were shut out of myself. So how do I get back in and put into my action what is no doubt already there, but unbeknown to me and beyond my control? How do I match the subject to the actual subject? To want myself fully, I have to want more than I have yet managed to find. Colliding with the supreme necessity of will, I therefore have to determine what I want, so that I can in all fullness *want* to want. Yes, I have to want myself; yet I cannot reach myself directly; between me and me there is a gulf that nothing has been able to fill. I cannot stop, I cannot go back, I cannot proceed on my own: out of this conflict, which arises in any human conscience, there inevitably emerges the admission of 'the only necessary thing.' BLONDEL, *L'action*, 336.

79 Writing from a different perspective, Hans Sluga arrives at the same conclusion. See SLUGA, *Searching for the common good*, 231-250.

Here we must bear in mind how profoundly our thinking is marked by materiality.[80] We spontaneously think about sharing a good as if what is obtained by one person is lost to another, as if it was biscuits or money. But the material element of social goods is only part of what is shared – and not the most important part. Of course, interaction does usually produce a material, tangible good; but its creation and, even more, its existence depend, as we have seen, on a communality of meaning: a common intention and will; a common benefit and a communal rationality; collective habitus. All this is intangible, but still real. And the sharing of intangible goods is marked by the fact that what is given to one person does not diminish what others receive. On the contrary, a broader distribution base (a greater number of people) tends to increase the total good. The classic example is a mother's love for her children. The birth of another child does not reduce her love for the previous ones. Similarly – and this is too often overlooked – my freedom is rather augmented than reduced by another person's freedom.

The law enriches my freedom with other people's freedom so that *together* we can be free. Only a very pessimistic view of human nature has made us forget this ancient conception of the law. The law is not primarily an instrument for repressing individual freedom. It is primarily the result of free collaboration, the expression of freedom that is increased and enriched by other people's. We are freer together than on our own. The human quality of this common freedom was the pride of the Greek city states, which is why antiquity saw the law not in minimal terms, but as the basis for a virtuous life, i.e. excellence in human action. This conception of the law, which is so hard to understand today, shows how the creation of a social good – in this case, the law – is both a personal good (individual virtue) and a social praxis (collective habitus). It is the intangible – ethical – nature of these social goods that makes this possible.

The expression 'basic social goods' is used in development literature to designate the minimum goods that should be available to all, such as food, housing, safety and all the fundamental human rights. Each of these basic social goods is what has been referred to here as a specific common good. What my analysis adds to this literature is an understanding of all the intangible elements that structure the real existence of these goods. The lasting creation of a 'basic social good' depends on the existence of a communality of meaning. None of these goods – food, housing, education, the law – can

80 Henri BERGSON, *Matière et mémoire*, Paris, Presses Universitaires de France, 2012 (1896).

be created on a lasting basis unless they are collectively seen as common goods that we want to create together.

Indeed, it soon becomes clear that even in the case of food the problem is not merely a question of production. Of course, in a famine there is a real shortage of food; but, as Sen has pointed out,[81] famines are not so much due to the lack of food as to the lack of will to distribute it to everyone. There are no famines in democratic regimes. What prevents the implementation of the right to food is that eating one's fill is not seen as a common good. Ultimately, it is because there is no communality of meaning surrounding the notion that no-one in a community should die of hunger that some people still do. The organisation of food production and distribution is based on such a fundamental consensus.[82] This is even more true of education, in which the intangible element of the common benefit – knowledge – is such that its distribution does not involve any reduction of shares. Teachers do not lose what they impart, or forget what they pass on to their pupils; on the contrary, their knowledge is enriched by being passed on to others.

It is because the common good is essentially moral that the good of the individual and the good of the community can coincide in interaction. One person's good is then increased by another person's, even though it is shared.

4.2 Wanting the common good

This conjunction, even though it is an intrinsic part of our social condition, does not occur without us. We have to *want* the common good. We have to work out how it *must* occur, and *can* occur, in the present circumstances. We have to work at wanting to live together, in order to maintain, reinvent and increase the common goods around which we are gathered together as a community. Although already found in their most basic forms within the

81 Amartya SEN, *Poverty and famines*, Oxford, Oxford University Press, 1981.

82 Recognition of the right to food as a human right is a first step towards the recognition of food as a common good. But in terms of the nexus of the common good, this human right clashes with other requirements, especially legal and economic ones. This goes to show the complexity of this nexus, and why its political governance is so essential.

family, clan or ethnic group,[83] actions for the common good are bound to become increasingly conscious and free, i.e. political. It is this process – this common good dynamic – that must determine which goods unite us, which ones we want to create together, and how to design, share or distribute them.

But since the conjunction achieved at the level of the nexus may be manifold and must be wanted, it is the central object of political deliberations and decisions. We must discern exactly what it consists of, what the conjunction requires in the present circumstances, determine the goods that bring us together as a community and what we want to promote in common (appreciation of common goods, setting of hierarchies, coherence, resolution of conflicts of meaning/production/distribution). The forms of these political agencies of deliberation and decision are many; but in contrast to the now prevailing idea, the legislature and the executive are not the ultimate source of this *order of the common good*, which they very often largely inherit and are simply called on to frame and develop.

Take customary law, which in all civilisations is one of the oldest forms of the common good. The reciprocity of customary rights and duties organises a community. Custom coordinates the good of individuals with the good of the community, and preexists positive law formulated by the legislature. The order of the common good is thus primarily a practical matter, and its political dimension only emerges gradually. The same applies to the executive which, in the vast majority of cases, is much more in the position to manage the nexus of the common good than to create it. The daily bread of executive is to assess and settle the many possible *conflicts* emerging between the good of individuals and that of the community. The origin and then the slow flourishing of the nexus of the common good thus escapes the republican ideal: that of an omnipotent assembly that sovereignly decrees the form of the state, decides the general interest and promulgates a constitutional order. The fact is that these decisions are not usually the result of an assembly, but of far longer processes, age-old experiences that form the wisdom of a people and found its political culture.

That is why the political perspective of the common good, while acknowledging the role of the legislature and the executive power in governing the common good, does not reduce it to them.

83 The conjunction of the common good is based on a certain logical and empirical correspondence between the existence of the individual and the existence of a community. The existence of an individual is always a social existence. This is self-evident in practice; it can be challenged in theory, but not in terms of action.

4.3 The dialectical dynamic of the common good

What explains the dynamic of the nexus of the common good is its *quality*. The quality of the common good is indeed measured by *the real conjunction created by a government between the good of individuals and that of the community they belong to*. This quality will first be judged by the existence and distribution of the material conditions needed for the survival of individuals and the community, but also – and mainly – by the quality of these goods that make a common life a human life (*humanitas*): peace, strength, justice, law, concord, magnanimity, forgiveness, prudence, wisdom, etc. These virtues are in this case collective virtues, a good of order as much as a shared practice. They are part of our freedom and an expression of it. They are values achieved through common practices: common behaviour that embodies values.[84]

Yet the quality of the nexus of the common good varies significantly. It may be more human, or less human; capable of organising more humanly the social relationships that unite us, or of degrading them in violence, injustice and perversity. Not every nexus of the common good is equally valuable. Some are basic, reduced to the simplest common goods; others are more complex and, like modern society, include many particular common goods. Yet it is not complexity that makes the quality of the nexus of the common good, but the quality of the relationships it creates between people. The freer these relationships, the more they will enhance our dignity. The truer they are, the more universal they will be. The more they are focused on values of the spirit, the more they will be able to accommodate our desire for the good life.

The quality of the nexus of the common good refers to its eschatological achievement horizon.[85] Here is a dialectic. Deepening and broadening the common good often involves a paradoxical stage in which the quality of the previous nexus is lost in order to broaden its base. The lost quality will then

84 For instance, a court will be unable to administer law and justice if the judge fails to respect the law and lets himself be bribed by the highest bidder. Similarly, the rule of law can only prevail if citizens spontaneously recognise, and comply with, the law. It is not prisons and the police that create the authority of the law, but fairness, justice and reason. The nexus of the common good is therefore eminently embodied in the *collective virtues on which the great social institutions and their authority are based*. Peace, justice, education, the law and health are thus essentially a communality of meaning embodied in social practice and habitus that strengthen the nexus of the common good. Were these practices to be lacking, our great social institutions would prove hollow and fragile, and could be overturned by a small group of determined people.

85 One of the most convincing points made in FESSARD, *Autorité et bien commun*, 98 ff.

have to be reconstructed, but this is a perilous undertaking that may also fail. The lost quality will then not be replaced, and the new equilibrium will be worse than the previous one. Aiming at the universal common good takes therefore the form of a dialectic.

In this connection the construction of Europe is a good example. There was a wish to integrate Europe's various countries, i.e. broaden and deepen the nexus of the European common good. The attempt is remarkable, makes sense, and is brave. It responds to the purpose of the common good. But will it succeed? The question remains entirely open. European integration was first seen in terms of economic integration, free movement of goods, services and people (the single market). But this is only one aspect of the common good – the creation of well-being – and it is quite clearly insufficient. Everyone is aware of this: the quality of the nexus of the European common good cannot be reduced to the merely economic good, a set of rights and standards, and a pretence at political governance of the Union. The difficulty is that the pursuit of integration, the deepening of a nexus of the European common good, entails transferring sovereignty to the European Commission and the European Parliament. So it is the very nation states involved in integration that are braking and rejecting it. The success or failure of Europe will depend on the nation states' ability to forge a European nexus of the common good with a quality similar to those they have already created at national level. If in the long term the quality is not the same – or, worse, if European integration reduces the national quality of the nexus of the common good – it is a fair bet that the democratic process in our countries will encourage a nationalist withdrawal and wreck the European project without adding anything but the slow decline of the national nexus.

Indeed, every determination of the nexus of the common good is historical, and hence incomplete and unfinished. First of all, the nexus is dynamic, and the equilibrium achieved in recent decades cannot claim to respond to all future changes. Populations change, economies are transformed, technologies develop; and the nexus of the common good must respond to these changes. Second, the size of the reference community varies and constantly tends to increase. The common good of a family is not that of a nation, or the whole of humanity. The nexus of the national common good is too narrow to cope with the various globalisation processes. It *must expand*, for many of the interactions that drive it up go beyond the governance of the nation state. If the dynamic of achievement of the common good tends towards universality, it is not just with reference to a moral imperative, but also on the basis of a gradual movement towards global integration of communities.[86]

Conclusion

If every historical determination of the common good is never more than partial and incomplete, destined to be revised and transformed, and if every achievement of the common good is conflictual, we can only say that what drives the wish for the common good is *hope – hope that this conjunction* of the good of the individual and the good of the community *is possible* and *will one day be real.* This hope is at the root of politics and political commitment. Should it ever be lost, the community will collapse. If the hope of the common good disappears, the solidity of the institutions that make up a society can do no more than delay the gradual dissolution of those that it groups together. The great question, of course, is whether this hope is well founded. Here the West depends on Christianity, which has found in the *parousia* of Christ in glory the ultimate foundation for this hope.

Which brings me to my final point: *serving the common good.* This hope provides the basis for a fundamental political attitude that will be, as it were, the soul of politics. Working for the common good means constantly seeking, despite the deficient nature of its determination, despite the obstacles and the conflicts, this conjunction between the good of individuals and that of their community. It means believing in the future value of the goods that make a political community into a human one. Working on the common good is a service that goes beyond thirst for personal power, one's own interest or that of a group, and even goes beyond national interest to focus on a horizon of achievement that must be accepted as eschatological. Political commitment in terms of service is therefore not an outmoded value, but the very soul of politics – the virtue that keeps a community within *humanitas.*

86 This argument is convincingly set out in HOLLENBACH, *The common good*, 212-229.

Christos N. Tsironis

The common good: historical roots in the Greek patristic texts and modern foundations

Introduction

What is the common good? This is how a historical analysis usually starts when the interest is focused in a strenuous effort to determine 'what is' and 'what is not' the concept in question. This approach echoes the voice of ancient Greek philosophy where the analytical route is assumed to be clearly delineated. As it is written, "The investigation of the meaning of words is the beginning of education" (Discourses of Epictetus, i. 17). However, the theological discourse to a significant extent has different premises. Although the Church Fathers used the rhetorical and philosophical methods, their homilies and their work served different purposes. They wanted to teach, to preach, and to offer their pastoral care. This means that they do use the terms and the methods of their own epoch, but only in the event that these are concurrent with their concerns.

Hence, the search of the meaning of the 'common good' concept in the wide area of Christian Ethics demands something more than a strict tracking of the notion in its historical development. In fact, it is rather rare that the Greek Church Fathers use the term 'common good' as such. Because they speak with a variety of cultural elements taken from their environment and their education they do not develop a definitive approach of the concept. Furthermore, they often use an apophatic approach[1] in their texts as they try to construct a sense of 'togetherness' in human *communitas* based on Christian premises. These premises are to be found in the teaching of Christ, when He indicates the active engagement in the realization of just relations in the society (1Cor 10: 33, Eph 4:28). In early Christianity, imitating Christ meant, among other things, the commitment in pur-

1 The social apophatic option is not to be confused with apophatic theology. In the first case the terminus *technicus* means that the Church Fathers speak on social issues without trying to create overwhelming social categories or frames of Social Theories. In the latter case the theological apophaticism refers on the knowledge of God. On the issue of the apophatic theology see: Andrew RADDE-GALLWITZ, *Basil of Caesaria, Gregory of Nyssa, and the Transformation of Divine Simplicity*, Oxford, Oxford University Press, 2009.

suing the good of all —both individually and collectively— in spiritual and social terms.[2] Under this scope, the Church Fathers continuously underline that the "fruit of the light *consists* in all goodness and righteousness and truth" (Eph 5:9). Therefore, they ask Christians —without the explicit reference of terms such as common good or common interest —to be agents in the realization of the common good (*koinofeles*) in their own specific social context (το χρήσιμον και κοινωφελές βλέπειν).[3] Seeking what is of common benefit for fellow people and their communities is the ethical basis of the Christians' view of civic participation in the early patristic literature.

The notion of the common good was a central issue in a variety of philosophical and theological inquires in Classic, Hellenistic and Medieval writers; and it is approached from diverse angles and points of view. Additionally, a wide range of terms has been used in this area: τὰ ξύμφορα καὶ τὰ κοινά (Thuc. 1.91), ξυνὰ (Aesch. Spt. 76), ξυμφέρον ([*koino*] *sumphéron*), καλόν (*kalon*), συμφέρον (1 Cor 7:35) χρηστότης/αγαθότης (*christotis*), ἀγαθόν, τἀγαθόν ("*agathon*" the good) etc. The term *koinon agathon* per se can be found in works dealing with political theory, metaphysics, theology and social ethics.[4] Although the origins of the concept can be traced to ancient Greek philosophy, its conceptual development and use in the Greek patristic is not widely explored. This issue recently re-emerged by Holman as she "explores how language about the common good in the Greek Fathers referred both to theological unity among Christians and to social unity among citizens".[5]

In general, it is always a challenge to decipher the meaning in every single writer and every single work since a relatively wide conceptual range of the notion 'common good' was available for use: From the 'Good' (*agathos*) as the maximum good (*summum bonum*) being as an end in itself, to the 'common good' (*koinon agathon*) as a principle that should govern the social relations with love and spirit of *diaconia*. In the case of the Greek patristic literature this task is even more challenging due to the distinctive features of the way the Greek Fathers expressed their theology. Very often they con-

2 Cf. "(...) they were looking not to their own but the common good" (οὐ τὸ ἑαυτῶν ἐσκόπουν, ἀλλὰ τὸ τῶν πολλῶν), in JOHN CHRYSOSTOM, *Homily IV on Matthew*, PG 57, 53.

3 See: ISIDORE OF PELUSIUM *Epistle: CLXXXV*, PG. 78,873D (κοινωφελές βλέπειν); *Epistle: CXXIII*, PG 78, 1197.

4 For an extensive study of the vocabulary in the Antique see: Peter HIBST, *Utilitas Publica - Gemeiner Nutz - Gemeinwohl*, Frankfurt, Peter Lang, 1991, 7-46.

5 See: "Introduction", in Johan LEEMANS, Brian MATZ, Johan VERSTRAETEN (Eds.), *Reading Patristic Texts on Social Ethics: Issues and Challenges for 21st Century Christian Social Thought*, Washington, Catholic University of America Press, 2011, xvi.

structed their arguments in the milieu of a Homilia, an epistle or a biblical commentary, while their main aim was to ensure the integrity of the faith, to answer topical challenges, and to guide ethically their flock. In that sense, they linked the idea of 'common good' with their pastoral reality instead of conceptually developing it.

In sum, the use of this term in Greek patristic has been developed on the biblical basis that God is *agathos* (Mt 19:17) and that God is love (1 John 4:8.10). In the Greek patristic texts some of the terms that used to express the notion of the common good were 'κοινωφελής' (*koinofelis*), 'κοινός' (*koinos*), 'κοινωνικός' (*koinonikos*) etc.[6] In general, the repetitive homilies on greed, usury, debt overhang, along with those on justice and philanthropy, create the canvas in the early patristic period, where the ideal of the common good is drawn.[7] Although reviewing extensively the literature on the common good exceeds the purpose of this analysis, a long interpretative walk both in history and in present times is necessary in order to understand better the origins and the main perspectives of the common good in the socio-ethical Greek patristic teaching.

The common good in the span of today's Christian Ethics: the Roman Catholic and the Orthodox theological traditions[8]

The 2008 global economic crisis brought once again to the center of public interest issues connected with the relationship between economic growth and social development. The "consumption-production-investment-maximization of profits" scheme as an internally re-enforcing system fails to integrate a significant part of the society: the weak, the excluded, the unemployed, the poor and all those who are not able to respond to 'glocal' challenges as global players.

6 Holman is working on the term 'κοινωφελής'. Cf. Susan R. HOLMAN, "Out of the fitting room: Rethinking Patristic social texts on the 'Common Good'", in Johan LEEMANS & Alii (Eds.), *op.cit.,* 103–123.

7 See among many others: GREGORY OF NYSSA, *On the love of the poor*; BASIL OF CAESAREA, *To the Rich*, *In time of famine and drought*, *I will tear down my barns*, *Against Those Who Lend at Interest*; JOHN CHRYSOSTOM, *2nd sermon on Lazarus and the Rich Man*; AMBROSE OF MILAN, *De Tobia* (PL 14,759-94), *De officiis 3,3* (PL 16,151).

8 A fair analysis of the multi-paradigm theological framework in the world of the Anglican, Protestant and Reformed Churches needs a special study. For the Anglican teaching Cf. Malcolm BROWN (Ed.), *Anglican Social Theology: Renewing the Vision Today*, London, Church House Publishing, 2014.

The importance of the notion of the common good has recently been underscored by Christian and non-Christian scholars. The global economic crisis placed in the epicenter of the public interest questions about how to maintain social integration, how and why the members of society sustain their social ties and how the relationship between economic growth and social development affects individually and collectively the wellbeing of people.

As it will be argued later in this essay, in the theological tradition the common good concept is shaped by the intersection of the question of equality, the pursuit of a just and fair society along with the protection of the weak and vulnerable as it is understood within the Christian eschatological frame.[9] It seems that, from this Christian theological point of view, the goods of creation given by the Creator to people are for the common benefit of all people.[10] As it is characteristically written in the anonymous work attributed to Basil of Caesarea entitled *On beneficence*[11]: "You, then, are disciples of God and hearers of the divine words, and we, who have been ordained to the teaching of the Word, we must serve the Word as much as we can and expound what is salutary for the audience with confidence and zeal for the good... Love is not unfruitful, nor did one who pretends to love his neighbor in word fulfill love's purpose. Let us listen to the apostle's saying, 'Let us not love in word nor in speech, but in deed and truth.' Let no one worry about his stewardship when he has obeyed God and sup-

9 Paul Schroeder notes: "In conclusion, it is important to emphasize that the 'newness' of Basil's new city is not so much an *institutional* newness as it is an *eschatological* newness... The new city is present wherever people live together in this way, waiting for the Kingdom of God even as they constitute a sign of its presence in our midst". BASIL OF CAESAREA, *On Social Justice*, (Trans. C. Paul SCHROEDER), Crestwood, St. Vladimir's Seminary Press, 2009, 38.

10 Ioanis PETROU, *Social Justice*, Thessaloniki, Paratiritis, 1992 [Gr]. See also: Paul SCHROEDER, *op.cit.*, 27: "Basil's ethic of sustainability is based upon an economic philosophy that might be described as a 'limited' resource paradigm: He believes that God has provided enough food, land, and usable materials to satisfy the needs of all; these resources, however, are limited commodities, and must therefore be shared out equitably".

11 See: "Although pseudonymous and extant (as far as we can determine)... De beneficentia, shares a number of characteristics common to social homilies preached in the late fourth and early fifth centuries (...)" in Susan R. HOLMAN, Brian J. MATZ, and Caroline MACÉ, "De Beneficentia: A Homily on Social Action attributed to Basil of Caesarea" in *Vigiliae Christianae* 66/5 (2012), 457-81.

ported his brother, for the Lord counts action done to brethren as done to Himself (...)"[12].

In view of this, there are critical questions to be asked and answers to be reflected on in the social and the theological discourse. In a world of polarized inequality, the common good can hardly be perceived as an average sum of all interests. Especially in the light of the unilateral conceptualization of economic freedom as limitless enterprising, that brings into the forefront crucial challenges such as Ecosystem sustainability[13] and the chances of the weak to live a dignified life. In this interconnected world Orthodox theology recently declared the need to define ways of common service with people of good will "for the sake of human society on the local, national, and international levels."[14] The aforementioned document of the Holy and Great Council of the Orthodox Church sets as a "presupposition for a wider co-operation...[the] acceptance of the highest value of the human person" (A.§ 3). It is obvious that for Orthodox theology the concept of the common good is strongly connected with the teaching on the "divine-human communion".[15]

The Social Ethics of Greek Orthodoxy have been developed as a polyptych formed by the interconnectedness among *Communio* (koinonia), *Martyria* (Witness), *Eucharistia* (celebration of God's new world) and *Diaconia.*[16] Through this polyptych, a variety of proposals have been shaped in light of the challenges evoked in the social arena.[17] On this account the purpose of

12 Ibid. 465-467.

13 For the link between the common good concept and ecological sustainability see: Pope FRANCIS. *Laudato si'* (2015); Ecumenical Patriarch BARTHOLOMEW, *On Earth As In Heaven: Ecological Vision and Initiatives of Ecumenical Patriarch Bartholomew,* New York, Fordham University Press, 2011.

14 See the document: *The Mission of the Orthodox Church in Today's World,* § 4 (accessed August 2017).

15 Aristotle PAPANIKOLAOU, *The Mystical as Political: Democracy and Non-Radical Orthodoxy,* Notre Dame, University of Notre Dame Press, 2012, 131-162. For a liturgical interpretation of human choices in the orthodox theology see also: Stanley HARAKAS, *Living The Liturgy,* Minneapolis, Light & Life Pub. Co, 1974; Ion BRIA, *The Liturgy After The Liturgy,* Geneva, WCC Publications, 1996.

16 Cf. Christos N. TSIRONIS, *Globalization and Local Communities: Social Ethics and Community Work,* Thessaloniki, Vanias, 2007 [Gr]; TSIRONIS, "Looking for the Causes of Economic Crisis from an Orthodox Point of View", in CCEE, *Economic Crisis and Poverty: Challenges for Europe Today. III Forum Europeo Cattolico- Orthodosso,* Bologna, EDB, 2013, 49- 68.

17 For the long theological elaboration on the interconnectedness of the Orthodox Social Ethics facets see: Metr. Pergamon John ZIZIOULAS, "Communion and Otherness", *St Vladimir's Theological Quarterly* 38/4 (1994), 347-361 in BRIA, *op.cit,* 1996; Georgios MANTZARIDIS, *Orthodox Theology and Social Life,* Thessaloniki, Pournaras, 1989.

the economic institutions —at least in the faithful's horizon of meaning— is considered to be the safekeeping of the world's integrity, the ensuring of life for all creatures and the respect of human dignity. Whereas spirituality and the ascetic life have a central role, the worldly goods are not disvalued if used for the good of fellow humans (*philadelphia*) or for the society at larger scale. Despite the fact that there is a certain tradition of relevant practices and teachings, there is not an Orthodox corpus of texts as an analog of the Catholic Social Teaching (CST) that deals with social and economic issues in generic, direct and authoritative way. As it is easy to understand, the non-systematic character of 'social *didache*' allowed the tension between the dynamic and the static qualities of community life. This tension and the respective ambiguity in the way the orthodox theologians frame the economic field of action has been recognized for a long time.[18] Yet, a wide range of letters and homilies, along with philanthropic deeds and welfare establishments, mirror in a non-systematic way the strong belief that the genuine care for the weak belongs to the core of the Christian Ethics.

The concept of the common good holds a central place in the Catholic Social Teaching (CST). As pointed out in the Compendium (§ 164) the common good indicates "the total sum of social conditions which allow people, either as groups or as individuals, to reach their fulfillment more fully and more easily... Just as the moral actions of an individual are accomplished in doing what is good, so too the actions of a society attain their full stature when they bring about the common good. The common good, in fact, can be understood as the social and community dimension of the moral good".[19] The significance of the concept was officially underlined in modern times with the encyclical letter *Rerum Novarum* (Pope Leo XIII, 1891). This encyclical started a chain of pontifical letters and exhortations

18 See: Alexandros PAPADEROS, "Orthodoxy And Economy: A Dialogue With Alfred Muller–Armack". *Social Compass* 22/1 (1975), 33-66 [here: 56].

19 Cf. "§ 165. A society that wishes and intends to remain at the service of the human being at every level is a society that has the common good — the good of all people and of the whole person— as its primary goal. The human person cannot find fulfilment in himself, that is, apart from the fact that he exists 'with' others and 'for' others." And it follows: "§ 166. The demands of the common good are dependent on the social conditions of each historical period and are strictly connected to respect for and the integral promotion of the person and his fundamental rights" and finally: "§ 169. To ensure the common good, the government of each country has the specific duty to harmonize the different sectoral interests with the requirements of justice. The proper reconciling of the particular goods of groups and those of individuals is, in fact, one of the most delicate tasks of public authority." See: PONTIFICAL COUNCIL FOR JUSTICE AND PEACE, *Compendium of the Social Doctrine of the Church,* Rome, Libreria Editrice Vaticana, 2004.

with a specific concern on issues of social and economic nature. There is a line that firmly connects the letter of 1891 with the papal writings and messages of the last century. The term "universal common good" emerged in *Pacem in Terris* (§ 100) while at the same period *Gaudium et Spes* (§ 26) linked it with the Human Rights perspective.[20] The concerns of the Orthodox Church on 'mutual love', 'common purpose' and 'mutual assistance' in works of welfare have been in modern times expressed firstly in the Patriarchal and Synodal encyclicals of 1902 and 1920.[21] To a certain extent, this parallel development of moral and social concerns continued —although asymmetrically— during the rest of 20th century.

Recently, Pope Francis emphasized the dimensions of responsibility and service in consistency with an integral understanding of the common good concept. He delineated his intentions in the Apostolic Exhortation *Evangelii Gaudium* in a way that allows a sort of bridging between theological, socio-ethical and political advocacy. As he notes: "I am firmly convinced that openness to the transcendent can bring about a new political and economic mindset which would help to break down the wall of separation between the economy and the common good of society" (§ 205). The core of this phrase deserves theological and societal attention: Is there truly a "separation between the economy and the common good?" This question is a good start for reflective thinking both in the wider society and within the Christian communities, and it is open for further discussion.

Indeed, it seems that all Christian communities are facing to a greater or lesser extent the same problems in the globalised world. In this perspective, the Pope Francis and the Ecumenical Patriarch Bartholomew I, met in Jerusalem (25 May 2014) and signed a Declaration where they affirmed, among other things, their will to work "together in the service of humanity,

20 See also: John FINNIS, *Human Rights and Common Good*, Oxford, Oxford University Press, 2011, 89-90.

21 Cf. Metr. Gennadios LIMOURIS (Ed.), *Orthodox Visions on Ecumenism*, Geneva, WCC, 1994; Rev. Theodoros MEIMARIS, *The Holy and Great Council of the Orthodox Church & the Ecumenical Movement*, Thessaloniki, Stamoulis, 2013.

especially in... promoting peace and the common good, and in responding to the suffering that continues to afflict our world".[22]

Naturally, the fact that the common good can serve as a common reference to the origins of the Christian Social Ethics, is not the only thing that attracts scientific interest. The concept itself is rooted in ancient Greek philosophy as an essential part of classic political thinking.

From ancient Greek philosophy to Christian Theology

The concept of the common good is not exclusively Christian. The idea that the city has precedence over the individuals is a kind of *locus communis* in the political theory of many philosophers in classic antiquity. In the moral and political theory of Plato and Aristotle, a good citizen is one who fulfils his social life by conducting a virtuous way of life and achieving aims leading to the common good, the overarching good of the City-State.[23] In his attempt to explore the conditions and the aim of this kind of citizens' active participation Aristotle examines *eudaimonia* as a concept linked with virtues that propel the personal *and* the social fulfillment. A citizen can flourish as a member of a flourishing political community and the *koinon sumpheron* expresses this prospect: "But all communities are like parts of the political community, for people come together for a certain advantage, namely, to provide some of the things conducive to life. And the political community seems to come together from the outset, and to continue to exist, for the sake of what is advantageous; lawgivers aim at this and claim

22 At this point, a clarification about the way the moral and social teaching occurs in the Orthodox Tradition is required. The notion of the common good can be found in the spectrum of the Orthodox social theology, but not necessarily in the form of a principle as it is in the CST. The construction of conceptual frames as systematized sets of fundamental principles by which key issues of social ethics might be interpreted is not a characteristic of the Orthodox Tradition. Yet, the different ways the Christian Traditions followed in elaborating and expressing their social ethics do not prevent them from working together in developing an ethics of responsibility. Under this scope, the most valuable Orthodox contribution on the common good concept is not so much that of a particular approach to a theoretical conundrum, but rather an expression of a tradition that focuses on *diaconia* and reconciliation.

23 See: Aristotle Pol. 31279a22–1281a10 "ὅταν δὲ τὸ πλῆθος πρὸς τὸ κοινὸν πολιτεύηται συμφέρον, καλεῖται τὸ κοινὸν ὄνομα πασῶν τῶν πολιτειῶν, πολιτεία" ("while when the multitude govern the state with a view to the common advantage, it is called by the name common to all"), in Aristotle (H. Rackhman trans), *Politics*, Cambridge, Harvard UP (Loeb), 1959, 207.

that the advantage held in common is what is just".[24] In this sense, the common good is something more than the sum of particular interests and presupposes reciprocal ties, civic participation and a sense of togetherness. The Aristotelian idea that "in cases when the one or the few or the many govern with an eye to the common interest (*koinon sunpheron*), these constitutions must necessarily be right ones (...)" (Aristot. Pol. 3.1279 a) deeply marked the way the Hellenistic philosophical schools and the Christians understood their civic identity and especially the way they described their vision of the earthly societies. Besides, the starting point of Aristotelian politics draws a picture of the City-State/*Politeia* as an interpersonal political body (partnership) that is "formed with a view to some good" (*agathou tinos heneken*).[25] Of special note is the concept of the common good elaborated by the Stoic philosophical schools that emerged in Hellenistic period. As Sandbach notes "For them [the Stoics] virtue is the only thing of which the possession is relevant to happiness (...). Moral action consisted in having the right preferences and it brought happiness (...). The actual acquisition or possession of external things, however valuable they might be, did not increase that happiness. This solution springs from the dogma that 'good' means 'morally good' ".[26] According to this perspective, the Stoics favoured the participation to the public life as long as it was directed to the common good (*sumpheron).* Some virtues were associated to this search of the common good, especially justice, and developed an idea of humanity as a universal family: "If, then, any action of yours has not its tendency... to the common-good as its end, this action disorders your life, and hinders it from being uniform, and it is seditious".[27] In this context terms such as good (*agathon*), happiness/fulfilment (*eudaimonia*), appropriate act (*to kathikon*), virtue (*arete*), righteousness (*dikaiosune*) were extensively used.

Based on the aforementioned references, the path from classical Greek ethics and political theory to Hellenistic philosophy and from there to

24 See: Aristotle Nic. Eth. 1160 a: "Αἱ δὲ κοινωνίαι ... συμπορεύονται γὰρ **ἐπὶ τινι συμφέροντι**,... καὶ ἡ πολιτικὴ δὲ κοινωνία τοῦ συμφέροντος χάριν δοκεῖ... τούτου γὰρ καὶ οἱ νομοθέται στοχάζονται, **καὶ δἰκαιόν φασιν εἶναι τὸ κοινῇ συμφέρον**", English translation () Aristotle (R. C. Bartlett and S. D. Collins), *Nicomachean Ethics*, Chicago, The University of Chicago Press, 2011, 177.

25 Aristotle Pol. 1.1252 a. See: Aristotle (H. Rackhman trans), *Politics*, Cambridge: Harvard UP (Loeb), 1959, 3.

26 Francis H. Sandbach, *Aristotle and the Stoics*, Cambridge, Cambridge Philological Society, 1995, 25.

27 Francis Hutcheson (Ed.)., *The Meditations of the Emperor Marcus Aurelius Antoninus,* Indianapolis, Liberty Fund, 2008, 112.

Christian Ethics is now more clearly visible. Aristotle insists that a citizen should aim at the common good of the City in order to achieve conditions of personal and collective wellbeing. A citizen is considered to be a part of a larger association; the circle of fellow citizens in the City-State. The geographical and the psychological boundaries in the description of the common good changed during the Hellenistic period. Especially the Stoics developed a new cosmopolitan idea that is assumed to be originated by the Cynics. As described by Diogenes Laertius (VI 63) the Cynic philosopher Diogenes answered "I am a citizen of the world" (*kosmopolitês*), when asked where he was from. The Stoics regarded human beings as members of a wider community that exceeds the characteristics of the City-State. The Cosmos ruled by the Logos is the biosphere where the wise understand that the best possible way to happiness is to pursue with all actions the common *sumpheron.* As Bryent notes "The Stoic telos of 'living consistently with physis' thus presupposes an awareness of the interdependence of self and universe —a fundamental and decisive shift from the traditional citizen-Polis axis".[28]

The idea of a virtuous life directed towards the realization of a flourishing community where persons individually and collectively can achieve their fulfillment, created a valuable legacy which was not insignificant for Christians in the following centuries. Especially for the Church Fathers of early Christianity, the ideal of the common good is at odds with a self-interested way of life and any political regulation that allows space for uncontrolled and greedy antagonism.

Being under the influences of the conceptual development of the common good and all the relevant terms in the context of philosophy, the Christian theologians explained the vision of their faith community for earthly affairs. At first the apologetics had to persuade the people of their times that the Christians were not an antisocial cult. The Christians were both citizens of the society and members of the Church. The Church (ἐκκλησία/*ecclesia*), understood in socio-political terms as the assembly of the faithful believing in Christ, was a community committed to the common good. By this they meant that the individual and the collective actions of Christians were by no means against the *koinon sumpheron.* From St. Paul's letters to the first Christian communities where the individuals were asked to put aside their private interests for the sake of the whole believing-in-Christ community, to the organized caritative /diaconical work,

28 Joseph M. Bryant, *Moral Codes and Social Structure in Ancient Greece: A Sociology of Greek Ethics From Homer to the Epicureans and Stoics*, New York, SUNY Press, 432.

the Christian theologians gradually associated their identity with the love and the stewardship of all humanity. In their own theological terms, the Church as the mystical body of Christ has an ecumenical character by definition.

The reception of various philosophical notions within early Christian writings is obvious. But while using terms that were well-known in his philosophical and socio-political context, St Paul, however mitigates their philosophicalmeaning in the light of his Christology and the pillars of the Christian faith. In the letters of St. Paul, the *sumpheron* is what is beneficial for the life of the faithful both as individually and as a member of the community. The use of these terms is central in the relevant studies. As it is noted in the Kittel *Theological Dictionary of the New Testament*:

"The profit at issue here is... the union of each Christian with the Lord and of the Lord with him (...) the other aspect which is much more prominent in Paul in determining what is profitable. συμφέρον is that which edifies the community. The profit of the individual is far less important than this. This ranks first for Paul himself and his apostolic ministry: μὴ ζητῶν τὸ ἐμαυτοῦ σύμφορον ἀλλὰ τὸ τῶν πολλῶν, ἵνα σωθῶσιν (1C. 10:33).... Similarly, the basic rule for the charismata granted to the whole community is: πρὸς τὸ συμφέρον, 1C. 12:7. In the middle of the discussion (c. 12–14) of the different value and profit of these gifts stands love".[29]

In this manner, doing good means choosing to do all that benefit others. Since salvation in Christ is what matters for the early Church, the Christians are called to be imitators of Christ (1Cor 11:1)[30] Thus, an essential difference between the philosophical and the theological meaning is that the concept of the common good *per se* was elaborated by the Christians not only

29 Karl Weiss, "συμφέρω, σύμφορος", in *Theological Dictionary of the New Testament*, Vol. 9., 1964, 76-77.

30 For the theological parameters of St Paul's teaching as perceived in the tradition of the Orthodox church see also: Petros Vassiliadis, "Equality and Justice in Classical Antiquity and in Paul: The Social Implications of the Pauline Collection.", *St. Vladimir's Theological Quarterly*, 36/1992, 51-59; Ibid., "Paul's Theologia Crucis as an Intermediate Stage of the Trajectory from Q to Mark", in *VII Simposio di Tarsosu S. Paolo Apostolo,* Roma, L. Padovese, 2002, 47-55; Charalambos Atmatzides, "Gregor Palamas und die Theorie über das Wahre Licht und dessen Begründung von der Heiligen Schrift. Das Beispiel des 2Kor 4,4.6", *Orthodoxes Forum*, 5-20; Moschos Goutzioudis, "The Entrance of Jesus in Jerusalem according to the Gospel of Matthew", in, Eugen J. Pentiuc - John Fotopoulos - Bruce N. Beck (Ed), *Studies in Orthodox Hermeneutics: A Festschrift in Honor of Theodore G. Stylianopoulos*, Brookline, Massachusetts: Holy Cross Orthodox Press, 2016, 80-94; Wayne A. Meeks, *The First Urban Christians: The Social World of the Apostle Paul,* New Haven, Yale University Press, 1983.

as an outcome of the citizen's political virtue, but mainly as God's gift and a challenge for humankind. This is a noticeable conceptual move from the realm of political institutions to the Kingdom of God.

Another issue of special interest is the comparison between the Stoic and the Christian teaching on fellowship/brotherhood. The call to work for the common good was in both cases a proclamation that has been orientated towards the cosmos and the *ecumene.* Although this may be true, the premises of the Stoic universality are not identical with those in the Christian ethic and social teaching. The Stoic cosmopolitan orientation was more of a political value. The social and hegemonic structures of the multi-colored Hellenistic world brought to the fore the idea of a cosmopolitan citizen who is not bounded exclusively with the benefit of a certain City-State. On the other side, the Church Fathers reinterpreted the existing philosophical ideas on the means and the ends of a good life through their theological, spiritual and pastoral teaching. In this way, the idea of the common good understood as the welfare of all humanity - was based on the ontology that emerged in the Christian faith with regard to one, almighty God, Creator and Father of all. While the Stoics' teaching recognizes the importance of being 'wise'[31] in order to gain a fulfilled life on earth[32], Christian theology focuses on the possibility of all to be "no longer strangers and aliens, but (...) fellow citizens with the saints, and members of God's household" (Eph 2:19-20). In this way, the Christian perspective was manifested as inclusive and eschatological *in Christ.*

In sum, the Church Fathers employed the rich philosophical tradition concerning the common good concept in terms of their own theological frame of reference. For early Christian Theology, life in *eudaimonia* is not something to be approached intellectually but it is rather a life *in communion* with Christ who *is* the Good. Through this framework, the Church Fathers restricted the theoretical inquiries of the *sumpheron* as they diversely appeared in political theory, and they focused on its ethical prospective. As Isidore of Pelusium explains in a way characteristic for Christian self-awareness, the distinctive feature of the Christian Ethics is the fact that love and

31 See also Algra KEIMPE, "Stoic Theology", in Brad INWOOD (Ed.), *The Cambridge Companion to the Stoics*, Cambridge, Cambridge University Press, 2003, 155.

32 Joseph M. BRYANT, *Moral Codes and Social Structure in Ancient Greece: A Sociology Of Greek Ethics From Homer to the Epicureans and Stoics*, New York, SUNY Press, 439.

philanthropy are addressed to all people and not only to the networks of kinship, community, etc. (Epist. to Bishop Lampetius PG 78, 765D).[33]

On the one hand, the ancient philosophical way of thinking was based on the political premise that the community is and should be the center of the human biosphere. As Aristotle underlines: "to secure and preserve the good of the city appears to be something greater and more complete" (Aristotle, *Nicomachean Ethics*, 1094 b).[34] On the other hand, Christian social teaching was structured on an ontological and theological basis.[35] The good of all humanity was to be understood as a life-goal for all those who believed that every single person has been created in the image and likeness of God. The turning of a new page in the meaning attributed to the common good was marked by an eschatological perspective: Because the Reign of God was the common reference point for Christian theology, it is obvious that the way eschatology was perceived within the historical context of Christian communities affected the conceptual development of the common good. Since the Church Fathers were simultaneously focused on the route to the Reign of God along with the historical conditions of their communities, the notion of the common good has never been conclusively and monolithically defined. It was rather approached as a concept of dynamic character, as an inclusive and universal response to the ethical and social challenges of human societies, and finally as the harvest of the faithful life. For this reason, the focus on caritative work went along with the eschatology of Christian faith and similarly the cultivation of the Christian socio-ethical *didache* was forged with the loving *diakonia* of all people within a frame of theory-praxis nexus[36]. The belief in the eschatological fulfillment of the life in Christ (Phil. 1:6) was fundamental for the Christian communities. Notions such as *sumpheron* and common good acquired a

33 See also: JOHN CHRYSOSTOM, *In Epist. Ad Hebraeos* Cap. XII Homil XXXII, PG 63, 224; Ibid., In Cap.VI *Epist. Ad Galat*, PG 61,677.

34 ARISTOTLE (Robert C. BARTLETT and Susan D. COLLINS), *Nicomachean Ethics*, Chicago: The University of Chicago Press, 2011, 3.

35 See: Charles AVILA, *Ownership: Early Christian Teaching*, Maryknoll, NY, Orbis Books, 1983; Georgios I. MANTZARIDIS, *Soziologie des Christentums*, Berlin, Duncker & Humbolt, 1981; Susan R. HOLMAN, *The Hungry are Dying*, Oxford, Oxford University Press, 2001; Robert P. MALONEY, "The Teaching Of The Fathers On Usury: An Historical Study On The Development Of Christian Thinking" , *Vigiliae Christianae*, 241-265; Verna HARRISON, "Poverty in the Orthodox Tradition," *SVTQ*; Blakein LEYERLE, "John Chrysostom on Almsgiving and the Use of Money", *The Harvard Theological Review*, 29-47.

36 See: St. BASIL, *Homilia I in Psalmum* XIV, PG, 256 A-D.

soteriological meaning while the service of the others was recognized as an obvious sign of following the teaching and the paradigm of Christ.[37] The ethics of early Christianity on the issues of self-giving and salvation reflected the reception of Jesus Christ's saying on the Good Shepherd. In this framework, the Christians could only understand the meaning of human action in light of the example of the Good Shepherd who decides to put Himself (John 10: 11-19) or the rest of the flock (Lk 15:1-7) in danger in order to go after the lost sheep.[38] Above all, Christ's 'self-emptying' (*kenosis*) as it is experienced in the early Church (Phil 2:6-10) is a chapter of major importance in patristic theology. The Church Fathers perpetually referred to the kenotic character of love in Christian Ethics and called Christians to limitless love and service for the others.[39]

As is mentioned earlier, the Christian scholars and Churchmen, while drawing on the basic facets of the Greek philosophical approaches, also incorporated basic premises of Christian faith. The common good in this context goes beyond the idea of the aggregation of particular, private goods and interests, and it is more about "the unique fulfillment afforded by mutuality, shared activity, and communion of persons(...)".[40] This view still has a central place in the Christian theological approaches while the pursuit of a 'symphony' between the individual and the social aspect emerged as a

37 St. BASIL, *Asceticon magnum* (Ὅροι κατὰ πλάτος), PG 31, 916D-917D [interrogatio iii].

38 For the eschatological perspective in the Early Church, see, among many others: Metr. John ZIZIOULAS, "Déplacement de la perspective eschatologique", in Giuseppe ALBERIGO et al., *La chrétienté en débat: Histoire, formes et problèmes actuels,* Paris, Cerf, 1984, 89-100; Patrick DE LAUBIER, *L'eschatologie*, Paris, Presses universitaires de France, 1998; Brian E. DALEY, *The Hope Of The Early Church*: A *Handbook of Patristic Eschatology,* Cambridge, Cambridge University Press, 1991.

39 See also in Maximus the Confessor the Chapters on Love: "When a person loves someone, he is naturally eager to be of service. So, if one loves God, he is naturally eager to do what is pleasing to him.... What pleases God is love, temperance, contemplation, and prayer... Therefore, "those who are in the flesh cannot please God. And those who are Christ's have crucified their flesh with its passions and lusts", in MAXIMUS CONFESSOR (George BERTHOD transl.), *Selected Writings*, New York, Paulist Press, 1985, 62.

40 In the same entry of the CPD the Aristotelian understanding of humans as social and political beings and Christian Trinitarian Theology are indicated as the sources for this kind of ethical perspective on common good. See: James B. MURPHY "Common Good", in Robert AUDI (Ed.), *Cambridge Dictionary of Philosophy*, Cambridge, Cambridge University Press, 1999², 161.

central issue in modern times when dealing with the "common good question".[41]

As the biblical echo was intensive in the communities of the first centuries, it was repeatedly and in various ways underlined that - by principle - every personal or social choice should be judged by the standards of the dual-love commandment (Mt 22:37-40).[42] Nevertheless, an everyday pragmatism has never been exiled from the earthly living, and therefore the tension between self-interest and *caritas* for all fellow humans remained throughout history one significant challenge in Christian Ethics.

The best-known works of St. Augustine of Hippo[43] and St. Thomas Aquinas[44] have a central place in the long chain of Christian interpretations of the common good, and they constitute, of course, an enduring legacy in the Roman Catholic tradition. It is justifiably noted that, "true love, as Augustine sees it, does not seek private advantages. It recognizes that the common good has greater worth than the private, merely individual good".[45] In this context the notion of the common good is strongly connected with the idea of a true and pure love as a way of existence that can embrace others and overcome the enclosure of selfish interests. In the same vein, "Aquinas's Summa Contra Gentiles reaffirmed Aristotle's statement that the good of the community is more 'godlike' or 'divine' than the good of an individual human being. Aquinas went on to identify the good to be

41 See for example in the first lines of the well-known work of Jacques Maritain: "Does society exist for each one of us, or does each one of us exist for society? Does the parish exist for the parishioner or the parishioner for the parish? This question, we feel immediately, involves two aspects, in each of which there must be some element of truth. A unilateral answer would only plunge us into error", in Jacques MARITAIN, *The Person and the Common Good*, Notre Dame, IN, University of Notre Dame Press, 1966, 1.

42 This issue remained topical in various time periods and even affects discourse on the common good in today's world. A note of Mary M. Keys on Aquinas's ethical thought points out the tension when dealing with the equality ideal and the challenge of the ethos of service: "Equality alone does not lead to an ethos of service, to placing oneself – even physically –below another person to attend directly to his or her needs, including their basic physical welfare. Such service, if sincere, requires a humility and a love (charity in its original meaning) that are central to Aquinas's ethical and political thought". See: Mary M. KEYS, *Aquinas, Aristotle, and the Promise of the Common Good*, Cambridge, Cambridge University Press, 2006, 98-99.

43 See esp. in Paul WEITHMAN, "Augustine's Political Philosophy", in Eleonore STUMP & Norman KRETZMANN (Eds.), *The Cambridge Companion to Augustine*, Cambridge University Press, 2001, 234-252.

44 See esp. in Mary M. KEYS, *Aquinas, Aristotle, and the Promise of the Common Good,* Cambridge, Cambridge University Press, 2006.

45 Eleonore STUMP - Norman KRETZMANN, *The Cambridge Companion to Augustine*, 218.

sought by all persons in common with the very reality of God".[46] Thomas Aquinas is truly a significant figure in the historical development of the concept of the common good.[47] It is also certain that he is the pillar in the theological elaboration of the Aristotelian tradition within the framework of the Roman Catholic teaching. In the cases of St. Augustine and St. Thomas Aquinas, the political perspective[48] of their work and teaching was important in the development of the common good theories in theological and political fields.

Situating the common good in Greek patristic texts and the paradigm of St Basil: Revisiting the missing bond

Most historical reviews trace the beginnings of the conceptual development and cultural deployment of the common good concept to Aristotle's work. Some attention is given to the Statesmen —mainly Cicero and Seneca— in Roman Antiquity. From there the analytical line goes on to Augustine and Aquinas and then straight forward to the Papal Encyclicals of the last two centuries. In most cases, only a few lines are dedicated to the long patristic history and, almost always, the work of the Church Fathers in the Greek patristic texts is absent.[49] In the Greek patristic texts and in the Eastern Orthodox tradition the concept of common good is present although the term as such is not often used. It is not a surprise for those who are familiar with the theological traditions of Christianity that there is no definition of the common good concept in its framing parameters. Indeed, the work of St. Basil of Caesarea forms a paradigm of a life and a legacy (pastoral and theological work) that illustrates *par excellence* the early Christian perspective.

The life of St. Basil is recognized as an example for Christian *philadephia* (brotherly love) because he was a highly influential theologian. He estab-

46 David HOLLENBACH, *The Common good and Christian Ethics*, Cambridge, Cambridge University Press, 2004, 4.

47 See: Matthew S. KEMPSHALL, *The Common Good in Late Medieval Political Thought*, Oxford, 1999, 76-129.

48 Peter HIBST, *Utilitas Publica - Gemeiner Nutz - Gemeinwohl*, Frankfurt, Peter Lang, 1991, 149-153, 185-189.

49 To my knowledge, it is only the work of Susan Holman that recently brought up the topic of the common good in the Greek "patrologia". See: Susan R. HOLMAN, "Out of the Fitting Room: Rethinking Patristic Social Texts on The Common Good", in Johan LEEMANS - Brian J. MATZ - Johan VERSTRAETEN (Eds.), *Reading Patristic Texts on Social Ethics: Issues and Challenges for 21st Century Christian Social Thought*, Washington, Catholic University of America Press, 2011, 103–123.

lished a welfare institution with a multipurpose service center that served as an archetype of care institutions. His life, theology and pastoral work form one of the main pillars of the social teaching of the Orthodox Tradition.[50] Nothing remained over the centuries so vividly warm in people's hearts as his remembrance as a man of *diaconia*, a person who bridged theory and praxis. His philanthropic establishment, the so-called *Basiliad*, his active solidarity with the poorest of the poor and the socially excluded of his time, his words of justice and his everyday service to the weakest, are still commemorated in our days.

The significance of St Basil's teaching on sharing the goods and ensuring the common good in society is of major significance for Christian Ethics. In a certain way, the severity of his response to the greedy can shed more light to his teaching. The modest bishop, sweet and moderate in his pedagogical way of speaking, becomes harsh in issues of consumerist affluence and irresponsible richness. St. Basil who had been ready to suffer —intellectually and physically— in order to avoid a trauma in church unity, leaves no chance for compromises when some people are in danger and others choose neutral comfort or indifference. Surprisingly enough, he states that people who do not respond to the needs of the others —the 'un-social' (ἀκοινώνητος), as he called them— will be in the first line of all sinners who are facing the eternal punishment (PG 31, 324B). Furthermore, he repeatedly states that people do not need but a few sets of clothing and some modest food. The food surplus is something that does not belong to the one who has it in his own storehouse; it belongs to those in need. What led a tempered bishop to speak about eternal punishment and to condemn this specific sin in such a way? For St. Basil, as for other Church Fathers, a desire for ownership beyond actual needs, a materialistic disposition, in other words greed and attachment to money, is a grave sin. The biblical basis is obvious: "For the love of money is the root of all evil: which while some coveted after, they have erred from the faith, and pierced themselves through with many sorrows" (1 Ti 6:10).

The social conditions and adversities of the late antiquity era are often demonstrated most graphically in St. Basil's homilies as he attends to matters of individual choice and of public values in terms of the Christian ethos. At the same time his eschatological perspective is present when he describes the duties and the levels of Christian civic participation. The

50 Christos N. Tsironis, "Peace-War-Ecclesia in Modern Greece: Fragments and Continuities", in Semegnish Asfaw, Alexios Chehadeh, Marian Gh. Simion (Eds.), *Just Peace. Orthodox Perspectives*, Geneva, WCC Pub., 2012, pp.128-151.

loving care for everybody and the service of the common good are the central points of his social *didache* because his vision of the faith community of fellow-heirs is gospel-rooted. As Azkoul notes "the Christian 'city' and its 'culture' prepares its citizens for 'the heavenly Jerusalem'... Christ dwells in the midst of the city, giving her stability, sending out on every side providential rays to the limits of the world (...)"[51] In the new – Christian – city the community bond is not based on blood kinship but on communion with God. Given that all people as God's creatures share a common nature, the call for merciful acts and rightful living originated from a theological understanding of the Divine Justice and the kenotic character of love in Christ.[52]

St. Basil uses the well-known frame of patronage and civic *philanthropia*[53] and imparts to them a Christian message. He underlines the moral obligations of all peoples with regard to those in need of social protection. The poor people are not just fellow endangered citizens, but also fellow human beings, all created by God and therefore an indifference to their life is a grave sin.[54] In this sense, he uses the term *communis utilitas* (κοινῆς τῆς ἀπ' αὐτῶν ὠφελείας ἅπασι προκειμένης, PG 31,384 C) in order to link the possession of wealth with the responsibility to protect and ensure other peoples' lives. Establishing the Evangelical principle of Love at the center of his perspective, he creates relevant moral standards around the social values and

51 Michael AZKOUL, *St. Gregory of Nyssa and the Tradition of the Fathers*, New York, Edwin Mellen Press, 1995 35-36.

52 As Susan Holman notes: "The justice of the common good, for Basil, is ultimately rooted in God's goodness for, he says (in *Hom.* 20), 'You have not known God by reason of your justice, but God has known you by reason of His goodness.' Common goodness is therefore based not only on ideals of harmonious community, but on all that goodness means for the individual within the very nature and person of God." Susan R. HOLMAN, "Healing the World with Righteousness? The Language of Social Justice in Early Christian Homilies", in Miriam FRENKEL and Yaacov LEV (Eds), *Charity and Giving in Monotheistic Religion*, Berlin, W. de Gruyter, 2008, 89-110 [here 102].

53 More on this: Susan R. HOLMAN, *The Hungry are Dying,* Oxford, Oxford University Press, 2001, 3-30.

54 See: "The spiritual value of these poor lay in their very corporal humanness as part of God's created world... he is guilty of homicide, Basil charges, who passes by the starving person without granting assistance. The poor are fellow servants, worthy of food whether they are young, old, kin, or enemy. The poor enter the Christian consciousness as a body which is part of the created order. They enter the civic and religious liturgy through the homiletic call to social change. By the imagery of infancy, repentance, and redemptive almsgiving, they become liturgy itself". Susan R. HOLMAN, "The Hungry Body: Famine, Poverty, and Identity in Basil's Hom. 8", *Journal of Early Christian Studies*, 337-363 [here 362].

actions: A wealthy person is to be pitied if he considers his affluence as a means to injustice. On the contrary, he becomes a positive paradigm for all if he administers his possessions virtuously in favor of the common good (Homilia XI de Invidia [on envy] PG 31,371-386).

The admiration for St. Basil's work is based on the fact that he did not simply speak about the common good; he tried to make it happen. He even shared his personal assets for the common good and he died redeemed from his wealth. However, he did not spent it nor did he give it away. He used it in order to make visible and tangible the paradigm of Christian life in social life.

His action-centered preaching[55] is one of the keys to his overall thinking. He knows that things in life do not just happen. This actually sheds more light on the question "what is and for whom is the common good?" For Basil of Caesarea believing is not only belonging but also dedicating one's life to the realization of the double commandment of love and understanding – the latter as the foundation of Christian identity. A human being is a loving human being in relation to God and others. Therefore, believing without acting, preaching without practicing, is nothing more than an illusion that devastates the core of the Evangelical message. The option for the poor is not an idea but a call to action[56] based on the very own words of Christ (Mt 25:31-46 [here 40]). In this manner, the option for the weak could also be considered as a pastoral approach to the common good. The choice of many Church Fathers to direct their words to the powerful is a choice defined by the realistic view of their social context. They tried to move all the necessary mechanisms in their society in order to establish a kind of a safety net for the endangered weak brothers and sisters of Christ (Mt 25:40). The rich and powerful could claim what they wanted even without the protection of such ethical principles.

As is shown in various texts and circumstances, the Christians are called to gain an awareness of their personal responsibility for their own vices.[57]

55 "St Basil the Great urged that monasteries not only should extend hospitality to occasional visitors but also should undertake organized charitable work on a long-term basis". See: bishop Kallistos WARE, "'Seek First The Kingdom': Orthodox Monasticism And Its Service To The World", *Theology Today*, 14-25.

56 See also: Susan R. HOLMAN, *The Hungry are Dying,* Oxford, Oxford University Press, 2001, 96.

57 St. BASIL, *Hexaemeron* 2, 5 PG 29, 37D-40A.

Furthermore, Augustine of Hippo[58], St. John Chrysostom, Asterius of Amasea[59] among others praised the act of giving, and underlined the importance of the disposition of the giver because philanthropic acts are important both for the rich and the poor. Be that as it may, the Church Fathers could not tolerate the scandalous indifference of those who had the *actual* power to take care of people and community with reference to the common good in its Christian understanding. As St. John Chrysostom notes: "Putting on the one hand golden necklaces on our servants and mules and horses, and neglecting on the other hand our Lord who's naked passing our doors and He is standing on our threshold and He is reaching out, facing Him often with relentless stare, what can be a worse kind of madness?"[60]

In this perspective, the homily on the saying 'I will pull down my barns' [61] of St. Basil exemplifies the Christian Ethics in its own time. An analysis of the aforementioned homily points out that according to St. Basil the meaning attributed to the common good might emerge from the active intersection of two ideas: Everything is given in common by God, and everything should be shared as a "*good for all in common (τὸ κοινῶς πᾶσι)*".[62]

58 "The heavens will proclaim his justice. … I was hungry and you fed me (Mt 25:34.35). What action could be so insignificant, so earthy as to break your bread for a hungry person? Yet that is the price of the kingdom of heaven. Break your bread for the hungry, and take the person with no shelter into your home. If you see anyone naked, clothe him (Is 58:7). But suppose you have no opportunity to break your bread for them, or have no house into which you can invite them, or no garment to clothe them with? Give only a cup of cold water, or put two tiny coins into the treasury. A widow purchased with two mites, and Peter purchased by leaving his nets, as much as Zacchaeus purchased by giving away half his fortune. What it costs is what you have. The heavens will proclaim his justice, because God is the judge." St. AUGUSTINE (John E. ROTELLE Ed - Maria BOULDING transl), *Expositions on the Psalms (33-50,) The Works of St. Augustine. A translation for 21*[st] *Century*, Part III, Vol. 16, New York, New City Press, 2000, 394 (Psalm 49, v. 6.13).

59 ASTERIUS OF AMASEA, *Homilia VIII in SS Petrum et Paulum*, PG 40 276 A-D.

60 *Homilia XXIII IN De Eleemosyna et Hospitalitate* in PG 63, 725 *Eclogae i-xlviii ex diversis homiliis*, PG 63, 567-902, see also: JOHN CHRYSOSTOM *De eleemosyna*, PG 51, 261-272.

61 Homilia in illud dictum evangelii secundum Lucam: "Destruam horrea mea, et majora ædificabo:" itemque de avaritia, PG 31, 261– 278.

62 Ibidem § 7, PG 31, 276B – 277A.

St. Gregory of Nyssa used almost the same words to describe a world where the beatitudes had been realized.[63]

St. Basil wants in this way pedagogically to emphasize that all the goods have been created by God and offered to all humans so they may serve human need. The belief in God as Creator and Father implies that everyone is a member of one family and that everything in the world is a part of this common inheritance. St. Gregory of Nazianzus frames this theological point in a very expressive way as he notes in his Oration 14, On the Love of the Poor: "Give a little to him from whom you have received much... and you are never giving away what is your own, since everything comes from God. And just as it is not possible to step over our own shadow, which moves along exactly as far as we do (...) it is impossible to outdo God in our giving. For we never give him anything apart from what belongs to him, nor beyond his munificence".[64] St Gregory of Nyssa agrees that "everything belongs to God, our common Father" (PG 46, 465B).[65] Based on this, the Christians have often been asked to imitate Christ and to share with others, even to serve by focusing on the common good in every act (*eis to koinofeles*) and not to prefer a narrow self-interest.[66]

The gospel-rooted proclamation of unity in Christ arrives at an understanding of love and loving care for all as the main characteristic of the Christian life. As the Cappadocian Fathers commonly insist, the compassionate acts of love are not just a matter of good social behavior, but rather they are a manifestation of faith inseparably linked to the prospect of salvation. In sum, God is the Creator of all and everything is given to all to accommodate their needs. Given that the injustice dominates the world, Christian identity is determined by a keeping of the love commandment and by a working for the common good. In this sense, St. John Chrysostom warned about the consequences of their disposition not only those who are

63 See: "...**All things would be common to all**, and equality of law and citizenship would prevail in human life, as excess voluntarily equalized itself with need", Hubertus R. DROBNER and Albert VICIANO (Eds), *Gregory of Nyssa, Homilies on the Beatitudes: an English Version with Commentary and Supporting Studies*, Leiden, Brill, 2000, 60. The original text: "πάντα γὰρ ἔσται πᾶσι κοινά" GREGORY OF NYSSA, *Orationes viii de beatitudinibus*, PG 44,1253A.

64 Brian E. DALEY, *Gregory of Nazianzus*, London, Routledge, 2006, 88; Saint Gregory of Nazianzen Oratio 14, *De Pauperum amore* (Λόγος ΙΔ Περὶ φιλοπτωχίας.), PG 35, 857-910, § 22.

65 GREGORY OF NYSSA, *De beneficentia* (Περὶ φιλοπτωχίας και ευποιίας. Λόγος Α'), PG 46, 453 – 469.

66 JOHN CHRYSOSTOM, *Homilia XV In Johanem*, PG 59,101.

choosing evil but also those who are not doing good, since "*God favors nothing more as to live for the common good*" (In Matthaeum Hom.LXXIII,714).[67]

In line with this, St. Basil criticizes those who are not willing to help people in need as he underlines in his Homily on the Saying '*I will pull down my barn*' that: "From God comes everything beneficial (...). But human beings respond with a bitter disposition, misanthropy, and an unwillingness to share. Such characteristics are what this man offered back to his Benefactor. He did not remember that he shared with others a common nature, nor did he think it necessary to distribute from his abundance to those in need. He did not keep even a word of the commandments: 'Do not neglect to do good for the needy'."[68]

In this homily, he actually drags everybody into a scene that is consumed by the question *What should I do?* At first, *What should I do?* is the question that the greedy rich man would ask himself in agony. The barns are not big enough for his accumulated wealth. He decides to pull them down and to build bigger ones. On the other side, the same question is asked by the poor man: *What should I do?* His family suffers from hunger and poverty. He is in a desperate condition and his unimaginable choices are beyond any logic —or at least beyond any thinkable choice for people who are not in this stance. He decides to sell one of his children to save the others. St. Basil also addresses throughout his homily the same question to the invisible listeners of his time and of our time. *What should I do?* someone might ask. The answer in St. Basil's social understanding and teaching is not easy and is not tepid. He says that the social action of humans should look like the earth's productivity. The fruits of the earth's fertility are offered to everybody and so the people's affluence ought to be. This is for sure a very inconvenient if not disturbing dilemma for people of all times, but if God gave everything in common, injustice is not a result of His will, it is a product of unfair social structures and misuse of social power.[69] *The rich men should have as their barns the poor peoples' houses* says the Church Father. Thus, the social vision of St. Basil frames human action as invested in the justice of all people, responding to the needs of the poor and the weak, satisfying

67 Cf. PETROU, *Social Justice*, 57-66.

68 In BASIL OF CAESAREA (Trans. C. Paul Schroeder), *On Social Justice*, Crestwood, St. Vladimir's Seminary Press, 2009, 60.

69 See in parallel the words of St Basil on his 12th Homily (on psalm 14) "This interest, which you take, is full of extreme inhumanity... Woe to you who say that the bitter is sweet and the sweet bitter, and who call inhumanity by the name of humanity", in Sister Agnes Clare WAY (transl.), *Saint Basil: Exegetic Homilies*, Washington, Catholic University of America Press, 1963, 181-191 [here, 191].

the personal needs with autarky, sharing what is beyond human needs, creating a communal spirit, fixing the problems, developing fair social structures, preparing the new World of God. As he said, any power and recourses have been given to certain people in order to manage and to redistribute them as common. Whatever we define under the concept of common good has to be directed to the community of all people, and it has to ensure the wellbeing of all people beyond any sense of moral neutrality. In a rhetorical dialogue with a fictional greedy person St. Basil writes: "But whom do I treat unjustly; you say, 'by keeping what is my own?' Tell me, what is your own? What did you bring into this life? (...) It is as if someone were to take the first seat in the theater, then bar everyone else from attending, so that one person alone enjoys what is offered for the benefit of all in common. This is what the rich do. They seize common goods before others have the opportunity, then claim them as their own by right of preemption".[70]

The balance between liberty and justice, an issue that is greatly debated in our time, seems to be a pseudo-dilemma in St. Basil's writings. In his very own life the scope of believing, wording, teaching and living were all parts of the same reality. It seems that for him the necessary constraints in the social and economic action of Christians should lead to a transformation of the economic, political, and the social reality for the benefit of all. As liberty and justice are forged into an indivisible chain, the common good cannot simply come out of pragmatism or political realism, national or private interests, etc., as it always remains a challenge to be faced through critical, active, self-giving, advocating, just and affective ways of life. In a way, the common good should not be understood as a situation to be achieved and established once and for all, but should be better conceived —at least in St Basil's terms— as a dynamic and synthetic process of caring for the others, a constant commitment to the vision of *communitas christiana.*

In Search of the common good on a windy trail

To summarize the aforementioned arguments, we can see at the very core of St. Basil's teaching the idea that theory and praxis, the *diaconia* of the word (Act 6,4) and the *diakonia* of the tables (Act 6,2), that spiritual and social service are nothing more than an integral orientation of man's life in the fulfillment of faith. Under these terms the common good as an ethical and social condition is an essential part of the earthly pilgrimage towards

70 Basil of Caesarea, *On Social Justice*, 2009, 59 -71 [here 69].

the Kingdom of God.[71] This is also the main reason why the common good can only be achieved if it is connected with justice and loving care for all, and does not reflect a prosperity that is based on other peoples' misery[72].

How should this teaching in the modern and religiously diverse world be received? It is not necessary to say how difficult it is to define the common good in the current socio-political[73] and economic situation.[74] Nowadays, the economy is a complex worldwide network.[75] This network, especially due to its impersonal and virtual character, seems to be so powerful and unapproachable to pro-human and pro-social views, that most people think that paradigms such as that of St. Basil are admirable but to no avail. Getting trapped into disappointment is as easy as it is for someone to think that by giving personal possessions to the poor nothing is not going to change. However, reflecting the choices that St. Basil made is a good point to start

71 See also: "But now it is for the poor that I make my supplication; nay, not so much for the poor, as for your sake who bestow the gift... Give unto thy Lord in His hunger: Put raiment on Him, going about naked; Receive Him,...I will not then be ashamed, but will say, and that boldly, 'Give to the needy'; I will say it with a louder voice than the needy themselves... for I vehemently set my heart upon your salvation". JOHN CHRYSOSTOM, *Homilies on First Corinthians.* Homily XLIII. Hom. XXV- XLIV, Oxford, MDCCXXXIX, 604-614 [here 607].

72 On the unity between Justice, Peace and Love as a quality that cannot be based on the unfair use of power see: ISIDORE OF PELUSIUM, XXXVI, *Petro Monacho*, PG 78, 1088 C.

73 It seems that there is a wider cultural change that affects the idea of identity at personal and community levels and challenges the endeavor for a common good perspective. The challenges were obvious quite early in the circles of the Catholic Social Theology. See: Karl GABRIEL, "Die neuzeitliche Gesellschaftsentwicklung und der Katholizismus als Sozialform der Christentumsgeschichte", in Karl GABRIEL – Franz-Xaver KAUFMAN (Hrsg.), *Zur Soziologie des Katholizismus*, Mainz, Grünewald, 1980, 201- 225.

74 For an overview of the political, economic, legal, Christian approaches see: Bruce CRONIN, *Institutions for the Common Good. International Protection Regimes in International Society*, Cambridge, Cambridge University Press, 2003; Amartya SEN, *Development as Freedom*, Oxford, Oxford University Press, 1999; Elinor OSTROM, "How Types Of Goods And Property Rights Jointly Affect Collective Action". *Journal Of Theoretical Politics*, 239-270; Lynn DOBSON, "Plural Views, Common Purpose: on How to Address Moral Failure by International Political Organizations", *Journal Of International Political Theory* 4/1 (2008), 34-54..

75 Paul DEMBINSKI, *Finance Servant or Deceiver? –Financialisation at the Crossroads*, London, Palgrave McMillan, 2009; Paul DEMBINSKI, Carole LAGER, Andrew CORNFORD, Jean-Michel BONVIN, *Enron And World Finance*, Basingstoke, Palgrave Macmillan, 2005; Lisa Sowle CAHILL, "Globalisation and the Common Good", in John A. COLEMAN, William F. RYAN, *Globalization and Catholic Social Thought: Present Crisis, Future Hope,* Ottawa, St Paul University, 2005, 42-54.

thinking in terms of Christian Ethics, because giving away his wealth was not the only thing St. Basil did. His paradigm actually made a change in his own society and affected other societies and people's lives with time.

If a methodological scheme is to be drawn from the faith-based response of St. Basil, a course of analysis may be largely outlined as a climax of the following steps: a.) observing and analyzing the social reality, b.) contrasting the ideal with reality and addressing their contradictions, c.) identifying the problems, d.) looking for the causes of the problems, e.) bringing to the fore the values that will direct human action, and f.) advocating the principle that everything in the world is given in common to all people by God.[76] One essential aspect of the common good is that the only way to understand it in the terms of the Church Fathers theology is in its interconnectedness with the living conditions of their Christian communities. In this case the *koinon agathon* —more than a concept— is a need, a call, a paradigm. In this perspective, the pre-eminence of the common good presupposes the pre-eminence of the Christian virtues, such as those of meekness, of moderation and kindness, the disposition of solidarity, etc. Terms such as 'sharing' and 'unity' have always been the context of the common good conception in patristic literature.[77] Having said that, the common good as it is conceived in Early Christianity is not a separate and distinct part of Christian Ethics but rather another hub in the network of the Christian identity.

The question of whether the patristic paradigm is nowadays only a narrative or a truly tangible frame of Christian action brings back into view the churches' role in the social ferments of modern societies. From a critical point of view the Christian Churches went sometimes too deep into the world of compromises. The moderation, that ancient virtue of the just management of social world, has often been interpreted as a tepid stance —at its best, a decision to stay in the middle of all possible interests in society. Meanwhile, the weakening of the normative character of Christian Ethics in modernity was propelled by various causes as the power elites distanced themselves from the spiritual guidance of Ecclesia. The separation of State and Church marked the public sphere, and economic interest

76 Cf. Ioanis Petrou, *Christianity and Society*, Thessaloniki, Vanias, 2004.

77 See the notes and the translation of "*Commentary on the Song of Songs*" of Gregory of Nyssa in Anthony Meredith, *Gregory of Nyssa*, New York, Routledge, 1999, 128.

became for many an end in itself.[78] In these circumstances it is quite difficult for Christians to determine the common good perspective and to integrate it in the political decision making.

Thus, the questions concerning the common good are complex. For sure, the common good in today's context has to be strongly connected with access to public goods and the realization of basic human rights such as food, water and sanitation, employment, housing and education for all, personal freedom and social integration, and even more. A social theological perspective in the current socio-political paradigm can only reflect on a multi-facet vision of the common good. As Maritain notes: "that which constitutes the common good of political society is not only the collection of public commodities and services (...). The common good includes all of these and something much more besides... a sum which is quite different from a simple collection of juxtaposed units (...). It includes the sum or sociological integration of all the civic conscience, political virtues and sense of right and liberty, of all the activity, material prosperity and spiritual riches, of unconsciously operative hereditary wisdom, of moral rectitude, justice, friendship, happiness, virtue and heroism in the individual lives of its members. For these things all are, in a certain measure, *communicable* and so revert to each member, helping him to perfect his life and liberty of person. They all constitute the good human life of the multitude."[79]

At this point a common basis for dialogue between Christian ethics, modern social ethics, social and political theories could be actively pursued. St. Basil refers to society as a community of persons based on loving care and compassion for all fellow humans. In like manner, there are a variety of non-Christian approaches in the history of ideas setting the communal well-being at the centre of public interest. Levinas,[80] Bauman[81], Etzioni,[82] Nuss-

78 The relevant discourse in the field of Economy is multimodal and contested. See: Barry SMART, "Good For Business, Good Without Reservation? Veblen's Critique Of Business Enterprise And Pecuniary Culture", *Journal Of Classical Sociology* 15/3 (2014), 253-269; Friedrich A. HAYEK, *The Road to Serfdom*, London, Routledge, 1944.

79 Jacques MARITAIN, *The Person and the Common Good*, Notre Dame, IN, University of Notre Dame Press, 1966, 52.

80 Roger BURGGRAEVE, *The Wisdom Of Love In The Service Of Love*, Milwaukee [Wis.], Marquette University Press, 2002.

81 Zygmunt BAUMAN, *Life in Fragments: Essays in Postmodern Morality*, Cambridge, Blackwell, 1995, 64-65.

82 Amitai ETZIONI, *Rights And The Common Good*, New York, NY, St. Martin's Press, 1995; Ibid., *The Common Good*. Cambridge, Polity, 2004; Ibid., "A Neo-Communitarian Approach To International Relations: Rights And The Good", *Human Rights Review* 7/4 (2006), 69-80.

baum[83] just to mention a few of the modern intellectuals, speak about responsibility for the others and try to describe ethical principles that might lead to the way of *communitas* that is based on the good of all people, especially those who are the weakest in our society. As Bauman writes: "Just as the carrying power of a bridge is not measured by the average strength of its pillars but by the strength of the weakest pillar, and grows together with that strength, the confidence and resourcefulness of a society are measured by the security, resourcefulness and self-confidence of its weakest sections and grow as they grow."[84] Notwithstanding that there is a soteriological perspective in Christian ethics clearly different from the political orientation of the social theories, the dialogue between the people of good will on the common good of all in society remains a vibrating challenge.

In any case, the search of the common good as a concept and ethical option for Christians and non-Christian citizens in modern societies is a demanding task. Particularly for Christian Theology there is no other way but to face the challenges with a firm knowledge of the social, political and economic parameters of today's world; especially because the balance between the personal and societal interests requires nuance without an expectation of easy answers.[85] For sure, conceptual interpretations are insufficient if not accompanied with the cultivation of the values of cooperation[86] and the support of relevant social practices.[87] In this light, a productive dialogue can only be constructed by asking a series of fundamental questions[88] such as: a. What *can* be the common good? b. How do we define the principles by which we are *searching* the common good? c. How do we *reflect* on and *evaluate* our proposals for the common good? and d. How do we *assess* the results of our proposals and *ensure* all levels of

83 Martha C. NUSSBAUM, *Political Emotions. Why Love Matters for Justice*, Cambridge, Harvard University Press, 2013.

84 Zygmunt BAUMAN, *Consuming Life*, Cambridge, Polity Press, 2007, 142.

85 Joseph HOEFFNER, *Christliche Gesellschaftslehre*, Kevelaer, Butzon & Bercker, 1965, 40.

86 The Ecumenical Patriarch Bartholomew I calls for a sense of "synergism", eg. "a close cooperation in order to address issues of common concern". See: H.H Ecumenical Patriarch BARTHOLOMEW, *Encountering the Mystery*, N. York, Doubleday, 2008, 218.

87 Ioannis PETROU, *Social Theory and Contemporary Culture*, Thessaloniki, Vanias, 2005 [Gr]; Emmanuel CLAPSIS (Ed.), *The Orthodox Churches in a Pluralistic World: An Ecumenical Conversation,* Geneva- Brooklin, WCC Pub.-Holy Cross Orthodox Press, 2004.

88 The challenges and the difficulties have been noted not only in the theological discourse. The philosophical and the socio-political analyses made repeatedly their remarks. See: Amitai ETZIONI (Ed.), *Rights And The Common Good: The Communitarian Perspective*, New York, NY, St. Martin's Press, 1995; Claus OFFE, "Whose Good Is The Common Good?", *Philosophy & Social Criticism*, 665-684.

accountability? One thing to be underlined contrary to the self-enclosed climate of our times and to the fear that the Welfare deconstruction causes is this: "We are not suffering from an overdose of an unreal idealism, but from a morally apathetic and fearful seeking for a safe niche in our present predatory society".[89]

In either case, the challenge is obvious: our social being structured by society is called to change our society. Whatever is given has been given in order to be changed in the eternal dynamic between structuring and restructuring the social reality. Hence, the most essential point in the search for the common good is not to find a definitive description of the concept. With regard to the above, the greatest challenge for Christians is to walk beyond the prospective social obligations, to learn the grammar of the lives of poor people, to encounter the excluded on their own terms (Mt 25:31-46), and to envisage a just world for all peoples.

89 Charles DAVIS, *Religion and the Making of Society: Essays in Social Theology*, New York, Cambridge University Press, 2009, 187.

Thierry Collaud

The names that theology gives to the common good

According to St Thomas Aquinas, any theological elaboration merely attempts to make complex what is in itself simple, to make explicit what is implicit.[1] It deploys what is contained in the heart of the unformulated believing experience, like the blooming rose opens out the petals that are enfolded in the bud. This simple heart of faith that is unfolded by theology is summed up in the affirmation of a God who intervenes for the salvation of humans: 'all the articles are contained implicitly in certain primary matters of faith, such as God's existence, and His providence over the salvation of man.'[2] If God's saving action is at the heart of faith, any theological reflection must set out from the place and means of this salvation. Indeed, this is what the Bible does. It does not present us a unified theoretical reflection on God, but a multitude of more or less exemplary human stories, and invites us to see how relationships with others and with God unfold in them – or fail to.

The common good as salvation

Here we will take *salvation* in its most literal sense: the fact that individuals or groups get out of a situation of danger that threatens their existence. According to the *Académie française* dictionary, it means 'Conservation in, or restoration to, a state of happiness, a suitable state'.[3] There is thus a strong semantic parallel between salvation and the *common good*, which bears witness to the latter's central position in the theological discourse.

However, continues the dictionary, salvation 'specifically designates, in religious language, the fact of escaping from damnation, of attaining eternal bliss.' Here we see a regrettable shift in meaning that dissociates salvation from the *good life* that humans seek by associating it with terms – damnation and bliss – whose semantic content has over the centuries become charged

1 "Hence things that are simple in themselves are known by the intellect with a certain amount of complexity". Thomas AQUINAS, *Summa theologica*, *Summa theologica* IIa-IIae, Q1, a2.

2 Thomas AQUINAS, *Summa theologica*, IIa-IIae, Q1, a7.

3 *Dictionnaire de l'Académie française*, 8th edition (consulted on 11 February 2017).

with representations that detach them from the reality of a human community. Such representations, especially iconographic ones – e.g. scenes of the last judgement – point to a false afterlife that escapes transcendence and lapses back into the immanence of a *post mortem* time, an imaginary, fantasmatic and endless heavenly or hellish eternal life. Yet the Bible associates salvation with the specific realities of *this* life; its places are a city (new Jerusalem), a kingdom or a festive meal, realities of human life that are densified to the extreme because they then yield all their potentiality.

In this reflection I propose to approach the *common good as salvation* in its broadest sense, i.e. as the *state of happiness* to which we are brought (or brought back), as described by the dictionary, or as the *good life* that a community can construct. The point is to see how theological reflection can associate this common good with various categories whereby it attempts to make complex, and hence unfold the meaning of, the heart of the conviction of faith that relates to this salvation and makes it depend on the community's recognition of, and relationship with, God. I will attempt a three-stage argument in the multiform hermeneutic field of theology – an argument suggested by Lonergan when, at the end of his *Method in Theology*, he states that the community is based on three principles: *moral*, *religious* and *Christian*.[4] This triad makes me propose a threefold hermeneutics that unfolds from the intersubjective field to that of Christology. The *moral principle* expresses the fact that '[human beings] individually are responsible for what they make of themselves, but collectively they are responsible for the world in which they live'. This is the place in which a *hermeneutics of coexistence* is unfolded, revealing the interplay of violence and non-violence. Here the common good can be seen as a seemingly illusory wish to break out of the circle of deadly violence. It is the impossibility of an intersubjective solution to violence that opens up the need for a *hermeneutics of transcendence* which restates the *religious principle* which, to Lonergan, is 'God's gift of his love, and it forms the basis of dialogue between all representatives of religion'. Finally, the *Christian principle* – which 'conjoins the inner gift of God's love with its outer manifestation in Christ Jesus and in those that follow him' – further densifies the pursuit of the common good, which will then be describes using the criteria provided by a *hermeneutics of presence*, i.e. the dwelling at the heart of worldly reality of a reality and temporality from

4 Bernard LONERGAN, *Method in Theology*, Toronto, University of Toronto Press, 1990, 360. See also Robert M. DORAN, 'Social grace and the mission of the Church', in Patrick HAYES and Nicholas RADEMACHER (eds), *A realist's church: essays in honor of Joseph A. Komonchak*, Maryknoll, Orbis Books, 2015, 169-184.

another dimension that allow the community to move towards, and at the same time already experience, the fullness of its *common good.*

It is these three kinds of explanation of the community that open up to a representation of the *common good* of growing intensity, ranging from a valuation of peace to a community that is aware of the transcendence that is constantly renewing it, to a community that lives on, and achieves, the Christic presence within it that we must now explore in more detail.

Hermeneutics of coexistence
The human community between war and peace

Reflecting on salvation means attempting to understand how a human community can unfold towards its *good* – i.e. how the community, and the people within it, can live a good life, and how they can value, pursue and implement whatever constructs and maintains this common life, as well as recognise and escape from whatever may threaten or destroy it.

It is from the specifics of community experience that we will become aware of the need for something beyond the impossibilities and concealments of a purely immanent community and the need for a transcendent opening that will lead us to realise that the good desired by the human community can only be achieved with, and in, God. The latter can only be considered in this dynamic of community building, not as a *deus ex machina*, but as a strength breathed into the most intimate part of human reality itself.

The community as a living body

A human community is a living body whose primary purpose is to be alive, i.e. to unfold its potentialities by escaping the ever-present threat of death.[5] The purpose of the community is not external to it but, as Aristotle said, is its very life.[6] So the *common good* can be seen in a community achieving its full development and blossoming as a community, just as an orchestra is called a *good* orchestra because it achieves a degree of excellence *as an orchestra*, rather than as a group of excellent soloists.

5 For more on the history of the political community as a body, see Suzanne RAMEIX, 'Corps humain et corps politique en France: statut du corps humain et métaphore organiciste de l'État', in *Laval théologique et philosophique* 54/1 (1998), 41-61.

6 *Politics* III, 9 1280 b.

A human community that forms a social body displays the same paradoxical attitude to the principles of thermodynamics as other living bodies. These are statistically improbable structures, always evolving, unfolding and growing. They constantly contradict the law of entropy, according to which they should tend to dissolve and gradually become disorganised, lapsing into chaos. This entropy that threatens to drag all living beings towards death could be seen in what Hannah Arendt describes as a threat to 'human affairs', i.e. the way in which humans build a common world. And for her, it is the human capacity to keep performing new, creative acts that contradicts this disintegrative movement.[7] It will be said that this *creative resistance to entropic disorganisation* is what differentiates a true human community from a functional organisation. A *good community* as a living body is one that can, in spite of all its determinisms, freely build an ever-new, ever-unexpected community.

It is important not to contrast the determinism of a living body that necessary depends on the world around it and the true freedom of a human community. If we cannot think the two in synergy rather than competition, we arrive at the a-communitarian dead end of the anarchist or libertarian philosophers or the sad resignation of a freedom whose wings have been clipped by social-contract philosophies.[8] The challenge is twofold. First, we must think of communitarian determinism as prior to freedom, as a necessary basis on which it can unfold.[9] It may be said the community itself is prior, insofar as humans' freedom to develop in the common world presupposes this common. Second, we must think of communitarian determinism in a sufficiently open manner for it to be a place from where freedom can emerge rather than an obstacle to it. The analogy of the freely improvising jazz band may be taken as one figure of freedom. Yet there are strong predetermined factors that influence the free improvisation: the composition of the band, the various musicians' mastery of their instruments, the fact that they play together, and some rules for interaction. All this is not a hindrance, but provides a framework in which creative freedom can produce ever-new music. The reflection on the community as a brotherhood, to which I will return in the third part of this paper, will be decisive.

7 Hannah Arendt, *The human condition*, Chicago, University of Chicago Press, 1958, 245-247.

8 See Mathias Nebel's paper in this volume.

9 In his reflection on consent, Paul Ricœur mentions the necessity that precedes freedom, '... my life that I have not chosen, but that is the condition for all possible choices'. See Paul Ricœur, P., *Philosophie de la volonté I: le volontaire et l'involontaire*, Paris, Seuil, 2009, 598.

The violence that threatens the common good

In the tension between construction and deconstruction in which any living organism necessarily develops, the movement towards excellence and the common good may be countered by disorganising forces that contradict the constructive forces that seek to build the community. I will use the term '*violence*' to describe any destructive force exerted on a living structure to prevent it from deploying its vital dynamism. Anything that causes destruction and death is violent, regardless of its immediate goal (the 'legitimate violence' that the State may commit during war, or the death penalty, is nonetheless true violence). The legal philosopher Sergio Cotta has pointed out that, in the human order, violence is *a-dialogal* inasmuch as dialogue presupposes reciprocity, respect and acceptance, which violence destroys. 'This state of affairs entails the *depersonalisation* of the other, *despised* by the violent person who literally no longer assigns a *price* to his adversary, whose human face he does not recognise: this is proved by the symbol of striking or spitting at him.'[10] Violence depersonalises the other, but at the same time it depersonalises the person who exerts it, thereby causing 'the abrupt breakdown of coexistence'. By the same token, Arendt contrasts violence with power, which to her is an ability to act in common. Violence prevents this, for it is a source of 'internal disintegration factors'.[11]

Violence is thus a key element that interferes with the dynamism of a community on its path towards the *common good.* The community is wounded by violence because it is vulnerable, but paradoxically this vulnerability is necessary, for it is linked to the opening that is essential to all that is 'common', an opening that makes it breakable but also makes it a community. Hence the deadlock for a community which responds to violence by hardening, over-immunising and immobilising itself – thereby losing the common good.[12]

10 Sergio Cotta, 'Violence', in Philippe Raynaud, Stéphane Rials (eds), *Dictionnaire de philosophie politique*, Paris, Presses Universitaires de France, 1996, 730.

11 Hannah Arendt, *Crises of the republic: lying in politics; civil disobedience; on violence; thoughts on politics and revolution*, New York, Harcourt, Brace, Jovanovich, 1972.

12 Thierry Collaud, 'La vulnérabilité nécessaire au bien commun', in Marie-José Thiel (ed.), *Souhaitable vulnérabilité?*, Strasbourg, Presses universitaires de Strasbourg, 2016, 33-48.

The common good as a resolution of the tension between war and peace

The human community try without success to move beyond these opposition between construction and deconstruction. Must we then abandon the common good – abandon full, complete peace? Must we resign ourselves to negotiating a contractual peace that ensures a halfway house, overcoming violence at the price of imprisoning the creative freedom of the common world in the straitjacket of the contract – what Levinas calls 'the sober cainesque coldness'[13] in which my contractual freedom takes priority over my possible responsibility for others? Is curbed freedom another dead end?

Interestingly, at about the same time, at the end of the first half of the twentieth century, three philosophers recognized the dead end of the inescapable tension of a 'finiteness' or an 'immanence' that fails to provide what it should. Significantly, none of them made any secret of his religious faith. In 1950, Paul Ricœur concluded the first volume of his *Philosophie de la volonté* with a reflection on consent as the ability to escape the 'sadness of finiteness' but needing for that move a 'leap from existence to transcendence'.[14] In 1953, the Italian Giuseppe Capograssi's *Introduzione alla vita etica* spoke of the 'despair of finiteness', to which he saw two responses: self-destruction by escaping into entertainment, or acceptance of an appeal to transcendental hope, an alternative he summed up as 'suicide or prayer'.[15]

Finally, in 1961, in his preface to *Totality and Infinity*,[16] Levinas focused on the tension between war and peace. In the brotherhood of human beings, he said at the outset (p. 5), there is 'the constant possibility of war'. The violence of war destroyed the community by interrupting the 'continuity of persons (p. 6). This depersonalisation dehumanised their action, making them perform 'acts that [would] destroy all possibility of action' (p. 6). This brings us back to the self-amplified deadly violence of the crucifixion or to other similar violence, such as that of the South American torturers mentioned by Mathias Nebel[17] who went out of their way to systematically destroy the continuity of the people that made up the social body. It is here that, to get beyond the despair of finiteness or the inconsistencies of a

13 Emmanuel LEVINAS, *De Dieu qui vient à l'idée*, Paris, Vrin, 1992, 117.

14 Paul RICŒUR, *Philosophie de la volonté I: le volontaire et l'involontaire*, Paris, Aubier, 1949, 584.

15 Giuseppe CAPOGRASSI, *Introduzione alla vita etica (1953)*, Opere, III, Milano, 1959, 159.

16 Emmanuel LEVINAS, *Totality and infinity*, Pittsburgh. 1969.

17 Mathias NEBEL, *La catégorie morale de péché structurel : essai de systématique*, Paris, Cerf, 2006, 66-81. See also William T. CAVANAUGH, *Torture and Eucharist : theology, politics, and the body of Christ*, Oxford, Blackwell, 2006.

hermeneutics of immanence, we must invoke a peace that does not call itself the end of war or the end of history (p. 9), but is an eschatological peace that superimposes itself on 'the ontology of war' (p. 6) – a certainty that contradicts the self-evidence of violence.

This lies at the heart of theological thinking on the *common good*, which cannot be expected from the historical accomplishment of gradually improving social practices. Instead, it is an *occurrence that subverts the course of history*, for it pervades what Levinas calls totality. Peace occurs when humans are able to utter *eschatological* words, i.e. words that explode the finite totality of history and are not 'anonymous words of history' (p. 8) – words that break the expected chain of historical events and become true human actions as understood by Arendt. They are able to create something new, as well as break the circle of violence and revenge by being words of forgiveness, i.e. by providing an exit from the trap of a negative event that cannot be undone.[18] We must note that the language and the act that bring about the common good are based on gratuitousness and freedom, beyond all determinism. Again for forgiveness, an essential ingredient if we are simply to live together, Arendt comments that, unlike revenge, 'forgiveness can never be predicted', for strictly speaking it is not a response, but always acts 'in a new and unexpected way'.[19]

Hermeneutics of transcendence love that builds

Theological thinking begins with this taking account of humans seeking to unfold their humanity as well as they can, and faced with the inconsistencies of immanence and the impossibility of escaping the destructive dynamics of violence. We have seen how opening up to transcendence enables us to move beyond these inconsistencies. We need to remember that this appeal to transcendence does not mean submitting to a higher power that would limit man's freedom, but that it is the very condition for this freedom, by providing an exit from the deadly trap of immanence.

If we follow on from Levinas, shifting from a *hermeneutics of coexistence* to a *hermeneutics of transcendence* means introducing the two fundamental elements of *desire* and *relationship* into the construction/deconstruction (peace/war) dialectic. To yield their full richness, both must move beyond egoistic, totalitarian withdrawal to open up to the dimension of the infinite.

18 Hannah Arendt, *The human condition*, 238-243.

19 *Ibid.*

The common good as desire

Desire must first be distinguished from need. The latter, like hunger or thirst, aspires to be – and can be – satisfied. It can be saturated and fulfilled. However, the need that is to be saturated is only concern for oneself or 'the anxiety of an ego for itself'.[20] If it opens up to the world, it does so only to take what it needs. Desire, on the contrary, is a departure from oneself, a movement towards the desired which is not there to complete something in oneself. Desire empties the self precisely because it cannot be saturated, and it maintains itself in a perpetual tension towards what it desires. It is 'beyond all saturation', 'the desirable does not fill up my desire but hollows it out.'[21] As early as the fourth century, Gregory of Nyssa had already sensed this. 'But every desire for the Good which is attracted to that ascent constantly expands ... as one progresses in pressing on to the Good. This truly is the vision of God: never to be satisfied in the desire to see him.'[22]

These are fundamental reflections when seeking to express the *good* of a community. They say something about its form and its dynamics. Formally, the overall satisfaction of needs as expressed, for example, in the language of rights (to food, water, housing and so on), however important and inescapable it may be, is not the last word on the *desire* of a community. This one, 'the infinite within the finite'[23], breaks through the closed walls of saturated need to tend towards the insaturable of goodness or transcendence, says Levinas.

The *good* of a community now takes the name of *Desire which is 'satisfied by the very things which leave [it] unsatisfied'*.[24] A *good* community is a community that desires; and, theologically speaking, what it desires is God and the elements associated with him: beauty, goodness, life, justice, faithfulness, tenderness, love and so on. It is a community that lives on, and desires, Beauty says Gregory. The *common good* as the life of a community must thus always remain in this dialectical dynamic of insaturability – it is to be experienced and desired at the same time.

20 Emmanuel LEVINAS, "The Trace of the Other" in M. TAYLOR (Ed.), *Deconstruction in Context,* Chicago, University of Chicago Press, 1986, 345-359, 350.

21 Ibid. p. 351.

22 GREGORY OF NYSSA, *The life of Moses*, II, § 238-239.

23 Emmanuel LEVINAS, *Totalité et infini,* 42. "The infinite within the finite, the more within the less that is accomplished by the idea of the infinite, is produced as desire. Not as desire that is quelled by the possession of the desirable, but as desire of the infinite that is aroused rather than satisfied by desire."

24 GREGORY OF NYSSA, *The life of Moses*, II, § 235.

On the other hand, in properly theological hermeneutics, such desire is a shared desired. Man's desire for God is a response to God's desire for man. In its divine side, desire can only appear in its purest form, as *desire that the other be fully himself, so that we can be together*. This is the definition of love. Hence once again the contradiction in thinking of a captative divine desire, God placing His hand on man and limiting his freedom is misleading. Because the act whereby He created man – already a manifestation of desire ('Let us make man!')[25] – ontologically constituted him as a free being.[26] The relationship to transcendence is then the relationship to the reception of a divine love, the figure of all true love. In the Bible, the first recipient of this loving divine intentionality is the collective figure of the people, which leads us to consider *the common good as the accomplishment of God's desire for the human community*. The whole Bible vibrates with this loving desire of God for mankind. The figure of the ardently desired bride recurs many times,[27] culminating in the Song of Songs.

The common good as relationship

This non-captative desire for the other, reciprocally exchanged, leads on to the second fundamental element that Levinas links to transcendence: *relationship*. Here again this is a relationship that opens up to the infinite of the other and the infinite distance between us. Then, speaking of transcendence, he can say 'This designates a relationship between a reality that is infinitely distant from my own, yet without this distance destroying this relationship and without this relationship destroying this distance, as would happen in the case of relationships within the Same.'[28] The relationship is all the more true and intense because the other remains mysterious to me. We must return to the way in which Levinas, and Buber from whom he drew his inspiration, discuss intersubjectivity. Their answers to this are perfectly clear. It is insofar as dialogue can break out of what can be controlled, planned and verified, i.e. what Buber calls 'I and It'[29] or Levinas the

25 Genesis 1:26.

26 Thomas AQUINAS, *Summa contra Gentiles*, III, Q73, "That divine providence does not exclude freedom of choice."

27 See the splendid, sometimes terrifying pictures drawn by the prophets to depict the interplay of seduction, love, betrayal and forgiveness between God and his people, including Hosea 1-3, Jeremiah 2:2 and 31:3, Ezechiel 16:1-43 and 59-63, and Isaiah 54:4-8.

28 Emmanuel LEVINAS, *Totality and Infinity*, 31-32.

29 Martin BUBER, *I and thou*, New York, Charles Scribner's Sons, 1937.

'dialogue of immanence'[30] that what happens between two human beings achieves its truth and its full density. We escape from the exchange of factual information to arrive at true dialogue, freed from determinism. It is the 'I and Thou' dialogue that appears when I cease trying to control the other and open up to his mystery and the mystery of what may happen between the two of us. Levinas speaks of the 'gaping transcendence' between the partners in the dialogue[31] – which means that, having moved beyond the determinism of immanence and opened up to an infinite dimension, they will see this appear between them, thus opening up their freedoms, which then themselves become infinite. There are infinitely more possibilities between an *I* and a *You* than between an *I* and an *It*. Transcendence is not enclosing, but liberating.

On the other hand, if we take seriously what Levinas says about the transcendence that appears *in the in-between of dialogue*, just as the infinite pervades the finite. This means that we cannot achieve transcendence without worldly relationality or without horizontal dialogue. We cannot achieve transcendence by escaping from the finite, but only by *consenting* to it – a consent that leads us to perceive, to feel with it, the infinite that pervades it. In community terms, it is in the consent to the finiteness of the community and to the materiality of interpersonal relationships that, if desire is there, the infinite of other relationships that break the closed world can emerge.

The *good* of a community as an insatiable desire can then be specified as a *desire for relationships that are nourished by infinite love*. A good community is one that can build itself a material base that emerges from pragmatic interactions, but whose materiality is constantly pervaded by the desire of the 'I-You', i.e. of a relationship with the other that is indissociably also a relationship with the 'Other' and receptivity to its benevolent desire.

The dynamics described here lay at the heart of the experience of the people of Israel and the testimony to it provided by the Scriptures. I will give two examples of how Old Testament authors expressed this fertilising presence of the infinite in the finite. First, by developing the notion of *blessing* considered as continual action of benevolent divine intentionality that touches men and is diffracted in the human community; second, by studying the description of social well-being in Isaiah 65:17-25, one of the

30 Emmanuel LEVINAS, "Le dialogue, conscience de soi et proximité du prochain." in Emmanuel LEVINAS (Ed.), *De Dieu qui vient à l'idée*, Paris, Vrin, 1992, 211-230, 214.

31 See also BUBER: "through contact with every thou we are stirred with a breath of the Thou, that is, of eternal life". BUBER, *I and Thou,* 63.

most characteristic passages of projections of the common good on the eschatological horizon.

The common good as blessing

This takes us back to the aforementioned theme of love. Blessing means speaking well of someone, a community or the world. It is a performative utterance in which the speaker commits himself to creating the wished-for good. It is the first word that God utters to Adam and Eve, the first micro-community that he has just created: 'God blesses them and says to them "Be fruitful ...".'[32] The performative word uttered by the blessing Creator opens to fruitfulness, i.e. to the capacity to unfold, to bear fruit – which for man goes far beyond biological reproduction – and take our place in the order of creation: 'Fill the earth!'. God's loving desire becomes a enlivening and fertilising force 'a forward-thrusting force that produce an effect into the future.'[33]

If we attempt to unfold the semantic content of blessing, we can identify the following four elements:[34] (1) it fosters life, (2) it allows possibilities to emerge, (3) it is also received in situations of suffering and difficulty, and (4) it circulates among humans, densifying the community.

(1) For believers, *life* is unthinkable without God. He did not simply perform a creative act at its origin, but he continually creates and maintains it. Biblical thinking links up with modern biology in thinking of life as constantly emerging, constantly overcoming the threat of disintegration and return to chaos. This instability of what is living and its dependence on the divine other are well expressed in Psalm 104: 'When you take away their breath, they die and turn again to dust. When you give them your breath, life is created, and you renew the face of the earth'.[35] Blessing corresponds to this life-bearing divine breath. A *blessed community* is then a community constantly recreated for life.

(2) Blessing, says Westermann, projects us into the future. It is a *promise of fruitfulness*, expressed in the agrarian cultures of the Old Testament by specific elements: wheat and wine are abundant, and cattle proliferate, as do

32 Genesis 1:28.

33 „*Vorwärtsdrängende, in die Zukunft wirkende Kraft*". Claus WESTERMANN, *Genesis Kapitel 1-3*, Neukirchen, Neukirchener Verlag, 1999, 222.

34 Thierry COLLAUD, *Le statut de la personne démente. Eléments d'une anthropologie théologique de l'homme malade à partir de la maladie d'Alzheimer*, Fribourg, Academic Press, 2003, 176-184.

35 Psalms 104:29b-30.

humans' descendants. In the dynamic of blessing, potential, burgeoning life can burst forth and be manifested, and all potentialities can be unfolded. This notion of opening ourselves up to possibilities is also found in the dynamic of the great biblical figures that God chooses as witnesses. They are promised blessing in the context of a sending. It arises from daring to set out on a journey: 'Go from your country ... and I will bless you,' says God to Abraham.[36] Blessing, i.e. life in abundance, is promised to him if he can take the risk of leaving material security and stability (Levinas's totalising enclosure) to move forward into the unknown with God.

The *good* of a community means therefore being *blessed and fruitful because it can hear a call that comes from beyond it* and, in responding to it, does not fear to be a community on the move.

(3) The biblical tradition makes no exclusive distinction between a perfect community and a sinful one. The people of God is the primary recipient of blessing, and at the same time the place where imperfections, wounds, betrayal and infidelity constantly recur. Yet blessing does not cease to be offered in such uncertain and ambiguous situations. At the individual level, the classic example is Jacob's struggle as described in chapter 32 of Genesis. After a night of combat with a divine figure, he is injured in his hip, but receives his mysterious opponent's blessing. He then continues on his *limping, blessed*[37] way, becoming the figure of a blessing that does not necessarily eliminate tribulation and human imperfection, but is nonetheless a source of energy for unfolding life.

A *blessed community* may sometimes seem unsteady and vulnerable, but at the same time have the inner strength afforded by the certainty of an acting blessing that enables it to carry on despite everything. I am thinking here of the monastic community of Tibhirine, which throughout its history has always been small, fragile and threatened; yet brother Christophe, one of the monks, could say 'Despite all the signs of aging, I feel we are alive and each exercising our freedom to live – until we die. *Rather, I feel we are being born ... the best can happen to us in the midst of the worst.*'[38]

(4) Finally, blessing circulates. Fruitful divine intentionality reaches the human community and, like light falling on frosted glass, it diffuses widely through the community. Blessing received incites us to be sources of

36 Genesis 12:1-2.

37 Genesis 32:30-32: "...he blessed him ... he was limping because of his hip ...".

38 Christophe LEBRETON, *Le souffle du don: journal de frère Christophe, moine de Tibhirine, 8 août 1993-19 mars 1996*, Paris, Bayard-Centurion, 1999, 157.

blessing ourselves. It thus becomes 'the manifestation of a relationship'.[39] When someone says 'Bless you!' to someone else, there is an implicit relationship with God. He is asking God to bless the other person. More broadly, however, he is acknowledging that he and the other are not only in a horizontal relationship – but that what they can weave between them depends on how they receive each other from God.

A *blessed and blessing community* is thus a community in which relationality includes the divine other, the saving other, for it prevents the danger of the captative, totalising confinement of the one-on-one relationship.

Blessing does not only circulate horizontally, but also returns to its author. Man who returns blessing to God 'is speaking well of God', for he has acknowledged in Him a creative, giving intentionality. Here again, the triangulation of blessing prevents the pretention of self-realisation and self-fulfilment.

In a theological reflection on the common good, we can see the opportunity of meaning provided by a conception of *blessing as an expression of a love and a giving intentionality that precede the community*. It is a force field from which the community can build itself and live its good life. The community is built on a *good* that is uttered and, at the same time, offered because the Word makes it possible. Unlike an imperative word, which creates a stable but confining normative framework, the *creative, blessing Word* opens up a space for the *good* to emerge from the free creativity of the community that is being built and finds its *good* way of being as it moves forward, constantly under this divine promise: 'Go, and you will be blessed!'[40]

The common good as a life unfolding its fruitfulness

What is a blessed, fruitful community? Biblical testimony often seeks to answer this question. The passage that does this most fully is very probably the eschatological description in chapter 65 of Isaiah (Isa. 65:17-25). Through the prophet, God promises to create new heavens and a new earth where peace, justice and joy will reign. This description is placed in the con-

39 Jean Daniel MACCHI, "La bénédiction dans la Bible hébraïque", in Marie Hélène ROBERT and Jacques MATTHEY (eds), *Figures bibliques de la mission: exégèse et théologie de la mission, approches catholiques et protestantes*, Paris, Cerf, 2010, 23-48, 25.

40 "The future of the hoping human person is largely unspecified in Israel's testimony and enormously open. Much may happen that is good, because the future is a gift of Yahweh." Walter BRUEGGEMANN, *Theology of the Old Testament: testimony, dispute, advocacy*, Minneapolis, Fortress Press, 1997, 480.

text of the return from exile, i.e. a time when a people that has experienced military defeat, deportation and social disintegration is wondering about its fragile, uncertain future. The so-called 'Trito-Isaiah' then turns the gaze of those who despairs towards the future, and revives their hope.

The first element of reflection concerns historical temporality. Our text avoids both the messianic and the apocalyptic pitfalls. Seen from a *political/messianic* angle, the common good is brought about by a political change initiated by the messianic figure at a time still to come in the historical future. *Apocalyptic* hope, in contrast, discredits any worldly organisation and sees salvation only in divine intervention, likewise historically dated, leading to the disappearance of this world and its complete replacement by a different reality.[41] The difficulty of both representations is that they shift the advent of the common good into the future – because they remain prisoners of a temporality conceived on the human scale, in which unambiguous historical events follow one after the other. The *prophetic* announcement blurs the boundaries of the worldly time by incorporating it into God's everlasting present.[42] By combining divine intervention *and* societal transformation, it shatters both the voluntarist construction of a politically organised society and its opposite, the projection of a flight into paradise outside a collapsing world. To be sure, history is positively reordered, but because God displays his acting presence in it. This corresponds to the aforementioned pervasion of the finite by the infinite. God repeats his creative act in a different temporality that concerns and, at the same time, goes beyond history. He *will make* all things new and *is already doing so* in a transcendent action that goes beyond the human separation between the present and the future. However, insofar as a worldly temporality remains something that humans cannot move beyond, they will necessarily need a set of semantic tools, for instance around the notions of *anticipation* and *beginnings*, to apprehend this coincidence of the already and the not-yet, this *common good* that is to be found in, but is not exhausted by, history.

The common good described here is not a *utopia*, i.e. 'no place'. It is part of everyday life. Ulrich Mauser points out that, even after the disasters experienced by the people of Israel, what is announced and desired is not a flight from the world to escape into 'spiritual values'. Love of the earth has

41 Revelation 21:1 or 2 Peter 3:13.

42 Verses 17 and 18 use a grammatical turn indicating an imminent future that lends a sense of immediacy to the announcement of the new creation; see Margaret D. BRATCHER, "Salvation Achieved. Isaiah 61:1-7; 62:1-7; 65:17-66", in *Review & Expositor*, 88/2 (1991), 177-188, 183.

not disappeared, the latter has not become bitter; there is still hope of finding oases in the desert.[43] The new world is a world in which houses must be built and fields sown, a world in which children are born and people are concerned about the conditions in which they die. This means that the *common good* is not built on a *tabula rasa*, but from the specific conditions of a community's existence by reviving them from within.

Finally, it should be noted that God is present as the main actor in this cosmic re-creation. He initiates it, but he also takes part in it, to the point where he shares its joy.[44] God's joy makes clear that not only worldly things will be transformed, but that the relationship with Yahweh will too, and radically.[45] This is now part of the *common good conceived of as the good of a community that incorporates the divine actor.* Joy being what indicates the accomplishment of a desire, divine and human desires come together in the same *good* of the community.

If we look at the details of Isaiah's description, we see a society in which the life of the community *can be unfolded so as to achieve its optimum blossoming.* This is done by the blossoming of the lives of each of the members who are closely bound up in the life of the whole. We are close to the contemporary notion of capabilities[46] with this description of existences that unfold their potentialities on the biological, psychological, social, ecological and spiritual levels.

Life is first of all accomplished in its *biologically* programmed duration; it is not prematurely interrupted (Isa 65:20). Death comes in due course in the image of the peaceful death of the patriarchs, who died like Abraham 'in a ripe old age, an old man and satisfied with life' (Gen 25:8).

Psychological blossoming is marked by the absence of weeping and crying (v. 19), the absence of perceived distress, of this sense of abandonment that the people experienced during its wanderings in exile. A weeping society is one that is utterly remote from its good. Whether or not it perceives it explicitly, it is deconstructing itself – its life as a group is in jeopardy. To the prophets, loss of social linkage is always systemic; the loss of the relationship with God entails the loss of social links, and vice versa. Thus, in his

43 Ulrich Mauser, "Isaiah 65:17-25", in *Union Seminary Review* 36/2, (1982), 181-186, quotation on p. 185. "*New heavens and a new earth are not at all the products of a tired turn to "spiritual values" but the fervent affirmation of the goodness of life and land.*"

44 Isaiah 65:19: "*I will rejoice over Jerusalem*". See in Isaiah 62:5 the description of God's joy as the '*the bridegroom [who] rejoices over the bride*'; also other passages in which God rejoices over his people: Deuteronomy 28:63 and 30:9; Jeremiah 32:41.

45 Bratcher, "Salvation Achieved", 184.

46 See the contribution of Michel Bonvin in this volume.

chapter 7, when condemning the paganisation of worship in the temple, Jeremiah associates the loss of contact with God with contempt for the law and one's neighbour, oppression of strangers, orphans and widows, theft, murder, adultery, perjury and worship of idols. These destructuring elements literally smash society, and hence 'the land will become desolate' and 'the sounds of joy and gladness and the voices of bride and bridegroom' will no longer be heard (Jer 7:34). If this deadly *common ill* can be reversed, then anguish and weeping disappear, for the present once more becomes a firm basis on which we can build. The past and its traumatising memories will no longer come to mind (v. 17) and the future can once more become the place of promise; children will no longer be brought to life for misfortune (v. 23).[47]

It can be seen that the elements of *social* justice and psychological comfort are closely linked. Houses will be built and vines planted – the two things that the Old Testament uses to describe human activity. This work will not be 'in vain' (v. 23), it will not be despoiled by others (vv. 21-22), but its fruit will be harvested by all. As thus described, individual work is a work of social construction; the text is always in the plural. Each person enjoys for himself the stone he brings to the social body. Thus the community that experiences the harmony of a seemingly ordinary, but full, life becomes 'a people blessed by the Lord, they and their descendants with them' (v. 23). Further, the life of the community recreated by God is only complete if it extends to the whole of nature. The violent, destructive conflicts in all the creation will also be pacified, 'the wolf and the lamb will feed together' (v. 25).[48] *The common good is necessarily an ecological, indeed cosmic, common good.*[49]

As already mentioned, a community cannot live the *good life* unless it is open to the infinity of a transcendence that bears it. We can then speak of the necessary *spiritual dimension* of the common good that is expressed in verse 24: 'Before they call, I will answer'. What is described here is the immediacy of the relationship with God. In the ideal therefore good community, God is here, and dialogue with him is easy. Calls and answers follow each other smoothly. It should also be pointed out that this dialogue will

47 "The renewal of existence becomes so radical that no painful memory survives".: Jan Leunis Koole, *Isaiah. Part 3*, Leuven, Peeters, 1997, 447.

48 Elsewhere in the book of Isaiah this pacification involves not only the animal but also the plant world, with the resolution of the desert/vegetation conflict: 29:17; 32:15; 35:6 and so on.

49 See Pope Francis's encyclical *Laudato si'* for emphasis on the indissociable links between social and ecological justice.

never initiate in a pietistic or liturgical escape, but is only possible when the other elements of the common good are present. Some chapters earlier, the prophet recalled that the closeness of God is linked to social justice: 'Then you will call, and the Lord will answer; "Here I am!" If you do away with the yoke of oppression, with the pointing finger and the malicious talk".' (Isa 58:9). The absence of justice divides the community, and it creates a distance from God: 'Your iniquities have separated you from your God; your sins have hidden his face from you, so that he will not hear' (Isa 59:2).

This transcendent presence mentioned by the philosophers, and witnessed by the Old Testament and many religious traditions, was to be further densified in Christian theology. What was manifested under the seal of invisibility as transcendence at the heart of the finite became visible when it took shape in the figure of Christ. St Irenaeus clearly expressed the historical moment when the hitherto 'still invisible' Word became flesh and made man divine by restoring the lost resemblance.[50] The visible and the corporeal then became places where God appeared and manifested his presence more precisely and densely. What has just been said about the divine presence and what it recreates at the heart of everyday reality takes its full meaning here. In the figure of Christ, dead and brought back to life, this presence became a victorious response to the destructive violence of any community and thus opened the way to the *common good*. Christian faith took a further step by asserting the persistence of this Christic body in the Church, a corporeal persistence that is constantly revived by the sacramental, and in particular eucharistic, practice. This brings us to the last three names that theology can give to the common good: the *community under grace*, *brotherhood*, and the *body of Christ*.

The common good as community under grace

Grace means 'the personal benevolence, the absolutely gratuitous – not due – favour that God grants to man.'[51] Rahner calls this 'God's self-communi-

50 "Mman was created after the image of God, but it was not shown; for the Word was as yet invisible ... When, however, the Word became flesh, He confirmed both these: for He both showed forth the image truly, since He became Himself what was His image; and He re-established the similitude after a sure manner, by assimilating man to the invisible Father through means of the visible Word." IRENAEUS OF LYON, *Adversus Haereses* V, 16, 2.

51 Karl RAHNER & Herbert VORGRIMLER, *Theological Dictionary,* Herder, New-York,1965.

cation'.[52] In the light of what has been said earlier about God's desire, it can even be described as God's *loving* self-communication to man: *a loving gift of himself that God makes to man for his salvation*, i.e. for his good life, for a life rid of any destructive, deadly dynamics. Christian faith sees the culmination of this self-communication in Jesus of Nazareth's life, death and resurrection. God's loving intentionality becomes a visible presence in history. It radically transforms history by opening up unheard-of possibilities for creating and undergoing communities that display specific signs of the eschatology announced by Isaiah.

In one of his sermons on the *Song of Songs*, St Bernard of Clairvaux, reflecting on the community, refers to the biblical parable of the two sons. The younger breaks the unity of the family because he wants only for himself 'a good that it was sweeter to possess in common'.[53] St Bernard could see how this captative greed, which broke what was shared in favour of self-interest, would be a source of violence: 'thus man becomes aggressive and his heart dries out; henceforth, incapable of affection, he despises everyone except himself'. He is then utterly remote from the common good and the grace that upholds it. 'He deprives himself of the unique sweetness of the social, common good', and his selfish preoccupations remove him from the 'sweetness of *social grace*'.

Christ's presence, as *social grace* par excellence, will shatter this deadly selfishness by radically changing envy into gift and selfishness into love going to the point of self-disappropriation: 'Greater love has no-one than this: to lay down one's life for one's friends' (John 15:13). The normative impact of this divine presence recognised by the community of believers makes the latter aware that man will only escape self-concentration, which at the same time is self-destruction, by opening up to the other, which takes the form of the commandment 'Love your neighbour as yourself.' As St Bernard says elsewhere, we must be able to 'share our goods with our companions'[54] rather than accumulate them. It is worth noting that the word translated as 'share' appears in the latin text as *communicare*. Yet, strictly speaking, *communicare* means putting in common, whereas *sharing* means creating shares and distributing them. Whereas sharing may suggest the impoverishment of the

52 Karl RAHNER, *Fondation of Christian Faith,* New-York, Seabury, 1978, 116-126. For more on the development of the social dimension of grace, Roger HAIGHT, 'Sin and Grace', in Francis S. FIORENZA, John GALVIN (eds), *Systematic theology: Roman Catholic perspectives,* Fortress Press, 2011, 375-430.

53 BERNHARD OF CLAIRVAUX, *Sermons on the Song of Songs*, 44,5.

54 *De diligendo Deo, § 23.*

person who originally holds the good, putting in common, in contrast, opens up an additional dimension of enrichment: construction of the community. St Bernard refers to this *'balanced and just' love of one's neighbour* as *social love*, since it can limit the individual's response to his own pleasure and open him up to his brothers' needs: 'carnal love becomes social when it enlarges for the common good'.[55] The term 'social' can then be understood as the extra that results from shared love, as the community created by the communication of goods *and* love. The possibility of its emergence comes from the ability to resist self-centred desire, i.e. greed. In theological words, the emergence of the *social* in its true dimension comes from the individual's ability to resist sin.

This brings us back to grace, since sin is what reveals grace *a contrario*. The 'cainesque coldness' (Levinas) of greed, i.e. the inability (or lack of will) to depart from oneself and live with the other in a brotherly relationship, reveals, as a contrasting effect, the necessity and sweetness of brotherhood, which is only fully manifested when it is 'fertilised by the breath of grace'.[56] To the question of the absence of the common good and the presence of evil that constantly destroys the community, the believers' answer is that of grace which, as St Augustine says, is necessary in order to correct free will and bring love into the community; for participation in the dynamics of grace 'gives human freedom a capacity for creativity that it does not have on its own',[57] a capacity for loving one's neighbour that goes beyond dual interpersonal structures to be truly an element of social construction. *The common good thus helped by grace is an ever-new free construction, but it is also the ability to resist the common ill, the structural sin*, i.e. to resist the forces of disintegration, just like any living organism.

The common good as recognised and accepted brotherhood

Theological reflection on the *common good as brotherhood* is crucial in order to place the common good, as understood by the Christian tradition, in contrast with modern conceptions of it, mainly those of contractualist writers. Considering brotherhood in its profound meaning, rather than the superficial expression of feelings of affection, inevitably entails taking account of its antecedence. Brotherhood precedes me and does not depend on me. At the same as it indicates a relationship with someone else, it places us in a

55 *Ibid.*

56 BERNHARD OF CLAIRVAUX, *Sermons on the Song of Songs,* 44,4.

57 HAIGHT, *Sin and grace*, 422.

common relationship to our origin. The Father from whom brotherhood comes precedes brothers. To Levinas, *being a brother* is not an ethical choice that could, or could not be made, but is given as a precondition for all morality. To him, brotherhood is pre-moral, pre-conscious, an-archic in the sense of being before all else: '*The human ego is posited in brotherhood: the idea that all men are brothers is not something that is added on to man as a moral conquest, but is his very selfhood.*'[58]

Brotherhood is not a kind of relationship like friendship, but is rather a determinant that calls for relationship. Thus brotherhood is always a challenge. It asks to be recognised and, even more, to be consented to and experienced. The aforementioned parable of the two sons in Luke 15:11-32 is perfectly eloquent on this. The young son recognises brotherhood, but no longer consents to it. Even though he can claim his inheritance and go far away, he nonetheless remains a son and brother. He cannot undo his filial or fraternal ties; all he can do is take a stance on them, either experiencing them or refusing to do so.

The common good can be seen as brotherhood, but as brotherhood that is *recognised and consented to.* Perhaps beyond what Levinas has said about the community of the Father, we must, within the Christian narrative, also emphasise the *community of the Brother*, in the sense that Christ dwells with us within this place of brotherhood and encourages us to make this effort of consent into which he draws us as an elder brother, 'the first-born among many brothers' (Romans 8:29).

The common good as body of Christ

These new possibilities of community are opened up by the historical event of the Cross on which a singular man faces, and disarms, violence. He acts as a revealer; the evil that is killing him becomes visible in him. And, confronted here with its opposite, infinite love, violence does not respond with anger or a desire for revenge, but is drained and disappears, as if absorbed forever. Now, violence he is suffering does not lead to any counter-violence, or injustice to a new injustice, but only to silence.[59] And it is from this overwhelming silence in the true sense of the term that the unexpected of a reconstructive attitude can emerge. It is a silence in which violence does not

58 LEVINAS, *Totality and Infinity*, 234.

59 Similar to the Suffering Servant's silence in Isaiah 52:13 and 53:12. Adrian SCHENKER, *Douceur de Dieu et violence des hommes: le quatrième chant du serviteur de Dieu et le Nouveau Testament*, Brussels, Lumen Vitae, 2002.

receive the expected response, and which opens up a 'creative interval', says the exegete Adrian Schenker, to whom 'introducing a pause, a gap or a space may turn out to be a creative attitude: it allows benevolent action, rather than retaliation, to take place.'[60] We can see such an interval in the suspended time of the Cross. Recognition of the transcendence of the dying man makes this a human pause that allows divine love to emerge. The believer perceives that only thus can violence be turned into love, through the mediation of God as man. And this makes visible, for a brief moment, in a purity never again achieved, the shift from the *common ill* to the *common good*, i.e. between the deadly community and the compassionate, healing community.

The death of Christ ultimately absorbing violence and its validation in the resurrection then became the driving force behind a completely unprecedented sociality. The Church performed this unique shift from the sacrificed, glorified body to its own body. The Christian community immediately understood that what should happen to it as a community, its *common good*, went beyond a fragile brotherhood that was always threatened by its very members. It had to perform this passage to the limit, this *transfiguration* of a human social body into the Body of Christ. It had to *become this Body in history* in order that its power to annihilate violence could also emerge. This is what Oscar Romero, the archbishop of San Salvador in the early 1980's understood in the midst of the extreme violence in which his country was plunged. The urgent need was not to make revolution, but to make El Salvador's Christians aware that they had to let themselves be transfigured as a community in order to become this peace-making, compassionate Body and a source of hope. He said this in one of his pastoral letters, written to mark the feast of the Transfiguration and entitled 'The Church, the body of Christ in history':

> Each year this Body of Christ in history, this church of the archdiocese, understands better that the August 6 feast day is something more than just a titular feast. It is rather the celebration of a covenant that binds all Salvadorans to each other, all Salvadorans baptised with the baptism of the world's Divine Saviour, even to the extent of an identification in thinking and in destiny. All of us who have been baptised form the church, and the church makes Christ present in the history of our country.[61]

60 *Ibid.*, 62.

61 "The Church, the Body of Christ in History", second pastoral letter, 6 August, 1977, in *Voice of the voiceless: the four pastoral letters and other statements*, Maryknoll, Orbis, 1985, 63-84, at 83.

Conclusion

Even if reflection on the *common good* is not explicitly stated as such, it fundamentally lies at the heart of any theological reflection, for theology has no subject other than the unfolding of the Life that is in God and is given by Him in his gracious creative externalisation. Man is then alive with a life that he does not give to himself, but that is always a life that is given to him and hence to be received, an experienced life, as Michel Henry says,[62] ultimately a life that we *wish to perceive as a good life.* I have attempted to point out that, from biological materiality to the highest spheres of spiritual life, life is only found in a constantly re-creating dynamism that fights against opposing ones, against a destructive violence that tends to reduce everything to undifferentiated chaos. Theology then thematises the conviction that birth and the unfolding of life are nonetheless possible if the Source of this life which comes closer to humans is recognised in and incorporated into the pursuit of the good life. St Augustine described the latter as 'heavenly peace', i.e. 'enjoyment of God, and of each other in God'.[63] It is this three-way, God/oneself/the other, relationship that, to theologians, is the true place of the common good. What we have seen is that, in a hermeneutics of *coexistence* the absence of God is cruelly felt and that, ultimately, coexistence inevitably calls for transcendence. This transcendence, recognised and consented to, thus becomes a strong driving force for community hope. The *common good* seeks to be constructed as an escape from destructive violence, nourishing itself with the received life of a *transcendence that is conceived of as blessing and loving.* There remains a dissatisfaction, that of a presence that is a promise[64] and nevertheless always eludes us. Christian theology then provides a final element: a *presence of transcendence embodied in history*, which both provides a final answer to violence and allows the community to live on the beginnings of a communion between man and God who,

62 "*As has been repeatedly shown, true man is not the empirical individual observed in the world, but the transcendental ego that is constantly self-experimented as living, as the ego that lives its life without ever being the source of that life ... Living as a living transcendental ego, given to us in a life that does not give itself to us, but is given to us in the donation to us of the absolute Life which is that of God: such is the Christian definition of man, his condition as a Son. This condition of man as a Son is precisely what allows his salvation.*" Michel HENRY, *C'est moi la vérité: pour une philosophie du christianisme*, Paris, Seuil, 1996, 192.

63 "*Fruendi deo et invicem in deo*", *City of God* 19, 13.

64 Bruegmann clearly shows the novelty and importance of this promise for Israel at the time of the exile: BRUEGMANN, *Theology of the Old Testament*, 170.

in the scriptural metaphors, assumes the figures of the kingdom of justice and a joyful feast.

Jean Claude Huot

The common good tested against the option for the poor: a perspective for the Church's social commitment

The strength of a people is measured by the well-being of its weakest members.
Preamble to the Swiss Federal Constitution

Introduction

The common good, 'the sum of those conditions of social life which allow social groups and their individual members relatively thorough and ready access to their own fulfilment',[1] is not defined once and for all. Its specific meaning is not specified in either *Gaudium et spes* or the social encyclicals. Pope Francis's *Laudato si'* is no exception. Yet it states 'In the present condition of global society, where injustices abound and growing numbers of people are deprived of basic human rights and considered expendable, the principle of the common good immediately becomes, logically and inevitably, a summons to solidarity and a preferential option for the poorest of our brothers and sisters.' In other words, the first condition for the common good is ethical rather than social, and concerns us all. The Pope highlights this in the final sentence of the brief chapter he devotes to the common good: 'this option [for the poorest] is in fact an ethical imperative essential for effectively attaining the common good.'[2]

This raises the question of how the common good relates to the preferential option for the poorest. To discuss this question, I will first set out from my own reality as a pastoral worker in the labour sphere, ecumenical work carried out jointly by the Catholic and Protestant churches in the Swiss canton of Vaud, in which I meet people who cannot find a job or, for lack of income, a place to live.[3] Second, I will consider how, given these people's actual experience, the common good can be constructed. We must then hear these excluded people's appeal to be part of society, to be recog-

1 Vatican II, *Gaudium et spes*, § 26.

2 Pope Francis, *Laudato si'*, § 158.

3 This background both limits and enriches my argument. Although I cannot claim to shed light on every aspect of the common good, what I have to say about it is based on my own actual experience.

nised. Third, I will look at what this appeal means to Christian faith and the Church's commitment in society. Fourth, I will use human rights, the cornerstone of today's world, to assert the inalienable dignity of every human being. Fifth, I will return to the importance of politics, the need to be and act together, collectively, so that the common good can come about, at least in part, and incorporate the weakest members of human society, as is called for in my own country's constitution. Finally, I will return to the pastoral field – for it is the Church's duty to act credibly for the common good in the social field.[4]

When the disadvantaged are excluded

To protect her privacy, I will call her Teresa.[5] When she was introduced to me, she needed help in drawing up a CV for a job application; but to help her I needed to hear her life story. So we went all the way back to her childhood, stage by stage.

She was born in 1973, in a rural area of a small Latin American country. When she was eleven years old her mother was diagnosed with cancer, and the family moved to the city in the hope of finding medical care. Since her father could not find work, it was the daughter that had to keep them alive. At the age of just twelve, she sold bananas and *empanadas* in the street, then she worked as a baby-sitter in private homes. This meant she could not go to school. In 1994 she emigrated to Argentina, where she found a job at a four-star hotel. 'The most wonderful period in my life – the boss treated me well and I earned a good living.' She was able to pay for her mother's treatment, and could afford gold jewellery, 'even a Rolex watch'.

In 2000 her mother died. The following year the *corralito* financial crisis hit Argentina. Parity between the peso and the US dollar was abandoned in 2002. Teresa explains 'The banks stayed closed for three weeks. Then the bank gave us a handwritten 100-peso voucher stamped with its name, which we could take to a department store and swap for food. We had to spend the whole voucher in one go – we weren't given change.' Subsequently Teresa lost her job and all her savings. In 2003 she sold her jewellery and her watch so she could travel back home. Then she moved to

4 I would like to thank the librarians at the *Centre pour l'information et la documentation chrétiennes* (CIDOC) and the Alliance Sud in Lausanne for their help in producing this paper.

5 All the people mentioned in this article are known personally to the author, but their names have been changed to protect their privacy.

Spain to try her luck there, and found work as a cleaner in private homes. She was allowed to bring her husband over, and gave birth to her first daughter. But she was not yet finished with financial crises. In 2008 came the global financial collapse. Although she by now had a Spanish passport, it was becoming harder and harder to survive in the Iberian peninsula. In 2012 she gave birth to her second daughter; at the time she was helping to run a welfare centre. In 2013 she left Spain for Lausanne, where she was initially employed by unscrupulous people. The first made her work for hours as a cleaner, for a mere pittance; another one didn't pay her at all. Finally, the third treated her decently. She was granted a residence permit and put her professional situation on an even keel. Meanwhile, however, she got divorced – she had had enough of being mistreated by and having to feed a husband who could scarcely find work. When I met her she was 43 years old, bringing up her two daughters on her own in Lausanne, on a monthly income of 2,500 Swiss francs (less than the half of the median gross salary)). 'Life hasn't been kind to me, but thank God I'm still here with my two daughters. It's for them that I keep going, and want to live. I love life.'

This life story shows to the extent to which upheavals in the financial world can determine individual people's fates. The global becomes the individual. But I could also tell the story of Isabelle, a Swiss university graduate who lost her job at a government office after a reorganisation. Despite her skills and experience, at the age of over 50 she can no longer find work. I also think of Elvis, an Ethiopian who arrived in Switzerland in 1998. He applied for asylum, and meanwhile found a job helping in the kitchen at a large hotel. But a change to asylum law following a national referendum meant he was no longer allowed to work, and he was dismissed. He has not been in fixed employment since 2005. Despite a change in his status that allows him to work once more, he has alternated every few months between precarious temporary jobs and periods of unemployment. One government department gave him two successive short-term contracts – but not a third one, as the law would then have required his employer to give him a permanent contract. Yet the work he was doing is still there.

These are just a few small examples of migration and access to the labour market. There are over 250 million migrants worldwide,[6] and the net rate of immigration into Switzerland is about 70,000 a year.[7] Most of the

6 World Bank (consulted on June 2017).

7 Staatssekretariat für Migration (consulted on June 2017).

newcomers, apart from asylum seekers, are from southern Europe.[8] And of the Swiss who are struggling to find a job, more than 60% of the long-term unemployed are over 55 years old.[9] Yet most of these people are simply trying to make a decent living somewhere in the world. This raises the following question: how can our economic system leave so many people in the lurch like this? Has it got so far off track that it mainly serves financial interests, worsening inequality? In April 2016 the International Labour Office (ILO) published an interesting study, which surprisingly has not been translated into English, on the impact of economic financialisation on the labour market.[10] The author describes how shareholders have taken control of businesses, turning managers into their agents, and wage-earners into the managers' agents. This 'shareholder primacy', which has become the governing principle since the 1970 s, has resulted in business management based on numbers – financial numbers, at the expense of labour. Since then, labour relations have become dominated by distrust, for workers are reduced to accounting figures – and, as we all know, labour costs money! This creation of more flexible, precarious employment due to the financialisation of the economy has clearly boosted inequality. The Crédit Suisse bank,[11] quoted by the originally British non-governmental organisation (NGO) Oxfam, has drawn the following alarming conclusion: 1% of the world's population now owns more wealth than all the rest put together. Admittedly, the poorest half of the world's population has seen its wealth increase by 1% between 2000 and 2015. This has helped to reduce extreme poverty (one of the millennium development goals); but the change is still tiny compared with the 50% increase in the wealth of the richest 1% of the world's population over the same period.[12]

Given all this, thinking of Teresa, Isabelle, Elvis and all the others fighting day after day to live dignified lives, I can only conclude that economic growth does not automatically spread wealth creation throughout the population – as a recent study by the International Monetary Fund

8 See Sarah Bouschiba-Schaer & Bernhard Weber, 'La situation économique dicte l'immigration', in *La Vie économique*, 55-57.

9 The 60 % share is calculated on the basis of the OECD and the ILO definition of unemployment. See OECD, *Vieillissement et politiques de l'emploi. Suisse: mieux travailler avec l'âge*, Paris, October 2014, 45 ff.

10 Olivier Favereau, *L'impact de la financiarisation de l'économie sur les entreprises et plus particulièrement sur les relations de travail*, Geneva, ILO, 2016.

11 Crédit Suisse, *Global Wealth Databook 2015* (consulted on 30 March 2016).

12 See Deborah Hardoon, Sophia Ayele, Ricardo Fuentes-Nieva, 'An economy for the 1%', OXFAM Report 1, January 2016 (consulted on June 2017).

(IMF) goes to show. If growth mainly benefits the 20% richest members of a population, the country's overall growth is lower, and the converse is also true: when growth mainly benefits the poorest fifth of the population, the whole country benefits more.[13] But all this depends on political choices. As the winner of the Nobel Prize for economics Joseph Stiglitz has made clear, the market alone does not ensure the common good.[14]

An appeal to respect human dignity

'I want to work!', 'I need a job!' – I've lost count of the times I have heard such cries from job seekers. Yet behind these initial appeals there often lies a deeper need: a need to be acknowledged, integrated, accepted. 'I want to contribute to the well-being of the society that I live in, that has welcomed me', 'I want to feel useful'. This is clearly expressed by Jonathan, who has worked on building sites all his life, and wants to keep doing so. He could soon be paid the 'bridging pension' that the Swiss canton of Vaud provides for people who are close to retiring but are no longer entitled to unemployment benefit. But he would sooner feel useful: 'perhaps by training young people, teaching them what I know'. The problem is that, as a mason, he has no formal qualifications; he has learned everything he knows 'on the job'. And who would invest in training a 60-year-old man as a teacher?

All these people who are excluded from the labour market want one and the same thing: to feel useful, and hence acknowledged. In other words, they want to contribute to the common good of the society they live in, regardless of their nationality, age or background. Of course, they need an income and housing, especially if they have children to look after; but even those that don't are looking for job or, failing this, voluntary work. Stefano, a cook, puts it very well: 'I can't just sit back and do nothing – but I can't find work. So I'm really happy to cook for Church events, I feel useful, and I help people enjoy themselves, however difficult their lives may be. And that gives my life meaning.' And Stefano's contribution to the life of the human community in the place where he lived was publicly acknowledged

13 Era Dabla-Norris, Kalpana Kochhar, Nujin Suphaphiphat, Frantisek Ricka, Evridiki Tsounta, *Causes and consequences of income inequality: a global perspective*, IMF Staff Discussion Note, June 2015.

14 See Joseph Stiglitz, *The price of inequality*, New York, W. W. Norton & Company, 2012 (on the United States). See also Joseph Stiglitz, *Globalization and its discontents*, New York, W. W. Norton & Company, 2002, in which he criticises the IMF's late 20th-century policies, arguing that the famous 'invisible hand' does not work, particularly in developing countries, owing to incomplete information and imperfect markets.

when he eventually received a signed document stating that he had indeed worked on such-and-such a date, and that his work had been appreciated.

An economy that can contrive to exclude 4% of Switzerland's population from the labour market, 7% of Canada's, 6% of Russia's, 8% of Brazil's or 25% of South Africa, and 200 million people worldwide,[15] an economy that forces much of the population to make shift in an informal sector without any social welfare protection, often with pitiful wages and the harshest working conditions,[16] is not serving humanity, but only itself. Pope Francis said this quite bluntly during the second pastoral journey in his papacy: 'When there's no work, there's no dignity! And this isn't just a Sardinian problem, but it strikes really hard here! It isn't just a problem of Italy, or some countries of Europe, it is the consequence of a world, an economic system that has its centre in an idol called money. And God has willed that the centre of the world is not an idol, but a man and woman with their work.'[17]

The focus of the Pope's words was respect for dignity – each person's dignity, regardless of his or her nationality, religion or occupational skills. And, since humans are social beings – which is what makes them person – respecting their dignity involves integrating them into a society. And how better to integrate than to contribute to the life of their communities through their work, the input of their knowledge and experience? It is then essential to organise the human community so that all its members can meet their own needs and contribute to the welfare of the societies they belong to. Human beings can only achieve fullness by contributing to the common good. No-one may shrug off this duty; nor may anyone be prevented from fulfilling it on the grounds that they are supposedly 'useless'. The social nexus is based on interpersonal partnership. There is nothing worse than being deemed 'superfluous',[18] unneeded, unwanted.

15 INTERNATIONAL LABOUR ORGANIZATION, *World Employment and Social Outlook – Trends 2016*, Geneva, ILO, 2016 (consulted June 2017).

16 In Africa the informal sector may involve up to 70% of the working population; the figure in Latin America is an estimated 50%. That is why, at its 2015 annual conference, the ILO launched a Recommendation concerning the transition from the informal to the formal economy (ILO, R204, 2015) as part of its decent work programme.

17 Pope FRANCIS, *Address of the Holy Father to Workers*, 22 September 2013.

18 The term is taken from Hannah ARENDT, *The Origins of Totalitarism*, New York, Meridian Books, 1967, 150-151.

From 'listening to the poor' to an 'option for the poor'

This tragedy of exclusion brings us back to God's choice of the poor to occupy the first place. Here I recall Father Dominique Barthélemy's splendid posthumous book *Le pauvre choisi comme Seigneur* ('The poor man chosen as the Lord'). In the lectures reproduced here he showed that God himself embraces the poor first and foremost, and unreservedly. He illustrated this with the parable of the poor man Lazarus (*Luke* 16, 19-31). Lazarus was a man without status. There was nothing to indicate he was better than the rich man passing before him. Yet the gulf was there, between the rich man who looked away and the man starving to death. 'The angels carried [Lazarus] to Abraham's side', whereas the rich man was buried. Father Barthélemy pointed out this discrepancy. Lazarus – the only person in the parable to be named by name – was welcomed into the kingdom, unconditionally, whereas the rich man was called on to be converted, to heed Moses and the prophets. Such was God's power and preference. 'The poor man's place was the first in the kingdom, and he did not even need faith to attain it, and this is explicitly asserted.'[19] For God knew the imperfection of human reality; he knew that some would have no chance of justice in this base world. 'The imperfection of human justice, which is partial, will inevitably entail God's preferential choice for the poor.'[20] So God granted the first place to the poor man Lazarus, for he was fair and omnipotent. He corrected human justice.

Cardinal Gerhard Ludwig Müller, today Prefect of the Congregation for the Doctrine of the Faith, has also addressed the reality of people living in often extremely precarious situations, for they require us to think about the Church's very mission. In his view, the question is not what Christians can say and do in response to poverty. The basic question is rather how we can 'speak about God, Christ, the Holy Spirit, the Church, the sacraments, grace and eternal life in light of misery, exploitation and oppression of people in the Third World, especially when we conceive of humans as the reality created in God's image, the reality for whom Christ died so that in all

19 Dominique BARTHÉLEMY, *Le pauvre choisi comme Seigneur: la bonne nouvelle est annoncée aux pauvres*, Paris, Cerf, 2009, 27.

20 BARTHÉLEMY, *op. cit.*, p. 98.

realms of life human beings would experience God as salvation and life itself'.[21]

Listening to people confronted with exploitation and the inability to contribute to the common good, quite simply excluded from the channels of economic and social life, is thus a challenge to faith itself, to the Church and its mission in society. For are these people not ultimately the ones Jesus identifies with when he says 'whatever you did for one of the least of these brothers and sisters of mine, you did for me' (Matthew 25, 40)? How, then, can we not hear God's appeal in their own?

If the proclaimed Kingdom of God, already contained in the sacrament of the Eucharist, is to be relevant to the human history we are now experiencing, it is clear that these people are invited to the feast. And 'if [God] first loved us' (1 John 4, 19), Christians must respond to this initiative. The preferential option for the poor thus entails listening to their words as well as the Word of God; the latter joins the former, and identifies with it. So the preferential option for the poor is not an addition to Christian life, but lies at the very heart of it: the recognition that God is God. It invites us to re-read the Bible in the light of the situation of the poor. 'The whole Bible is imbued with God's preference for the weak and the mistreated in human history. It reveals us the Gospel's understands of blessing, and tell us that the priority given to the poor, the starving and the suffering is based the Lord's goodness.'[22] This option, stated clearly in liberation theology in Latin America, thus becomes an integral part of our understanding of the Church's mission as a whole. Pope John Paul II clearly states it in referring to the parable of the poor man Lazarus: 'This is an option, or a special form of primacy in the exercise of Christian charity, to which the whole tradition of the Church bears witness. It affects the life of each Christian inasmuch as he or she seeks to imitate the life of Christ, but it applies equally to our social responsibilities and hence to our manner of living, and to the logical decisions to be made concerning the ownership and use of goods.'[23] This is the driving force, in faithfulness to Christ's teachings, behind the Church's commitment to the common good.

21 Gerhard Ludwig MÜLLER, 'A critique of liberation theology: its merits and limits', in Gustavo GUTIÉRREZ, Gerhard Ludwig MÜLLER, *On the side of the poor: the theology of liberation*, Maryknoll, Orbis, 2015.

22 Gustavo GUTIÉRREZ, 'Where will the poor sleep?', in GUTIÉRREZ, MÜLLER, *op. cit.*, 119-120. Gutiérrez states that preference does not mean exclusivity, and writes of 'the great challenge coming from the need to maintain the universality of God's love and, at the same time, God's predilection for those.

23 Pope JOHN PAUL II, *Sollicitudo rei socialis*, § 42.

Human rights as a lever for action

In their historical development, human rights are among the essential fruits of the Enlightenment and the American (1776) and French (1789) revolutions.[24] 'Men are born and remain free and equal in rights. Social distinctions can be founded only on the common good' (*Declaration of the rights of man and of the citizen*, 1789).

Owing to these largely anticlerical historical origins, the Catholic Church had difficulty in accepting human rights. The boost given by John XXIII (*Pacem in terris*) and then the Vatican II Council (particularly the *Dignitatis humanae* declaration that recognised religious freedom), and finally Paul VI's and above all John Paul II's resolute commitment to human rights, greatly strengthened the commitment of the faithful on every continent to promote and defend human rights, sometimes at the risk of their own lives.

According to John Paul II, human rights are the very guarantee that development is not confined to economic development, but includes every aspect of human life: 'Nor would a type of development which did not respect and promote human rights – personal and social, economic and political, including the rights of nations and of peoples – be really worthy of man.'[25]

But, as far as the Church is concerned, human rights are not based on the isolated individual, cut off from his social, cultural or religious ties. As Alain Thomasset SJ points out, the linchpin of the Church's interpretation of human rights is the conviction that behind these rights lies natural law, and that human beings are by nature social beings. 'Human rights are not rights of the isolated, autonomous individual, but rights of the human person living in a community. The individual and the community are interdependent.'[26] This is very clearly brought out by the Vatican II Council's reflections on the common good. The Council states that this 'involves rights and duties with respect to the whole human race'. Noting that 'there is a growing awareness of the exalted dignity proper to the human person, since he stands above all things, and his rights and duties are universal and inviolable', the Council Fathers say 'therefore, there must be made available to all men everything necessary for leading a life truly human, such as food, clothing, and shelter; the right to choose a state of life freely and to found a family, the right to education, to employment, to a good reputation, to

24 Not forgetting the 1689 Bill of Rights.

25 Pope John Paul II, *Sollicitudo rei socialis*, § 33.

26 Alain Thomasset, '*Droits de l'homme*', at CERAS.

respect, to appropriate information, to activity in accord with the upright norm of one's own conscience, to protection of privacy and rightful freedom even in matters religious.'[27]

They then call upon everyone to 'consider his every neighbour without exception as another self, taking into account first of all his life and the means necessary to living it with dignity (see James 2, 15-16), so as not to imitate the rich man who had no concern for the poor man Lazarus (see Luke 16, 19-31).'[28] Respect for human rights is a requirement in order for all people to live in dignity. These rights are the basis on which the rights of the poorest can be asserted and the foundations laid for what the common good may specifically mean.

In practice, the 1948 Universal Declaration of Human Rights and the treaties and conventions derived from it have become instruments that are regularly used by all the movements and groups fighting for the rights of the poorest: indigenous people's and peasants' rights against land grabbing, black people's rights against the apartheid regime or racial segregation, religious minorities' rights against claims by the majority to impose their beliefs and the associated rules. This fight is far from over, and is found at all levels of society. In the specific field of pastoral work, it is also found when asserting homeless people's right to housing, or the right to a living wage when little or no payment is made for work that has been done.

Even if we are aware of the limits to a positive formulation of human rights, or indeed challenge it in the name of the very nature of these rights, it is nonetheless an essential instrument that can be used by the most vulnerable to obtain respect for their dignity. In the words of Father Henri-Dominique Lacordaire, 'between the strong and the weak, between the rich and the poor, between the master and the servant, it is freedom that oppresses and the law that sets free.'[29] When condemning the excesses of individualism, capitalism and financialisation of the economy, when criticising the disproportionate exploitation of our common home the biosphere, we should not forget that modernity has created usable international law and focused attention on the victims to a degree never before seen in history, a formidable lever used worldwide to defend what lies at the heart of the common good: human dignity.

27 Vatican II, *Gaudium et spes*, § 26.

28 Vatican II, *Gaudium et spes*, § 27.

29 Henri-Dominique Lacordaire, *Œuvres du R. P. Henri-Dominique Lacordaire des frères prêcheurs: conférences de Notre-Dame de Paris (1835-1843),* Vol. II, Paris, Poussielgue de Gigord, 1912.

Imperfect, provisional and subject to constant revision though they may be, human rights are a device that – at least in theory – prevents us from relapsing into arbitrariness, and above all provides a lever for action throughout the world. 'All human beings are born free and equal in dignity and rights.'[30] This statement is crucial, and substantially reflects the biblical creation story, according to which every human being is created in God's image.

The personal is political

This expression, which dates from 1970, was used by the feminist movement in the United States. The idea was that analysis of personal situations could be the starting point 'for an understanding of political relationships'.[31] The theologian Denise Couture refers to this movement to explain the relationship between liberation theologians and the World Social Forum; for, she explains, in order to imagine a possible different world to which the World Social Forum and the theologians associated with it aspire, we must start out from actual experience and find new concepts and ways of doing things. She believes we are in a kind of *entre-monde* – a transition 'between what we know but no longer accept, and what lies ahead but we do not yet know'.[32]

Recent events bear this out: from demonstrators in Paris's Place de la République to *Podemos* in Spain and *Syriza* in Greece, a whole series of movements are attempting to approach politics in a new way, in a process of inevitable trial and error. 'The true politicians are those that do not know, and hence seek ways and procedures in the best – i.e. the least bad – social arrangements.'[33] More today than forty years ago, uncertainty reigns about how to build a society geared to the common good. What we now need are *Mutbürger*: courageous citizens.[34]

But getting started means taking risks. Politics is precisely the area in which the content of the common good is worked out, in debate and con-

30 Universal Declaration of Human Rights, 1948, Art. 1.

31 Denise Couture, 'Théologies chrétiennes et mouvance altermondialiste', in *Théologiques*, 55.

32 *Ibid.*, 49.

33 Vincent Cosmao, *Changer le monde*, Paris, Cerf, 1981, 179.

34 The German expression *Mutbürger*, in contrast to the rhyming term *Wutbürger* ('angry citizens'), was recently used in Switzerland to sum up popular opposition to a proposal that all foreign law-breakers should be permanently deported. The proposal was rejected in a national referendum on 28 February 2016.

frontation between differing opinions and interests. As Pope Francis said to the young people of the 'Communities of Christian Life' in Italy in April 2016, 'Blessed Paul VI, if I'm not mistaken, said that politics is one of the highest forms of charity, because it seeks the common good.' And he added 'What do you want to say, that engaging in politics is a little like martyrdom? Yes. It is a kind of martyrdom. But it is a daily martyrdom: seeking the common good without letting yourself be corrupted. Seek the common good by thinking of the most fitting ways for this, the most fitting means. Seek the common good by working for the little things, the small ones, it gives little return... but one does it.'[35]

This brings us back to the basic criterion: participation by the weakest groups of people in society to define the common good. This does not just entail 'making the poor the subjects of a new society based on solidarity',[36] but above all recognising them as subjects, which they are in themselves. The main thing is not to see them as poor people, but as human beings – and to organise the public debate and the political scene, in order to avoid the cultural and social obstacles to participation. In Switzerland, foreigners' right to vote in local government elections, tools designed to help young people vote (the national 'Easyvote' website), the debates organised in clubs and the instruments of direct democracy all open up the debate to as many people as possible. However imperfect, this is essential, for the common good cannot be built without everyone being involved.

As for Pope Francis, he has suggested a useful criterion for guiding 'the development of life in society and the building of a people where differences are harmonised within a shared pursuit':[37] the whole is greater than the parts. Noting that the global conflicts with the local, the Pope invites us to work 'on a small scale, in our own neighbourhood, but with a larger perspective'[38]. As he sees it, in contrast to the sphere, '[the model] is the polyhedron, which reflects the convergence of all its parts, each of which preserves its distinctiveness. Pastoral and political activity alike seek to gather in this polyhedron the best of each. There is a place for the poor and their culture, their aspirations and their potential. Even people who can be considered dubious on account of their errors have something to offer which must not be overlooked. It is the convergence of peoples who, within the universal order, maintain their own individuality; it is the sum total of per-

35 Pope Francis, *Address of the Holy Father to the Communities of Christian Life*, 30 April 2015.

36 Agenor Brighenti, 66.

37 Pope Francis, *Evangelii gaudium*, § 221.

38 Ibid., § 235.

sons within a society which pursues the common good, which truly has a place for everyone.'[39] Thus, according to the pontiff, this three-dimensional geometrical shape illustrates unity in diversity and the contribution of all in both the sociopolitical realm and that of the church.

Pastoral perspectives

It is significant that the Pope includes political and pastoral action in one and the same reflection – as far as he is concerned, there is no distinction. He is thus faithful to liberation theology – or rather its Argentinian version, theology of the people.[40] This theology emerged from actual experience in grass-roots church communities. Bringing together slum dwellers, small farmers and landless peasants in rural areas, these communities read their social reality and daily lives through the Word of God as discovered by the community.

At this point we are no longer talking about acting *for* the poor, but *with* the poor. The Church is then no longer *for* the people, but *of* the people. 'The people of God themselves become the subject who, through its action, enable history to advance towards its goal of total liberation.'[41] Here we come to the opening statement in the pastoral constitution *Gaudium et spes*: 'The joys and the hopes, the griefs and the anxieties of the men of this age, especially those who are poor or in any way afflicted, these are the joys and hopes, the griefs and anxieties of the followers of Christ. Indeed, nothing genuinely human fails to raise an echo in their hearts.'

Social pastoral work thus means 'experiencing an embodiment of faith, in terms of transformation',[42] with two separate aspects: within the Church, so that it can truly be a Church of the poor, faithful to God's predilection for the most vulnerable; and outside it, by contributing to a society that includes its weakest members in building the common good.[43]

Which brings me back to my personal experience of the field I know. I meet people who are in very difficult situations. Take the undocumented Senegalese woman who has been living in Switzerland for six years. She still

39 *Ibid.*, § 236.

40 Nicolas SENÈZE, 'La théologie du peuple en Amérique latine, source d'inspiration du pape François', in the French Catholic newspaper *La Croix*, 3 July 2015.

41 Gerhard Ludwig MÜLLER, 'A critique of liberation theology: its merits and its limits', in Gustavo GUTIÉRREZ, Gerhard Ludwig MÜLLER, *op. cit.*, 107.

42 Agenor BRIGHENTI, 68.

43 See Claude ROYON, Roger PHILIBERT, *Les pauvres, un défi pour l'Eglise*, Paris, Les Editions de l'Atelier, 1994.

finds the strength to enjoy even the smallest things, and puts up with temporary jobs for which she is paid just eight Swiss francs an hour (for a job that should be payed eighteen CHF). I also think of all the single mothers that have to cope with a cruel labour market, usually in the lowliest of jobs. The cleaning, basic health care and hotel industries could not care less how their employees are supposed to look after their children, which makes it extremely difficult for them to find work that will enable them to do so. Yet these women are remarkably resilient, and incredibly creative in finding practical solutions. I also think of the men working on building sites for only partly official wages, or for companies that pay them little or nothing. If they fight for their rights, as they explain, it is often to prevent others from suffering the same injustice.

We cannot remain neutral in the face of such realities. We must provide support, sometimes going to court with the plaintiff, and backing trade union action or political claims such as applications for residence permits by domestic employees with jobs in Switzerland.

But this too must be part of a broader approach to pastoral work. The Church cannot just send outreach missionaries into the streets, among migrants and prisoners and into the labour market, without committing the whole institution in it. That is why community initiatives whose very dynamics include people in precarious situations are so valuable. 'A community that has the opportunity to write its story with these people carries the Good News into its flesh – not as a message that can merely be expressed in words, but as a proclamation reflected in attitudes and ways of experiencing relationships. It also acts in institutions that open up society to a different political view of how we live together, and more fraternal relationships between the nations of the world.'[44]

A good example may be the patronage program created by the Swiss canton of Vaud. This involves encouraging local residents to 'sponsor' refugees from Syria, Ethiopia or elsewhere to help them find a footing in their host society. Launched in late 2015, the scheme supplements government efforts; the aim is to familiarise the newcomers with the local language (French), customs and practices, and how to go about finding housing, getting a job or obtaining health insurance. But the most important aspect is the social links that are created between residents and newcomers. The latter become more independent and develop their own social networks.

44 Conference of the bishops of France, 'Allons de l'avant en Eglise avec les pauvres', at Comité de Suivi Théologique Diaconia 2013 (consulted december 2017).

The driving forces behind the scheme are the Catholic and Protestant Churches, but it is not their monopoly. It involves other civil-society actors, including local authorities. Politically, it is an act of resistance to the xenophobic isolationism encouraged by scare-mongering nationalist parties. It shows by practical example that the common good, built in an inclusive way, can be achieved despite social, cultural or religious barriers. When we see that similar schemes are being launched in other parts of the country, and other parts of Europe, it is clear that many *Mutchristen* and *Mutbürger*, courageous Christians and courageous citizens, are acting and opting preferentially for the poor – in order that the common good, as called for by Pope Francis in his social encyclical, can truly be achieved.[45]

45 See Pope FRANCIS, *Laudato sí'*, § 158 (quoted in the introduction to this article).

Mathias Nebel

A Theological Conclusion

This conclusion is not a summary of the articles in this book. It is designed as a sort of theological continuation to some of the remarks made in the introduction. In a way it reflects the thinking of the editors themselves, both of them moral theologians who at the conclusion of this book would like to continue the discussion a little further.

Why a theological conclusion? This book resulted from an observation: the contribution of theology to contemporary ideas of the common good is widely misunderstood. Although the ancient traditions of the common good are often cited, the diversity and the originality of the patristic and Scholastic reinterpretations elude most contemporary authors. Therefore a renewal of the theological logic of the common good seemed to be an interesting thing to try, especially if it could be contrasted with some present-day political and economic paradoxes [*apories*]. This was what the book intended to do; this epilogue wishes to attempt again.

Thus these concluding pages aim to make clear how a Christian perspective can not only dialogue with political philosophy but also possibly serve to point out the blind spots that may be present in our political certitudes. Thought can be blinkered, too. Often university types have been incapable of perceiving any reality that does not fit into the categories of their convictions. Theologians have often been accused of this, but they are not the only ones. Aren't the political scientists and the economists the biggest blind men of our time?

This conclusion is structured on three remarks that were made in the introduction. The first takes up the question of the boundaries of nation-states; the second reflects on the rapid political polarization of the populations in the West; finally, the third inquires about the governance of "global common goods." Each of these three subjects will prompt a discussion of some of the elements of a theology of the common good.

Therefore we intend to start a dialogue, but a daring dialogue, because political philosophy — a worthy heir of the Enlightenment thinkers — is often slow to accept its theological heritage and believes that it is "obliged" to dispute its value immediately, the better to guarantee its own autonomy. But for what motives should theological reasoning be excluded from public reasoning?

The closure of the commons and the dynamic of the common good

This book addresses the fact of a rapid transformation of our societies characterized by the loss of the hegemony that economic and political liberalism enjoyed following the fall of the Berlin Wall. One of the crucial questions in this development is the question of the *limits of the commons*[1] inherited from the twentieth century. No other place reveals more clearly their fragility than national boundaries, those tangible limits of the positive law, of the power of the state and of democratic governance. The common goods created by liberal democracies are enclosed by these national boundaries. This *closure of the commons* is being shaken today by the combined forces of economic globalization and the new mass migrations.

What these two forces are testing is the ethical quality of the commons achieved by liberal democracies. How can one justify morally the fact that this migrant, from the other side of the boundary, does not have the same rights as I do? And here of course arises once more the imperative to pursue the common good as the demand to extend the commons universally.

- In a theological reflection, the inability of the nation-states to enlarge the commons that they guarantee to their own population seals their

1 The term *common* [French: *commun*], a singular noun, designates a shared resource to which each of the stakeholders has an equal interest. The origin of the term is connected with English common law, in which it designates a shared ownership and management of agricultural lands, forests, and meadows by a community. As such, this juridical notion contributes directly to a concept of the common good that was widespread during the Middle Ages (*cf.* Robert STEIN, "Whose community? The origin and development of the concept of *Bonum commune* in Flanders, Brabant and Holland," in Elodie LECUPPRE-DESJARDIN and Anne Laure VAN BRUAENE, (Eds), *The Discourse and Practice of the Common Good in the European City*, Turnhout, Brepols, 2010). It was adopted and updated by the nascent ecological movement to describe natural resources as being limited and shared goods which are "owned" in a way that cannot be likened to individual or collective property. But the Nobel Prize in Economic Sciences awarded to Elinor Ostrom in 2009 for her work on the management of material and immaterial commons was probably what put on the agenda the very real existence of these shared resources and the specific manner of their political and economic management. *Cf.* Elinor OSTROM, *Governing the Commons,* Cambridge, CUP, 1990. This kind of management is not adequately grasped by the classic definition of public goods in economy (non-rivalry of consumption, non-exclusivity) which does not inquire into the political definition of these shared goods.

fate in the long term.[2] For historically the dynamic of the common good is never achieved or definitively attained.[3] On the contrary, it must constantly be renewed in a tension that opens every particular common to a more inclusive and more universal common good. To freeze that dynamic in one of its historical forms—the Roman Empire, Christendom, liberal democracy, the United Nations system—is to condemn that form to implosion in the mid- to long term. From the theological perspective, when a particular form of common cannot fit into a nexus of the broader common good that potentially brings the universal, then it withers and ends up perishing. For the requirement of the common good, its normative character, unfolds *from the future* and not from a previous fact—theodicy, myth, natural law, social contract, or original consensus. This unfolding therefore starts from *what will be*.[4] This perhaps is the most specific mark left by the patristic reinterpretation of the ancient traditions of the common good.[5]

- Indeed, as it reinterpreted some ancient traditions of the common good, Christianity would introduce a point of capital importance: that of the fundamental *ambiguity* of human history, an ambiguity that is merely the more profound ambiguity of the human heart.[6] For Saint Augustine, a tension between good and evil runs through the history of our societies.[7] Left to his own devices, man seems incapable of following constantly and consistently any good that he sets for himself. His very intention always remains ambiguous and will unfailingly pervert the

2 David Hollenbach, *The Common Good and Christian Ethics*, Cambridge, CUP, 2002, 200-201. *Cf.* Patrick Riordan, *Global Ethics and Global Common Goods*, London, Bloomsbury Academic, 2014.

3 Gaston Fessard, *Autorité et bien commun*, Paris, Aubier, 1944, 54-55, 94-97.

4 Revault d'Allones, borrowing from Arendt, popularized the idea that authority is contained in the relation to the origin insofar as the narrative about the origin authorizes the present reality. *Cf.* Myriam Revault d'Allones, *Le pouvoir des commencements: Essai sur l'autorité*, Paris, Seuil, 2012. But already in Arendt's writing, this thesis stems from antiquity and does not integrate the specifically Plotinian then Christian contribution in a concept of temporality that is entirely centered on the return of everything to a transcendent One, in other words, centered on the finality of history, on what will be, and not on what was at the origin. True authority flows then from that which anticipates this absolute future in history.

5 Peter Hibst, *Utilitas Publica, Gemeiner Nutz und Gemeinwohl*, Frankfurt am Main, Peter Land, 1991, 142-156.

6 *Ibid.*, 149.

7 Augustine of Hippo, *The City of God*, Book 12, Book 18. *Cf.* Etienne Gilson, *Les métamorphoses de la cité de Dieu*, Paris, Vrin, 1952, 47-80.

course of his action, whether it be private or public.[8] But conjointly with this broadly sapiential *anthropological pessimism*, patristic Christianity also affirms a *fundamental hope in the happy outcome of human history*. This is Augustine's theology of grace. Despite the ambiguity, or more exactly at the very heart of this ambiguity of the human will, a world is emerging —a Kingdom, to put it more precisely—*which will be and will be absolutely*. There are in present human history some elements, acts, words which have an absolute value, which *will be eternally*, which *will not pass away* because what they signify and what they bring about belongs already to the world that is coming.[9]

- This is a Christian understanding of time, and this eschatological fulfillment of history is based on faith in Christ.[10] But this faith is translated existentially into a hope, which of course remains a theological virtue, but now joins another sapiential element that is just as marked as the radical ambiguity of human history. This second sapiential element is the existence in the human heart, at the heart of the common history of mankind, of a *hope* that nothing can permanently thwart.[11] This hope is that my good and the good of others are not irremediably opposed, that they do not diminish each other but on the contrary increase one another. This hope is at the origin of all social life. It is the impulse of life in its most primitive and unconscious expression;[12] it is cooperation and common action in its conscious expressions, particularly the political ones.[13] This is the hope that joins the theological virtue of hope, not as something that replaces or distorts it, but as a *force*, a *power to act that fulfills hope*, in other words in theological language as a *grace*. Again it is necessary to understand correctly what Christianity means by this: not some superhuman powers—avatars of the childish desire for omnipo-

8 AUGUSTINE OF HIPPO, *De libero arbitro* [*On Free Will*], Book 2.

9 This indefectible value should not be understood as the value of an ethical principle, but as the eternal value of an act or event that will be forever. This is the point of Matthew 25 and its eschatological judgment. Having visited the prisoner, having clothed the naked, having given food to the hungry are acts having a value that does not pass away. Based on the ultimate significance of these acts, a life is declared good or bad: "As you did it to one of the least of these my brethren, you did it to me" (Mt 25:40). *Cf.* Vincent LECLERCQ, "Le royaume de Dieu comme horizon d'une éthique sociale," in: Olivier ARTUS, (Ed.), *Eschatologie et morale*, Paris, DDB, 2009, 203-220.

10 *Cf.* Juan Ruiz DE LA PEÑA, *La otra dimensión: Escatologia Cristiana*, Santander, Sal Terrae, 1986, 18-29.

11 *Cf.* Maurice BLONDEL, *L'action*, Paris, Alcan, 1893, 326.

12 Cf. Henri BERGSON, *L'évolution créatrice*, in *Oeuvres*, Paris, PUF, 1959, 708-710.

13 Cf. Henri BERGSON, *Les deux sources de la morale*, in *Oeuvres*, 995-998.

tence—but rather a determination, a confidence, a goodness that nothing will be able to thwart, neither failure nor betrayal nor death.

- Now the *sure confidence* of hope generates a *constancy*, and this constancy —a *continuity* which is that of the common good. And so in theology, the stability of the political is connected not so much with the power of the authority[14] as with this essential, fundamental continuity of the pursuit of the common good. It is *the stability of the commitment to the common good that guarantees stability for the political authority*. Only the continuity of the common good—because it tends toward a future—makes it possible to go beyond the conservatism inherent in all political society by opening it to a horizon that surpasses it. The stability of the political power and its authority are derived from the nobility of what it aspires to. That is why this *hope* is to be understood as a very real historical and political force[15] and not just as an interior disposition—an irenic spirituality that is as benign as it is foolish. Hope for the common good is a political force that structures common life and continually renews it.
- From this eschatological perspective—which is realistic and sapiential as well as theological—the pursuit of the common good is therefore conceived theologically as a constant work, or even more, as a struggle to bring about the emergence of commons in the social and political conditions in which we find ourselves. To work for the common good is a task that is never accomplished or attained. In social circumstances that are ever new, it is necessary to reinvent the common goods that unite us and constitute us as a society tending toward the universal common good. Patristic Christianity conceptualized in this way the finality and the structure of the political power in the form of a dialectic between the particular and the universal; this is its misunderstood accomplishment, one of the fundamental contributions of theology to the concept of politics in the West.

Allegiance to the commons: social habitus and shared virtues

Another contemporary fact mentioned in the introduction is the breakdown of classic political categories and the emergence of new political movements. Thus we see voters from the opposite extremes of the political

14 That is to say, a kind of stability through the conservation and reproduction of the authority and of its institutions by ruse, prudence, force, and violence. *Cf.* Niccolò MACHIAVELLI, *The Prince: On the Art of Power*, London, Duncan Baird, 2007.

15 *Cf.* Gustavo GUTIÉRREZ, *La fuerza historica de los pobres*, Lima: CEP, 1979.

spectrum pass, apparently without difficulty, from one camp to the other, and a growing number of parties make their principal or exclusive motto a break with the existing "political system." The classic oppositions between right and left, conservatives and liberals, socialists and capitalists are no longer capable of representing *the political allegiance of an important part of Western populations.*[16] It would seem therefore that democratic reasoning is no longer capable of containing within the *liberal ethos* the political development of our societies.[17]

- The question is therefore one of the allegiance of a population to a particular political regime. Now two things must be distinguished: intellectual allegiance and practical allegiance. The first is conscious and (supposedly) reasoned. This is the domain of political convictions. The second is often unconscious and habitual. This is the domain of political practices.
- Now as far as allegiance to a political regime is concerned, political practices are indisputably the more important. For these *habitus*—in the meaning that Bourdieu gives to this term[18]—are the ones that assure the stability of our democratic institutions. The *practical continuation* of these institutions is what attests to their *real value* in a population. But there you have it! As conscious as it may have been of the importance of these *social habits*, political liberalism cannot give a good account of their origins.[19] Rousseau points out the importance of education, Comte proposes a State religion and a State morality, Rawls refers to rationality. The manner in which practical allegiance to the "social contract" is generated and reinvented is simply not explained at all realistically by the various proponents of political liberalism.[20]

16 Antony GIDDENS, *Beyond Left and Right*, Cambridge: Cambridge University Press, 1994, 4-19.

17 Hans SLUGA, *Politics and the Search for the Common Good*, Cambridge: CUP, 2014, 203-205.

18 Pierre BOURDIEU, *Esquisse d'une théorie de la pratique*, Paris: Seuil, 2000, 272.

19 *Cf.* Alasdair MCINTYRE, *After Virtue*, Notre Dame, University of Notre Dame Press, 2007, 36 ff.; Michael WALZER, *Sphere of Justice,* New York, Basic Books, 1983, 1-10.

20 Michael SANDERS, *Liberalism and the Limits of Justice*, Cambridge, CUP, 1998, 104-132, 195-218; Mary KEYS, *Aquinas, Aristotle and the Promise of the Common Good*, Cambridge, CUP, 2006, 29-58.

- In contrast, the Scholastic theologians always acknowledged that *habitus*[21] play a key role in the dynamic of the common good.[22] Following the ancient traditions, they do not conceive of the formal institutions of politics independently of the social *habitus* that actualize them. The one does not work without the other. The Agora of Athens is inconceivable without the democratic virtues that allow its proper functioning.[23] There is a kind of circularity between institutions and social *habitus*. The institutions are actualized in behaviors and these behaviors support the existence of these institutions. Thus, determining the *virtues proper to politics* is a recurrent theme in the debate in the works of Plato, Aristotle or Thomas Aquinas.

But whereas in Antiquity the determination of these collective virtues easily takes a *totalitarian* turn—think of Plato, but also of the Stoics—this is not the case in the medieval reinterpretation. Antiquity, indeed, advocates an *absolute superiority* of the common good over the particular good by virtue of its (divine and prior) origin.[24] Moreover, the virtues required for the common good will tend to be imposed in an absolute manner on the citizens, particularly in the form of a juridical obligation to be virtuous (law and common good thus becoming in practice identical among the Stoics).[25] Christianity, in contrast, would argue in favor of a fundamental *reciprocity* between particular good and common good in which the latter has only a *priority* over the former which could never be absolute (*ordo duplex*).[26]

This reciprocity is affirmed particularly in the classic distinction between *habitus* and virtues. The Scholastic authors usually make a distinction between the *habitus*, which can be promoted by institutions like the law or the government, and the *acquisition* of virtues, which depends on the internal forum, in other words, personal freedom. A social *habitus* really exists only in the shared virtue of the individuals which actualizes it. We see

21 A *habitus* is a stable disposition to act in keeping with a certain good. It can be individual, in which case we speak about a "habit," but it is usually structured socially, induced as a common "custom" by the structured field of common action.

22 *Cf.* Matthew KEMPSHALL, *The Common Good in Late Medieval Thought*, Oxford, Clarendon Press, 1999, 102-129; Mary KEYS, *op.cit,* 143 ff.

23 Guido KIRNER, "Polis und Gemeinwohl: Zum Gemeinwohlbegriff in Athen vom 6. bis 4. Jahrhundert v. Chr." in Herfried MÜNKLER and Harald BLUHM, *Gemeinwohl und Gemeinsinn*, vol. 1, Berlin, Akademie Verlag, 2001, 31-63.

24 Peter HIBST, *op. cit.*, 141-142.

25 *Ibid.*, 131-138.

26 Matthew KEMPSHALL, *op. cit.*, 92-101.

here how this reciprocity between common good and particular good is envisaged.

Furthermore this reciprocity will have to be *worked for freely* by each individual, because the universal common good is now no longer an Idea but a Person, Christ in glory situated in history and at the end of history.[27] The common good then is not achieved by way of reproducing an archetype, but rather by way of a living, historical, and progressive relationship with a person. The *habitus* and the virtues therefore no longer have to be imposed as much as they have to be sought and promoted together.

Ever since antiquity, a series of *habitus*/virtues have been associated with the common good. Among them we find the virtues connected with *peace or with the good life*, such as wisdom, justice, magnanimity, temperance, or more prosaic virtues like those connected with *order and prosperity*, such as fortitude, generosity, foresight, prudence, or even diligence. But to these virtues associated with the common good, patristic reflection would permanently associate another: *charity*. This theological virtue is thought of not only as being private and interior but also as a social virtue. At this level, the virtue of charity means the excellence of action which should unite a people; it means the action that creates a communion. In its different secular metamorphoses, this idea of the political role of love remains to this day one of the axes of Western thought (in the form of a requirement for fraternity or solidarity). But it has lost a lot. It is no longer a shared virtue that actualizes the pursuit of the common good and dynamically unifies society, but rather the most elusive of the three principles of the republican order: equality, liberty, fraternity. This demand for fraternity quickly dwindled into a demand for solidarity. Our common humanity no longer makes us brothers—that is still an essentially theological postulate—but merely members *in solidum* of the same human nature. Yet it is not obvious that this same nature forms the basis of a duty, the duty to recognize each other as members of one and the same community; in other words, as someone responsible not only for those who are close to me and with whom I live, but also with those whom I do not know and who are not close to me through any institution. We see clearly therefore that the demand for secular solidarity cannot be equivalent to the social role of charity. What is this role, then?

We must recall that Christianity does not consider charity to be a sentiment. Charity—the divine grace of divine love—operates in a human being in a space of freedom in which the human person and the Divine Person

27 Mathias NEBEL, "El bien común teológico: Ensayo sistemático," in *Revista Iberoamericana de Teología*, 7-32.

can meet, give themselves, and receive each other. This is not a natural space. It is the work of two freedoms (divine and human). It is a space of communion in which both of them, man and God, find each other and give themselves without either one losing what he is (the superabundance of the gift). Here there is a unity in the diversity; a symphonic, plural unity. Finally it is a space of fulfillment in which the relational creature that is man becomes progressively more fully himself in relation to God.

But charity is not an exclusive space. The I-Thou relation between the person and God is also open to all other human beings. Just like friendship, charity can be shared and is increased by this sharing. A new friend who joins our circle does not diminish the friendship that binds the earlier members. The same is true of charity: the more it is shared, the more it increases and is enriched. Only in charity can humanity be perceived as a community united by a bond of fraternity.

It is not surprising, then, that charity has been considered the virtue that actualizes the pursuit of the common good. Indeed, the common good is essentially a hope, the hope of a possible coincidence between the particular good and the good of the community. To work for the common good is to strive to achieve this coincidence.

John Paul II depicts this social role of charity under the form of a virtue *of solidarity*, which he defines as: "a firm and persevering determination to commit oneself to the common good; that is to say to the good of all and of each individual, because we are *all* really responsible *for all*."[28] For John Paul II, the search for the common good is a virtue, a collective and eminently political virtue. Solidarity is this constant search for a plural, free liberty that eminently actualizes the common good. There is no real, living, and stable political community without such a virtue. This is a second crucial contribution of theology to the concept of politics in the West.

We can legitimately ask ourselves today: What *habitus* and virtues are indispensable for the existence of our liberal democracies? The minimal liberal common denominator declares that we are all equal by the fact that we are different—but is that sufficient to maintain a living (and not just professional) political community? Doesn't the radical redefinition of the contem-

28 John Paul II, *Sollicitudo rei socialis*, § 38. Does John Paul II really return to the level of secular ethics? That is doubtful. His virtue of solidarity is dependent on strong theological presuppositions. Thus the responsibility that he spells out following Dostoyevsky—I am responsible for all, for everyone, everywhere—is not human (an unlimited responsibility is the negation of our finitude). Such a responsibility can only be Christological, as is the case incidentally in *The Brothers Karamazov*.

porary political spectrum depend on the fact that a deep gap has been created between institutions and behaviors, between *habitus* and shared virtues? Can practical allegiance to the republican values do without all references to a pursuit of the common good? Can social solidarity be considered as a natural, indefectible, and inexhaustible good in every population?

Global common goods and governance for the common good

It seems to us necessary to mention a third point also. We are currently witnessing a rebirth of interest in the idea of the common good in a variety of fields. This renaissance is complex and seems to be connected with the search for rationales other than those of the contract or of utility in order to describe the emergence of new commons. This is the case especially for those *global public goods* such as peace, the environment, nutritional security, or the preservation of cultural goods.[29] To the classic difficulty of the production and distribution of public goods is now added at the international level the crucial question about their governance.[30] Who will define these goods and how? Who will supervise their production and make sure that they are distributed in a just manner? Who will sanction the failures and abuses, and how? There is no "World State," nor any "universal legislator" capable of imposing its decisions on the different "parties." Multilateral diplomacy today is a matter for sovereign states, and their common decisions are negotiated and not imposed on the members (except for the Security Council). Hence the question: what political governance should be given to these global common goods?

In the Catholic theological tradition the question of good governance is closely connected with that of the common good. Pope Francis takes up this tradition and develops it in a way that is at the same time new and anchored in his own experience. In his typically pragmatic way, he seeks to find out how to govern so as to build a lasting peace, how to develop a place for social coexistence "where differences are harmonized within a shared pursuit" (*Evangelii gaudium*, § 221). As an answer to his question, he then offers in §§ 217-237 four principles of government for the common

29 *Cf.* David Hollenbach, *op. cit.*, 213-228; Patrick Riordan, *op. cit.*, 61-82, 131 ff.; Eric Brousseau, Tom Dedeurwaerdere, and Bernd Siebenhüner, (Eds), *Reflexive Governance for Global Public Goods*, Cambridge, MIT Press, 2012, 1-17.

30 See the report of the United Nations Development Programme that launched research into public goods: Inge Kaul, Isabelle Grunberg, Marc A. Stern, *Global Public Goods*, Oxford, Oxford University Press, 1999.

good, which are also criteria for decision-making. These principles guide practice. In the insurmountable ambiguity of circumstances, they make it possible to make decisions in favor of a pursuit of the common good.

These principles are based on the recognition of four bipolar "tensions" (§ 221) that run through all of social reality: a) The tension between the limitation of space and of the moment as opposed to the unlimited character of processes and of time; b) the tension between the search for unity and a recognition of the conflicts connected with the irreducible diversity of reality; c) the tension between reality and ideas; and finally d) the tension between what is local and concrete and what is future and universal.

To think of social reality as being crisscrossed and structured by these four fundamental tensions[31] is to affirm the existence of a dynamic inherent in the building of politics. But this dynamic is a complex dialectic, a dialectic of the common good that oscillates between the terms of each of these four binomials. There is no linear or constant development, the Pope declares. The building of a people, the search for peace and justice follows a dialectical movement in which conflicts, failures, and setbacks are part of the progress itself. What the act of government has to maintain is the perspective, the pursuit of the common good.

Let us recall here two of the principles of any governance for the common good proposed by Pope Francis: "Time is greater than space," and "Unity is greater than conflict."

a) a) First practical priority: time is greater than space.[32] The expression is surprising and yet clear. Francis recognizes here the existence of a priority of action, of the long term over the mastery of events and the ability to control. Any governance for the common good must privilege the long term, the creation of new dynamisms in a society, the launching of participatory and open processes over the constant will to dominate and to master space. It is a question of privileging long-term fruitfulness

31 In each of these binomials Francis assigns a priority to one of the two terms in tension. But this priority is by no means the negation of the necessity of the earlier [*sic*] term, which constitutes social reality just as much as the second does. Therefore it is not a question of choosing one of the terms *as opposed to the other* (exclusion) but of recognizing *the priority of one over the other*. It is thus a matter of recognizing the dynamic of fulfillment that runs through these tensions which belong to all social reality.

32 "People live poised between each individual moment and the greater, brighter horizon of the utopian future as the final cause which draws us to itself. Here we see a first principle for progress in building a people: time is greater than space." (*Evangelii gaudium*, § 222). Note that he mentions the importance of the future (the final cause that draws) for the practice of any governance for the common good.

over immediate efficiency. For social reality is changing and full of unforeseen circumstances. Any governance for the common good must therefore provide for a margin of indeterminacy and flexibility that allows it to accept change or to experience failure without losing its dynamic as a result.

Such governance implies a *fundamental trust in the future of common history* as well as a *faith in human freedom*. This trust is the basis of the priority assigned to the *long term* and to the launching of the *open processes* that others can join, that others will have to perfect and develop "to the point where they bear fruit in significant historical events" (§ 223). This is why to judge the quality of the present common good is *to judge the realization of the hope that animates the social processes*: "The only measure for properly evaluating an age is to ask to what extent it fosters the development and attainment of a full and authentically meaningful human existence, in accordance with the peculiar character and the capacities of that age."[33]

b) b) *Second practical priority: unity is greater than conflict.* The diversity and the irreducible limitation of reality constantly generates conflicts. For Pope Francis, conflict must be assumed resolutely. But that does not mean that it must be considered as the insoluble horizon of human sociality. The reason why it can be assumed is because it is possible to overcome it. This is why priority must be assigned to the *search for unity* in and despite the existence of conflict.

Indeed, to decide to engage in conflict, or to attempt merely to avoid it, to circumscribe it, or to contain it, is ultimately to remain a prisoner of the world created by the conflict. It is to limit one's action to the shrunken horizons of the conflict and to its fragmented, complex reality. For the conflict causes us to lose the vision of the horizon of fulfillment of human sociality; it causes us to lose sight of the profound unity of the social reality. This is why any governance for the common good assigns a constant priority to the search for unity. To confront a conflict, Francis writes, "is the willingness to face conflict head on," so as "to resolve it and to make it a link in the chain of a new process" (§ 227). The unity aimed at is therefore a *unity that is becoming*. Such a pursuit of unity implies the conviction that it is possible to arrive at a true peace between persons and between peoples, because humanity, Francis asserts, is not an abstraction but one goal and one possible goal (§ 228).

33 Here Pope Francis quotes Romano GUARDINI, *Das Ende der Neuzeit*, Würzburg, Werkbund Verlag, 1965, 30-31.

Such a priority assigned to the search for unity amounts also to recognizing that *solidarity is a challenge and a work*. To make unity prevail over conflict is to work for human solidarity in present history. Francis thus asserts that "solidarity... becomes a way of *making history*" (§ 228, emphasis ours). It is the work of "great persons" who aim beyond the limited horizon of the conflicts at a multiform unity in which the dignity of each individual is respected (§ 228). In other words, a unity in which the present conflicts are able to lead to a "new and promising synthesis," a "reconciled diversity" (§ 230).

This concept of *governance for the common good* is the third crucial contribution of theology to the concept of politics in the West. Its rediscovery seems today to be indispensable if we are to regain a dynamic of politics at the international level. Two points are particularly sensitive.

First, it will not be possible to determine new *global common goods* without also envisaging the *processes capable of producing and conserving them.* The current international approach by way of agreement and consensus between States remains the prisoner of a logic of exchange and of national egotisms.[34] Only another type of governance, a governance for the common good, will be capable of generating a *political definition* of these new commons, a definition which will have to resolve in particular the question about their *community of reference.*[35]

Secondly, it is necessary to recognize and to maintain that *this governance will not always or necessarily assume a democratic form.* Democracy is not the whole of the common good, and democratic processes are not the sum and substance of governing for the common good. We saw this previously. The legitimacy of a political decision, from the perspective of the common good, does not come solely from observing the procedures of democratic decision-making, but from *processes of governance of the common*, from the *quality of the realized common good* and from *its openness to the universal common good.* Although they may be democratic, some political decisions can very clearly be opposed to the common good. More often than not, the majority in a parliament perpetuates collective egotisms, and it is not rare for a popular referendum to give priority to the national interest over the fundamental human rights of other populations on earth.

It is widely admitted nowadays that the international institutions resulting from the Second World War are no longer adapted and must be reformed if

34 Patrick RIORDAN, *op. cit.*, 97 ff.

35 Inge KAUL, "Rethinking Public Goods and Global Public Goods," in Eric BROUSSEAU, (Ed.), *op. cit.*, 49.

they intend to fulfill their mandate. But even though observers unanimously agree on this, the proposals for reforms are timid. They seem to boil down to *more democratic procedure* (break the hegemony of the Security Council) or *management by objective* (development goals). For our part, it seems to us that any international governance that wishes to pursue peace, justice, and fraternity will necessarily have to be thought of as governance for the common good.

Authors

Jean Michel Bonvin; Full professor in Social Policies and Vulnerabilities at the University of Geneva. His research interest cover labor and health policies, organizational innovation, labor sociology and the theories of justice, especially the capability approach.

Thierry Collaud; Full Professor of Moral Theology and Christian Social Ethics at the Faculty of Theology, University of Fribourg Switzerland and is also a medical doctor. His research addresses topics of Cristian anthropology, especially our condition of fragility and vulnerability and the connected theological questions of compassion and love, sacraments and social justice.

Paul Dembinski; Full Professor at the University of Fribourg, Switzerland, where he teaches International Competition and Strategy, he also teaches at the Tischner European University in Krakow, Poland. His research spans a broad spectrum from finances, business ethics, International competition and

Jean Claude Huot: Jean-Claude Huot is Pastoral Assistant in the Catholic Church in the diocese of Lausanne, Geneva and Fribourg. He worked previously for the Justice and Peace Commission of the Swiss Bishops' Conference, the Swiss NGO Public Eye and the Swiss Catholic Lenten Fund.

Matthew Kempshall; Cliff Davies Fellow in History and Clarendon Associate Professor at Wadham College, University of Oxford. His research concerns the reception of Aristotle's ethical and political ideas, the connections between Ciceronian rhetoric and medieval historiography, the ideology of medieval kingship, and the understanding of classical republicanism by scholastic theologians and early Renaissance humanists.

Mary Keys; Associate Professor at the Department of Political Science, University of Notre Dame. Mary M. Keys holds a BA from Boston College and a MA and PhD from the University of Toronto. Her research and teaching interests span a broad spectrum of political theory, with a special focus in Christianity, ethics, and political thought.

Mathias Nebel; Full Professor of Christian Social Ethics and Research Director IPBC, Department of Political Sciences, Universidad Popular Autónoma del Estado de Puebla (MEX). He has worked on structural sin, collective forms of responsibility and agency in justice theories.

Christos N. Tsironis; Assistant Professor in Social Theory of Contemporary Culture and Christianity, Department of Theology, Aristotle University of Thessaloniki. His main research focus on poverty and education.

Stefano Zamagni; Adjunct Professor of Political Economy at the University of Bologna and is a member of the Pontifical Academy of Social Sciences. He has published extensively on the history of economics and won international appraisal for his work on civil economy.